ROUTLEDGE LIBRARY EDITIONS: 18TH CENTURY PHILOSOPHY

Volume 10

LANGUAGE, SUBJECTIVITY, AND FREEDOM IN ROUSSEAU'S MORAL PHILOSOPHY

LANGUAGE, SUBJECTIVITY, AND FREEDOM IN ROUSSEAU'S MORAL PHILOSOPHY

RICHARD NOBLE

LONDON AND NEW YORK

First published in 1991 by Garland Publishing, Inc.

This edition first published in 2019
by Routledge
2 Park Square, Milton Park, Abingdon, Oxon OX14 4RN

and by Routledge
52 Vanderbilt Avenue, New York, NY 10017

Routledge is an imprint of the Taylor & Francis Group, an informa business

© 1991 Richard Noble

All rights reserved. No part of this book may be reprinted or reproduced or utilised in any form or by any electronic, mechanical, or other means, now known or hereafter invented, including photocopying and recording, or in any information storage or retrieval system, without permission in writing from the publishers.

Trademark notice: Product or corporate names may be trademarks or registered trademarks, and are used only for identification and explanation without intent to infringe.

British Library Cataloguing in Publication Data
A catalogue record for this book is available from the British Library

ISBN: 978-0-367-13518-8 (Set)
ISBN: 978-0-429-02691-1 (Set) (ebk)
ISBN: 978-0-367-18338-7 (Volume 10) (hbk)
ISBN: 978-0-367-18340-0 (Volume 10) (pbk)
ISBN: 978-0-429-06089-2 (Volume 10) (ebk)

Publisher's Note
The publisher has gone to great lengths to ensure the quality of this reprint but points out that some imperfections in the original copies may be apparent.

Disclaimer
The publisher has made every effort to trace copyright holders and would welcome correspondence from those they have been unable to trace.

LANGUAGE, SUBJECTIVITY, AND FREEDOM IN ROUSSEAU'S MORAL PHILOSOPHY

Richard Noble

GARLAND PUBLISHING, INC.
New York ——— London
1991

Copyright © 1991 by Richard Noble
All Rights Reserved

Library of Congress Cataloging-in-Publication Data

Noble, Richard, 1958–
Language, subjectivity, and freedom in Rousseau's moral philosophy/
Richard Noble.
p. cm.—(Political theory and political philosophy)
Includes bibliographical references.
ISBN 0-8153-0136-7 (alk. paper)
1. Rousseau, Jean-Jacques, 1712–1778. 2. Subject (Philosophy)—History—
18th century. 3. Liberty—History—18th century. 4. Ethics, Modern—18th
century. I. Title. II. Series.
B2137.N63   1991
194—dc20   91-10201

Printed on acid-free, 250-year-life paper.
MANUFACTURED IN THE UNITED STATES OF AMERICA

Contents

1. Introduction 7

2. Speaking Apes 13
   - 1.2 *The "Ape Debates"* 17
   - 1.3 *Apes and Humans in the Chain of Being* 20
   - 1.4 *The Cartesian Position* 26
   - 1.5 *The Materialist Position* 30
   - 1.6 *Lockean Sensationalism* 35
   - 1.7 *Conclusion* 39

2. The Problem of Language Origin 46
   - 2.2 *Rousseau and Condillac on the Origin of Language* 50
   - 2.3 *Conclusion* 58

3. Original Nature 64
   - 3.2 *Natural Liberty* 68
   - 3.3 *The Faculty of Perfectibilité* 72
   - 3.4 *Perfectibilité and the Species' Evolution* 75
   - 3.5 *Conclusion* 81

4. Rousseau's Arcadian Ideal 90
   - 4.2 *Sexuality and the Origins of Natural Society* 96
   - 4.3 *The Problem of Amour-Propre in the Golden Age* 106
   - 4.4 *Natural Language and Authenticity* 109
   - 4.5 *The Decline of Arcadia and the Possibility of Freedom* 118

5. The Metaphysics of Freedom — 133

5.2	*The Vicar's Metaphysic of the Self*	142
5.3	*The Vicar's Dualism*	147
5.4	*The Voice of Nature*	158
5.5	*Moral Freedom*	164
5.6	*Conclusion*	169

6. An Education According to Nature — 178

6.2	*The Pre-moral Education*	183
6.3	*The Infant Self*	185
6.4	*The Acquisition of Language*	188
6.5	*Natural Liberty*	191
6.6	*The Acquisition of Judgement*	195
6.7	*Natural Consciousness and Moral Relations*	198

7. A Moral Education — 209

7.2	*The Doctrine of Pity*	213
7.3	*The Consistency of Rousseau's Doctrine of Pity*	214
7.4	*The Coherence of the Doctrine of Pity*	217
7.5	*The Moral Contract*	225
7.6	*Sexuality and Love*	228
7.7	*Conclusion: Moral Freedom*	234

8. Bibliography — 243

Introduction

This book has two related goals. The first is to explicate Rousseau's conception of subjectivity; the second is to trace the influence of that conception on his theory of freedom. I want to argue that Rousseau's conception of subjectivity provides us with a basis for understanding both his analysis of the "social problem" of advanced civil societies, and the solutions he proposes to this problem. The work is therefore largely expository. The first part attempts to recover the often implicit assumptions informing Rousseau's conception of the subject, from his philosophical anthropology and his philosophy of language. I argue here that Rousseau maintained a consistent theory of the subject that can be understood to provide the groundwork for his moral theory. The second part of the work involves a discussion of Rousseau's conception of freedom. This follows from my exposition of his theory of the subject, which shows that for Rousseau, human beings were defined in virtue of their capacity for freedom. In Rousseau's view, our nature as subjects provides us with the potential to be free, but our existence in advanced civil societies has so distorted our nature that freedom seems to have vanished from our moral landscape. His theory of the subject provides us with a way of understanding his view of how the potential inherent in our original nature could be reconstituted in society. For Rousseau, freedom represented the recovery of nature because it consists in the full realization of our potential as human beings. An important part of what I want to claim then, is that Rousseau's theory of the subject shows us why freedom is the centrepiece of his moral theory. It represents for him the linchpin of any solution to the alienation and oppression endemic to contemporary societies, because it represents the only condition he believed to be consistent with a fully human life.

My interest in Rousseau's conception of the subject arose from what appeared to me a fundamental contradiction in his philosophical anthropology. This involved the assertion on the one hand that humans are naturally free, and on the other that human nature is formed in and through our experience the natural and social worlds. The view that we are naturally free and defined as human in terms of that freedom, is central to Rousseau's moral theory. It gives moral significance to his insistence that as social beings we are alienated from our original nature, and that this alienation constitutes the central problem of our social life. If human beings were not free *by nature*, the claim that we have lost our freedom under the influence of society would be entirely vacuous. It would preclude Rousseau's use of nature as the standard against which to judge the extent of the corruption and dependence engendered by our social institutions. Yet to claim that we are naturally free is to assert that we have an essential character which exists independent of the press of environmental contingency, and this seems to stand at odds with Rousseau's attempt to explain human consciousness and motivation in terms of the structure of civil societies.

The first part of what I want to claim about Rousseau's conception of subjectivity is that it derives from his attempt to overcome this contradiction in his philosophical anthropology. I argue that his theory of the subject attempts to reconcile elements of both Cartesian rationalism and Lockean sensationalism, in order to meet the conflicting requirements set for him by his account of the species' evolution. His anthropological interests led him to the conviction that as a species, humans had acquired most of the characteristics that define them, such as language, rationality, and social life, over the course of a long evolution. This entailed the assumption that human consciousness was constituted by the subject's experience of the world, a view that was most adequately explained in terms of empiricist epistemology. Yet at the same time Rousseau also wanted to argue that there was a reason specific to the species itself that had led to its acquisition of a consciousness suited to morality and freedom, (and that this is what we had lost in the course of our evolution). In order to argue this, Rousseau attempted to graft onto the empiricist account of the subject the Cartesian principle of the self as a simple subject of experience, defined by essential characteristics, and unaffected in its essence by its experience of the world. The result, I want to claim, is a theory of subjectivity which is unique in the context of the mid-eighteenth century, and in some respects important for our own understanding of the relation between subjectivity and morality.

My account of the epistemological basis of Rousseau's moral theory is in the very broadest sense "neo-Kantian", at least insofar as it attempts to explain Rousseau's theory of freedom in terms of his conception of the subject. It demonstrates that in some respects Rousseau's account of the subject rather strikingly anticipates Kant, and therefore strengthens the claim made by Cassirer and others that Rousseau's conception of moral freedom should be conceived in broadly Kantian terms, as a form of self-legislating autonomy.[1]

However, my reading of Rousseau also shows that neither his account of the subject nor his theory of freedom can be assimilated to Kant's philosophy. There are crucial differences, and these account for the enduring importance and influence of Rousseau's moral theory. More specifically, the "neo-Kantian" reading of Rousseau has overplayed the importance of reason in his conception of freedom. By viewing Rousseau's theory of the subject as an attempted synthesis of Cartesian rationalism and Lockean sensationalism, we are able to see how Rousseau attempted to integrate reason and the passions into his moral psychology of freedom, and why, beyond this, the possibility of freedom depends for him upon our living a certain kind of communal life. Neither of these positions is consistent with the Kantian conception of autonomy. For Rousseau, the self is not conceived in transcendental terms. If it is ever independent of the contingencies of experience, it is so only as potential. Reason can therefore only ever be exercised under the influence of the passions, and the central problem of his moral theory was to find a way of integrating the two in a conception of freedom.

In arguing that we should read Rousseau conception of the subject as an attempt to reconcile Descartes and Locke, I am also attempting to offer an antidote to a number of interpretations which rest on the view that Rousseau was a radical empiricist, or even a materialist.[2] This position is typically argued by political theorists who have been influenced by the writings of Leo Strauss. Regarding Rousseau as a radical empiricist enables them to portray his moral theory as a strategy for managing the passions in order to bring about moral and civic virtue. For the Straussians, it is virtue, rather than freedom, which is the central moral value in Rousseau's writings. A being whose consciousness is wholly dominated by sensation is one whose actions are determined by emotive or passionate responses to those sensations. Consequently, it becomes possible to regulate human behaviour by means of controlling human passions.[3] As a radical empiricist, Rousseau can be accommodated to the Straussian view of politics as an activity directed at imposing order upon the unruly and anti-civil passions of the masses. If my reading of Rousseau is correct, this places too much emphasis to the role of the passions in Rousseau's moral psychology. In doing so it fails to account for the interdependence of passion and reason in Rousseau's conception of moral freedom, and because of this leaves us with a false opposition between freedom and virtue in Rousseau's thought. I want to argue that for Rousseau, freedom and virtue are synonymous: that it is impossible in the context of his moral theory to conceive of one without the other. They represent for him the fullest realization of our natural potential as subjects. As a consequence, his prescriptions for reversing the moral and political decay he saw around him were aimed at creating the social conditions under which human potential could be maximized.

It will be evident then, that I think Rousseau's conception of the subject has important implications for his moral theory. My discussion of these implications attempts to show why Rousseau conceived the opposition between nature and culture as the

Introduction

fundamental problem of civil society. It then attempts to demonstrate why he conceived moral freedom as the solution to this problem, and finally to discuss what I take to be the problems inherent in the solution he proposes. These problems are by no means negligible. In viewing the subject as something defined by its innate potential for freedom, but which nevertheless acquires the constituent features of its consciousness from its social experience, Rousseau left himself the task of explaining how that innate potential could be realized within a social milieu that was both its condition and what made it *impossible*. This was certainly no small task. My claim is that his solution to the paradox is a conception of moral freedom conceived as self-legislating autonomy, in which reason, natural passion, and free will are said to be fully integrated into the motivational structure of the subject's moral psychology. This conception of freedom is not without difficulties, as we shall see, but I want to claim that it sheds important light on the problem of how we should think about the relation between our notions of what it means to be a subject, and the possibility of freedom.

No work of this nature and length could be written without the generous support of both friends and institutions. I owe my greatest debt of thanks to Maurice Cranston, for asking me to submit this work to Garland's series on political theory and philosophy. I would also like to thank John Charvet for his unfailingly acute criticism and advice, and George Feaver and Bill Buxton for their intelligence and their friendship. I am also grateful to the University of Winnipeg for its support.

Endnotes

1. Ernst Cassirer, *The Question of Jean-Jacques Rousseau*, Peter Gay trans., (Bloomington: Indiana University Press, 1976).

2. See for example, Joel Schwartz, *The Sexual Politics of Jean-Jacques Rousseau*, (Chicago: The University of Chicago Press, 1984); Marc Plattner, *Rousseau's State of Nature*, (Dekalb: Northern Illinois University Press, 1979); Peter Emberley, "Rousseau and the Management of the Passions" in *Interpretation*, May 1985, vol.13, #2.

3. Emberley, "Management", pp. 159-60.

1

Speaking Apes

1.1 Introduction

In the preface to the ***Discours sur l'inégalité*** Rousseau makes a radical assertion: if we want to understand the origins of inequality between human beings, we must first discover their original nature. We must distinguish what was original in our nature from what has been added by our development through time and circumstance, before we can hope to discern the origins of the differences that now distinguish us.[1] Rousseau assumes that we were by nature equal, and claims that to find the source of our present inequality we must look to the successive changes in both our environment and our nature over the course of our species' evolution. This was a radical, if not entirely original proposition in the context of the eighteenth century, because it shifted the inquiry into human nature away from the theological presumption of original sin, towards an entirely secular anthropology of human evolution.[2] Rousseau's inquiry carries with it the implication that humans are not properly understood as beings whose nature is fixed according to immutable and defining characteristics. Rather, we are beings who have evolved in and through our environmental circumstances, and whose present nature is radically removed from our original one.

This methodological proposition posits an opposition between nature and culture which remains a constant and often paradoxical theme throughout Rousseau's writings. In the context of the *Discours sur l'inégalité*, nature represents man in his original form: a hypothesized beginning point against which his present condition must be both understood and judged. The claim is that if we can trace man back to his origin, "tel qu'il a du sortir des mains de la nature", we can then retrace his development from a condition of equality and freedom to his present one of inequality and oppression. The explanation of our present condition lies in this development, and most crucially in the point at which we began to transform ourselves from natural to social beings. But there is a tremendous distance between our existence in nature and our existence in society. What we have become as social beings simply precludes our return to the state of nature, and in this sense nature and culture are opposed to each other. They represent two fundamentally different modes of human experience.

The opposition gives rise to a paradox, because the prescriptive dimension of Rousseau's thought demands that they be reconciled. Rousseau's analysis of the social condition depends upon an image of nature as society's other; a way of life completely opposed to and therefore exclusive of our present condition, which enables us to distinguish between the real and the artificial in our nature. Yet, as we shall see, this analysis yields a moral imperative to recover that lost other. As Rousseau conceived it, the social problem lay in our complete alienation from nature, and while a solution to it could not involve a return to that original condition, it had to entail of recovery of certain aspects of it. But if nature is society's other, if the two are mutually exclusive, how is this possible? This question remains a constant source of difficulty in Rousseau's thought which I hope, in the course of this work, to shed some light upon.

In Rousseau's philosophical anthropology then, the causes of our present condition lie in the course of our species' evolution from nature to culture. The most obvious starting point for such an anthropology is man as he exists according to nature.

But such an account, as Rousseau readily admits, while being necessary can be at best conjectural,[3] and this raises another question of importance for the entire enterprise. How can Rousseau hope to make accurate conjectures about man in the state of nature, when there is no reliable way of verifying them? The question is fundamentally important because, as we noted, Rousseau's account of natural man is to serve as the other against which social man is to understand himself: the standard against which we can distinguish between the natural and the artificial in our present nature, and on this basis attempt to rejuvenate our moral and political life. His account of our original nature is central to both his analysis of our present social condition and the solutions he proposes to it. In what follows I offer an account of the sources of Rousseau's portrait of natural man, which I want to claim find their basis in his conception of human subjectivity.

Jean Starobinski has suggested that Rousseau's portrait of natural man is the product of an "anthropologie negative". This is to say that Rousseau defined natural man as the absence of all those "artificial" (or acquired) characteristics that define civilized man; a being who lacks language, rationality, social relations and industry.[4] This "negative" portrait was bolstered by a certain amount of ethnographic information regarding "savages", whose primitive existence seemed to indicate that original man was far removed from our present condition; and also by the testimony of Jean-Jacques' uncorrupted heart, which validated his imaginative reconstruction of the natural human state.[5] Thus rather than project civilized man back into a hypothetical state nature, the mistake for which he criticized Hobbes, Rousseau projected the negation of civilized man into an imagined (though not in his view hypothetical) state of nature, and began his account of our evolution from there.

Starobinski was certainly right to characterize Rousseau's portrait of natural man as negative. It is clear from Rousseau's account that natural man's existence is virtually indistinguishable from an animal existence, and so constructed in terms of what social man is not. However, to assert that Rousseau conceived natural man as the negation of social man, is also to raise the question of how he conceived the species' evolution from its origins to its present state. For if natural man is simply whatever social man is not, how is it possible that the two are linked on an evolutionary continuum? Another way of posing this question is to ask: if natural man is nothing more than an animal, why did the human species in particular evolve beyond its natural state?[6] An "anthropologie negative" cannot answer this, because it does not spell out in enough detail what Rousseau took to be the constituent features of natural man, which could in turn explain why our species has evolved as it has. In Rousseau's view, natural man shares two constituent features with social man, both of which help to explain our species' unique evolution. These features are free will and *perfectibilité* (the faculty of self-improvement).

Part of what I want to claim is that Rousseau's account of natural man involves more than the simple negation of social man. It is also based on a set of assumptions regarding the constituent features of a human subject per se, independent of that subject's existence in an environment, and prior to its development into a self-conscious moral being. The first of these assumptions, which Rousseau's anthropology projects onto an historical screen, is that human beings are constituted cognitively, psychologically, and morally through their experience of the environment in which they live. In this respect Rousseau's conception of subjectivity was heavily indebted to Lockean sensationalism, particularly as it was articulated and refined by Condillac. Rousseau's account of natural man as a pre-rational, pre-linguistic, isolated being, depended on his being able to conceive the human mind as something that evolves over time under the influence of its environment. Condillac's "sensationalist" epistemology, as we shall see below, provided Rousseau with a way of conceiving the human subject as a being whose cognitive faculties and self-consciousness evolved in precisely this way.

Yet at the same time, as we noted above, Rousseau also assumed that the human species possessed certain innate characteristics which defined it as human by bridging the yawning gap between nature and culture in its evolution. This constitutes a second basic assumption about the constituent features of a human subject. For Rousseau, free will and *perfectibilité* are also necessary to explain our species' evolution, and as constituent feature they were not acquired in the process. But this view, as we shall see, draws on a very different philosophical tradition, which attempts to define the human subject in terms of its innate characteristics, most notably rationality and language. The philosophical tradition that argued most powerfully for a conception humanity marked off from all other species by its innate characteristics was Cartesian rationalism. Descartes had defined the self as a thinking essence, *Cogito ergo sum*, and his followers had maintained the conviction, against the rising tide of empiricism, that the apparently unique characteristics of human beings, in particular language and rationality, could not be explained solely in terms of their sensory experience of the physical world.

1.2 The "Ape Debates"

We noted above that Rousseau's imaginative reconstruction of the state of nature was fed in part by his reading of travellers' reports of primitives living in the non-European parts of the planet. However, these reports also raised a number of very serious scientific and philosophical problems in the eighteenth-century, two of which were particularly significant for Rousseau's philosophical anthropology. The first of these was how should we understand ourselves in relation to other, apparently less developed members of our own species? And the second involved the question of what distinguishes humans from other species in the so-called "Chain of Being"?

Rousseau's interest in these travellers' reports is evident from his assertion in "Note X" of the *Discours sur l'inégalité* that our knowledge would greatly benefit from a truly scientific study of the men and morals of non-European lands. He suggests sending a Condillac or a d'Alembert on such a mission, to sort out the facts from the prejudices and exaggeration of "les voyageurs grossiers".[7] For Rousseau, these reports constituted scientific evidence that the human species had evolved to its present state. The wide range of anthropomorphic species found in the outreaches of the planet, and their extremely diverse behaviour, indicated that the species was at various stages of its moral, social, and physical evolution. To study Europeans exclusively was to study humankind at only one stage of its development; and to presume that other anthropoids were animals simply because they did not behave or speak like Europeans was to be guilty of the crudest ethnocentrism. It was also to leave unanswered an extremely important question, i.e. what does their level of development tell us about our own. Thus Rousseau writes,

> Toutes ces observations sur les variétés que mille causes peuvent produire et ont produit en effet dans l'Espèce humaine, me font douter si divers animaux semblables aux hommes, pris par les voyageurs pour des Bêtes sans beaucoup d'examen, ou à cause de quelques différences qu'ils remarquoient dans la conformation extérieure, ou seulement parce que ces Animaux ne parloient pas, ne seroient point en effet de véritable hommes Sauvages, dont la race dispersée anciennement dans les bois n'avoit eu occasion de développer aucune des ses facultés virtuelles, n'avoit acquis aucun degré de perfection, et se trouvoit encore dans l'état primitif de Nature.[8]

Rousseau's doubt led him to a method of inquiry which strikingly anticipates modern anthropology. He came to the view that the study of primitive forms of life was crucial for Europeans to arrive at an adequate understanding of themselves. He writes in the *Essai sur l'origine des langues*:

> Quand on veut étudier les hommes il faut regarder près de soi; mais pour étudier l'homme il faut apprendre à porter sa vue au loin; il faut d'abord observer les différences pour découvrir les propriétés.[9]

The traditional ethnocentricism would no longer suffice. "Le grand défaut des Européens est de philosopher toujours sur l'origine des choses d'après ce qui se passe autour d'eux."[10] This has prompted some, most notably Claude Levi-Strauss, to name Rousseau as the founder of modern anthropology,[11] and there is an important sense in which Rousseau did anticipate the modern anthropological enterprize. He was interested in less developed forms of human life for what they told us about ourselves, though it must of course be remembered that his conception of the 'primitive' was grounded more in his imagination than empirical observation. His interest in apes, and in particular the orang-outang, arose in part from his desire to place his speculative history of the human species on a more scientific footing. He believed these apes might be human beings of a very primitive kind, and if this were true, it would provide us with a concrete idea of just how far we have evolved beyond our original state.

The debate over whether apes were human, and it should be noted that Rousseau had only a peripheral role in this debate, really turned on the question of what could count as legitimate criteria for establishing their humanity, or lack of it. It was, in otherwords, more a debate about the boundaries of the human than the similarities between apes and men. Its significance for Rousseau was partly, as I just noted, that these apes offered potential empirical support for his speculative anthropology. However, it also provides a backdrop against which we can understand the genesis of Rousseau's conception of the human subject, and indeed his philosophical anthropology as a whole. The "Ape Debates" were really about what, if anything, differentiated humans from higher order animals like apes. They consequently brought into focus two opposing conceptions of the human subject, both of which, I want to claim, Rousseau drew upon for his own account of our subjectivity. The issues these debates raised with respect to the origin of language, rationality, and ultimately society, arose from the necessity of explaining the apparently distinctive features of human beings, and so became of fundamental importance for Rousseau's philosophical anthropology.

1.3 Apes and Humans in the Chain of Being

The debate over whether higher order apes were humans arose within the context of a set of assumptions regarding the order of the universe. It was widely assumed by the educated public of eighteenth-century Europe that the universe could be understood as a Chain of Being, a rational and hierarchical order in which every existent thing had been assigned a place. Underlying this conception, as Lovejoy has shown, was the assumption of an omnipotent and omniscient God, Who had created the universe as a cosmos in which everything was given a pre-ordained place.[12] Thus in respect of organic nature, each form of life from the lowest to the highest, could derive its justification and significance from its place in the great Chain of Being. The Chain was thought to be hierarchical and continuous. The principle of plenitude implied that each species was regarded as a distinct essence with an equal claim to existence in virtue of their common ontological ground in God's will. These essences were thought to be of unequal dignity, but nonetheless linked together in a continuous and hierarchically graduated scale, in which each form, mineral, animal and spiritual had its place.[13]

The question of man's place in this great Chain was pretty much settled by the eighteenth-century. The old view, held over from the early modern period, was that man is the centre of creation, from which it followed that all other beings exist for his sake.[14] However, by the end of the seventeenth-century, the anthropocentric view of man's place in the Chain of Being had been largely supplanted by a somewhat more modest conception of our position. The anthropocentric view seemed to many out of line with the limitations of human nature (and therefore orthodox Christian doctrine), but besides this simply not in accordance with the facts. Descartes for instance, pointed out that there were innumerable species which exist or have existed without our knowledge.[15] This made the strong anthropocentric view seem somewhat absurd. What utility could an unknown species have for man?

The new view was that human beings held a middle or transitional position in the hierarchy of being. Our significance in the chain stemmed from our peculiar transitional position between the merely material/sentient forms of life and the more sustained, spiritual life-forms. Like animals or even lower forms of life, humans were material, sentient creatures. However, unlike lower forms of life, humans also possessed of metaphysical properties: free will, rationality, and eternal souls, which made them qualitatively different and superior. Language became an increasingly important attribute in this respect, because it seemed to be evidence of our superiority over the mute and therefore mindless beasts. However, this was not taken to mean that humankind inhabited the highest rung on the ladder. Above us were any number of wholly spiritual beings: those inhabiting other planets for instance, as well as angels, and ultimately God Himself.[16]

By the eighteenth century medieval or early modern anthropomorphism, with its presumption that all life exists for the purpose of serving man, was beginning to break down. As it did, the Chain of Being began to be conceived rather differently. Part of the reason for this was simply that human knowledge of the natural world, and in particular of biology, began to expand rapidly towards the end of the seventeenth century. It became evident, as the above allusion to Descartes indicates, that the Chain was simply to vast and too complicated to be understood in terms of its value for man. What came to be stressed instead, was the continuity and completeness of the Chain as a whole, quite independent of it use-value for man. In this respect the writings of Leibniz were particularly influential. In Leibniz's view, the universe had by virtue of its Creator to be as complete and as perfect as logic would allow. This was consistent with his view that the universe was a "real unity", which as such had to be the best of all possible worlds. In Leibniz view:

> ...essence tends by itself toward existence. From this it follows, furthermore, that everything possible, that is, all that expresses a possible essence or reality, tends with equal right toward existence, the degree of this tendency being proportionate to the quantity of essence or reality, that is, to the degree of perfection of the possible involved. Perfection, indeed, is nothing other than the quantity of essence involved.[17]

Insofar as the Chain of Being is a descriptive framework for understanding the natural order, Leibniz's conviction that the universe reflects its Creator's perfection leads him to the conclusion that the Chain must be as full and complete as possible. There can be no gaps or breaks in it, as this would imply irrationality in the Creator's plan and a denial of His perfection. As a matter of logic then, the Chain of Being requires the maximum quantity of essence, and therefore the maximum quantity of existent beings or species.

On the Leibnizean view, which, it is interesting to note was shared in its essentials by Locke, the Chain as a whole seemed an immensely graduated and continuous scale, each rung in the hierarchy barely distinguishable from those above and below it. Locke expressed the Chain's continuity in this way:

> [I]n all the visible corporeal world we see no chasms or gaps. All quite down from us the descent is by easy steps, and a continued series that in each remove differ very little one from the other.... There are some brutes that seem to have as much reason and knowledge as some that are called men; and the animal and vegetable kingdoms are so nearly joined, that if you will take the lowest of one and the highest of the other, there will scarce be perceived any great difference between them.... we shall find everywhere that the several species are linked together, and differ but in almost insensible degrees.[18]

This conception of the Chain of Being as a continuous and graduated scale which reflected God's perfect design, gave rise to its own scientific project: the search for missing links. If, as Leibniz had asserted, the universe was as full of life or existence as was logically possible, then as Locke notes, there cannot be gaps. This prompted Leibniz to predict, before their discovery by Trembley in 1739, species which seem to straddle the plant and animal kingdoms. "Thus there is nothing monstrous in the existence of zoophytes, or plant-animals, as Badaeus calls them; on the contrary, it is wholly in keeping with the order of nature that they should exist. And so great is the force of the principle of continuity, to my thinking, that....I am convinced that there must be such creatures..."[19]

If the Chain of Being was an immense and infinitesimally graduated scale, it was unlikely that species just above and below man would differ a great deal from him in either their physical or cognitive characteristics.[20] Furthermore, as Locke among others pointed out, the Aristotelian-inspired notion of natural species, that God had created each species as a distinct and definable essence, was possible but not in principle something the human mind could know directly. The classification of species in nature was merely a convention of language, and the classifications distinguished merely in terms of nominal essence.[21]

The "continuity thesis" stressed the importance of physical criteria in distinguishing between species, and in this way drew into question the radical demarcations between species in terms of their ontological purpose, which had been typical of medieval and early modern thought. The claim that any species' ontological purpose was simply beyond human ken, left natural historians and biologists with physical properties as the basis of their analysis of the order of nature. This drew man into the natural order in a way inimical to medieval anthropomorphism. It did so because of increasing empirical evidence that in physical terms at least, human beings were more alike than unlike those species close to them in the Chain of Being. Such evidence that did exist in otherwords, seemed to support the case for our continuity with other species rather than our radical distinctness from them.

We noted above that emphasis on continuity between species in the "Chain of Being" gave rise to a new scientific project, which preoccupied naturalists well into the eighteenth century. If continuity was the assumed order of nature, there were still gaps, especially at the transition points between the plant and the animal and the animal and the human. This gave rise to much searching for "missing links", which would empirically verify the rational order of nature. Thus Abraham Trembley's discovery of the polyp Hydra in 1739 (it had animal characteristics but could reproduce asexually) seemed to establish the missing link between plants and animals.[22] The discussion of apes and their relation to humans was important for this very reason. For obvious reasons, apes seemed to constitute a 'missing link' between rational, linguistically competent human beings and the mute, unthinking beasts. Of course, as a missing link in the Chain of Being, apes could not be human. However, some of these anthropoids were very similar in anatomical structure to human beings, and this raised the inevitable question of whether or not some varieties of ape hitherto thought to be animals, were in fact human. Rousseau, as we have seen, was among the first to suggest that this might indeed be the case.

But while the suggestion that some kinds of ape might be human presupposed a much broader, more flexible notion of species than had been current in the sixteenth and even seventeenth centuries, it did not entail the notion, at least until the late eighteenth century, that there were no fixed boundaries at all between species. The principle of continuity in the Chain of Being did not in otherwords imply evolution in the Darwinian sense of one species evolving from another. But what it did do was divide natural historians and philosophers over the criteria used to demarcate species from one another, as well as to bring into focus the question of what unique features could be said to distinguish the human species from those below it. This is why a reading of Rousseau's position in this debate helps us to grasp his own definition of the human.

The discovery of anatomical similarities between apes and men, especially in respect of their organs of speech and cranial measurement, raised the troublesome issue of whether these two ostensibly very different creatures, were not actually of the same species? For most eighteenth century Europeans, the affirmative answer to this question involved a radical extension of the category human, which is why it was strongly resisted. But what is also important here is the significance of physical characteristics for determining the difference between species. In general terms physical evidence seemed to support the principle of continuity in the Chain of Being; the anatomical similarities between apes and humans being just another example of nature's subtly graduated order. For thinkers like Condillac or La Mettrie, who believed human knowledge was limited to phenomena that had its origins in our sensations of the material world, the physical continuity of ape and man suggested that our definition of the human species could be made broader and more flexible, possibly to include some species of ape. Their view of the human species presupposed an account of human subjectivity, (an epistemology) which had a profound influence upon Rousseau's reconstruction of human evolution.

However, before we consider this influence, we should note that the opposite conclusion was also drawn from the apparent physical similarities between apes and men. There were important natural historians, Tyson and Buffon among them, who believed that the physical similarities between apes and humans proved the qualitative superiority and distinctness of human beings vis à vis all other animal species.[23] Their position also presupposed a particular conception of the human subject that influenced Rousseau.

In the context of the "Ape Debates" then, the significance of physical similarities between apes and humans depended on the antagonists' assumptions regarding the nature of the human subject. The two main positions in respect of this issue stemmed from two different and generally opposed epistemological traditions. The first tradition, of which Condillac and La Mettrie are representative examples, was empiricism.[24] While the second, particularly as it was expounded through the writings of Edward Tyson and le Comte de Buffon, we can refer to as Cartesian essentialism. Each of these epistemological positions provided different criteria for distinguishing the animal from the human, and consequently tended to give rise to different accounts of the relation between apes and men. The disputes about the status of apes in the early to mid-eighteenth century are important for understanding Rousseau, because his conception of what defined the human species, and beyond that his account of our evolution, was formed in relation to the conflicting conceptions of subjectivity informing these debates. I want to claim that much of the originality and importance of Rousseau's philosophical anthropology derived from his critique of these conflicting conceptions of the subject, and his consequent attempts to conceive the self in a way that incorporated what he took to be the insights of both, without falling prey to what he took to be their limitations.

1.4 The Cartesian Position

The publication of two anatomical studies of apes in the late seventeenth century: Perrault's *Memoires pour servir à l'histoire naturelle des animaux* (1676) and Edward Tyson's *Orang-outang, or, the Anatomy of a Pygmy* (1699) established the basis for the debate concerning the relation of apes and humans in the Chain of Being. Both studies indicated that there were striking physical similarities between apes and men, especially, as we noted, in respect of vocal cords and cranial structure. These studies raised two related questions: first, what does this physical similarity tell us, as humans, about our traditionally privileged place in the Chain; and second, if we are so similar physically, how do we explain the obvious differences between ourselves and apes?

Natural historians and philosophers influenced by Descartes' metaphysics, and in particular by his assertion of the innately rational character of human subjectivity, tended to draw similar conclusions from the apparent physical similarities between apes and men. Tyson is a case in point. He concluded, as Robert Wokler has shown, that the physical continuity of apes and men proved that apes could not be human. In Tyson's view, the fact that apes possessed vocal cords and cranial measurements nearly identical to those of humans, and yet lacked any apparent capacity for either speech or reason, strongly suggested that they lacked the fundamental animating principle of human beings, which is to say a rational soul.[25] Tyson's position was not without its difficulties. In particular, the apes' possession of superfluous organs of speech seemed to contradict the principle of continuity in the Chain of Being. On the assumption that the Chain of Being is a continuous hierarchy in which each species is most fully itself, a species possessed of superfluous organs is an embarrassment. Superfluity contradicts the principles of continuity and plenitude. Nonetheless, it seems that Tyson held to a basically Cartesian position. The Cartesian dualism of mind and body, and the presumption that no material construction could produce rationality, enabled Tyson to assert the physical continuity of apes and humans while at the same time asserting the essential distinctness and superiority of humans in virtue of their metaphysical properties. We will find echoes of this dualism in Rousseau's discussion of natural man's relation to animals in the original state of nature.

A rather more influential Cartesian position, especially in respect of Rousseau,[26] was argued by the great French natural historian Buffon. In Buffon's view, the anatomical similarities between apes and men proved only that one could not explain the operations of the human soul by reference to any form of material configuration. The fact of our linguistic competence and our rational nature could only be explained in terms of our spiritual essence.

> L'homme intérieur est double, il est composé de deux principes différends par leur nature, et contraires par leur action. L'âme, un principe spirituel, un principe de toute connaissance, est toujours en opposition avec cet autre principe animal et purement matériel: le calme et la sérénité, une source salutaire dont émanent la science, la raison, la sagesse; l'autre est une fausse lueur qui ne brille que par la tempête et dans l'obscurité, un torrent impétueux qui roule et entrain à sa suite les passions et les erreurs.[27]

Animals on the otherhand, were to be understood according to the Cartesian model, solely in terms of "cet autre principe animal et purement matériel". In otherwords as machines. And while they are relatively complicated machines, possessed of sensations and sentiments, a consciousness of their experience and even some degree of memory, they lack the uniquely human capacity to reflect upon their experience, and to produce ideas in the form of language.[28]

Buffon was not insensitive to the implications of the findings of comparative anatomy for natural history. However, like Tyson, his dualism gave him a way of reconciling the physical continuity between humans and apes with his view that humans were qualitatively different from and superior to all known creatures in the Chain of Being.

> En comparant l'homme avec l'animal, on trouvera dans l'un et dans l'autre un corps, une matière organisée, des sens, de la chair et du sang, du mouvement, et une infinité de choses semblables; mais toutes ces ressemblances sont extérieures, et ne suffisent pas pour nous faire prononcer que la nature de l'homme est

semblable à celle de l'animal.[29]

For Buffon, the difference lies in the fact that human beings are capable of actively associating ideas, which he takes to be the essence of rational thought, and evidence of an eternal soul. As Tyson's study showed, some animals have the physical capacity to speak, yet they are at best capable of mimicry, which gives no evidence of thought and therefore suggests that they lack the animating intelligence of a rational soul.

> [I]l paroit certain qu'ils sont incapables de former cette association d'idées qui seule peut produire la réflexion, dans laquelle cependant consisté l'essence de la pensée: c'est parce qu'ils ne peuvent joindre ensemble aucune idée, qu'ils ne pensent ni ne parlent; c'est par la même raison qu'ils n'inventent et ne perfectionnent rien.[30]

Buffon's influence on Rousseau can also be traced in their respective answers to the question of whether a species is a fixed essence. In Buffon's view, each species is a distinct entity, defined by a unique set of characteristics. He defines it as "une succession constante d'individus semblable et qui se reproduisant".[31] For Buffon, the crucial indication of the fixity of species was the apparent fact that hybrid animals, like mules, were sterile.[32] Fixity meant that each species was endowed with its own unique essence, and this precluded the possibility of one species evolving into another, as well as the notion that mankind was composed of different species of humans. However, it did not deny physical or cultural variation within the human species. In *Histoire naturelle* Buffon discusses this variation in great detail, but he explains human diversity in terms of our degeneration from an ideal/originary type, rather than differential rates of evolution.[33] The influence of climate, of environment, disease and so on were crucial to Buffon's explanation of human variation, but their influence was wholly exterior or superficial as regards the defining characteristics of the species itself.[34]

Rousseau drew on Buffon's conception of species, and through this upon Descartes' conception of the subject. Their most important point of agreement was over the principle of the fixity of species, and its corollary that human beings are defined by a distinct essence. For Buffon, who in this respect followed Descartes more closely than

Rousseau, human essence consisted in an innate capacity for rational thought, which is most clearly evident in our (natural) capacity for language.[35] Rousseau on the otherhand, while accepting the view that humans possess a distinct essence, ascribed that essence to our free will and our faculty of *perfectibilité*.[36] As we shall see in some detail below, for Rousseau neither reason nor language distinguished man from animal in the original state. It was rather our innate potential to acquire these characteristics that distinguished us.

The significance and extent of Buffon's influence on Rousseau in this respect is evident in "Note X" of the ***Discours sur l'inégalité***. The tenth note to the 'Discours' is Rousseau's most extended discussion of the possibility that the orang-outangs might be humans living in their natural condition. His discussion of this issue draws on Buffon's conception of species in two important respects, and goes beyond it in one other. At the beginning of the note Rousseau remarks that he cannot understand why, given the evident diversity of human types, travellers seem have taken *all* creatures resembling humans to be beasts. He suspects it is because they don't look like us and also that they don't use language; but for Rousseau, neither of these characteristics precludes their being human. In fact, he claims, some of them, in particular orang-outangs, may be "... véritables hommes Sauvages, dont la race dispersée anciennement dans les bois n'avoit eu occasion de développer aucune de ses facultés virtuelles, n'avoit acquis aucun degré de perfection, et se trouvoit encore dans l'état primitif de Nature."[37]

Rousseau's rejection of "conformation extérieure" as a reason for denying the humanity of orang-outangs follows Buffon's argument in *De l'homme* that climate, environment, etc., profoundly effect the *physical* appearance of human beings. But since the essence of humanity has to do with the character of our soul rather than physical construction, differences of appearance are simply beside the point in the question of the humanity of apes. However, none of this actually demonstrates that orang-outangs are human. To do this, Rousseau claims, one would have to determine whether the offspring of an orang-outang and a known human were fertile, thus again invoking the authority of Buffon, who as we saw above believed the sterility of hybrids to be proof of the fixity of species.[38]

Where Rousseau departs from Buffon is in his conception of the extent and manner of the human species' cognitive and cultural evolution. In Buffon's discussion of orang-outangs in *Histoire naturelle* the question of their humanity is not raised. The reason for this is that Buffon simply accepted the Cartesian dualism of mind and body, and as we noted above took the presence of speech organs in mute animals as evidence that they lacked rational souls. For Rousseau on the otherhand, the issue is not so straightforward. He did not endorse the Cartesian account of the subject as uncritically as Buffon did, and so did not view the absence of rationality and linguistic competence as a reason for excluding orang-outangs from the human species. To Rousseau their apparent silence and stupidity suggested only that these creatures were at a lower stage in their cognitive and cultural evolution than Europeans. The difference then is that while Rousseau accepted Buffon's account of human diversity in respect of our physical appearance or construction, which is to say in terms of our physical *degeneration* from an original/ideal race of human beings, he did not conceive our cognitive and cultural diversity in the same way. In Rousseau's view, the cognitive and cultural diversity of human beings indicates that the human species is at various different levels on an evolutionary continuum: Europeans at the most advanced end, orang-outangs (perhaps) at the most primitive end. This view can be traced to his basic criticism of Cartesian metaphysics, which is that human beings are not innately rational and therefore not innately capable of using language.

1.5 The Materialist Position

The doctrine of materialism represents the most extreme Enlightenment reaction to the Cartesian project, and in many respects it can be regarded as the most radical epistemological project of the period. The central aspiration of eighteenth-century materialism was to extend the mechanical philosophy to the study of man. It sought to extend the governing metaphor of the new mechanical philosophy, the notion that nature is a material order that must be described in terms of the operation of mechanical laws governing the motion of material bodies, into an account of human subjectivity. In one respect it shared an important article of faith with Descartes' philosophy, which employed the mechanistic model to explain animal and physical phenomena.[39] However, materialism broke fundamentally with the Cartesian project by extending the mechanistic model to man himself, proclaiming him a material entity whose physical and mental activity could only be explained in terms of efficient material causes. It amounted, in otherwords, to an attempt to purge philosophy of metaphysics.

The question of materialism's influence on Rousseau is a complex one. In the main, it must be said that its significance for Rousseau was largely negative, which is to say that Rousseau found it impossible to accept the materialist implication that nature and freedom were incompatible, and so sought to establish a conception of the subject independent of materialism. However, it must also be said that certain aspects of materialism, in particular its attempt to recast the problem of human nature in an anthropological form, certainly did influence Rousseau's thinking. The assumption that human consciousness and behaviour are directly attributable to material causes made it difficult to provide an account of free agency . Nevertheless, it opened the way to a developmental or evolutionary conception of our subjectivity, which could account for the influence of material and social factors upon human nature in a way that the Cartesian conception of subjectivity could not.

La Mettrie's *L'Homme machine* (1749) was an early attempt to extend Descartes' notion of animal machine into a full-blown materialist epistemology. The essay is an elaboration of one basic idea, that man is material entity explicable in terms of mechanical causation. For La Mettrie, there is no mental activity, and hence no human characteristic, independent of human physiology. This follows from the fundamental materialist tenet: that physiology determines mental states; or as La Mettrie puts it: "Les divers états de l'ame sont donc toujours corrélatifs à ceux du corps"[40] What makes this claim radical in the context of the eighteenth century is not merely the assertion that the body influences the mind. It is rather that there is no real distinction to be made between them.[41] Mental states are physical states, and this in turn validates the idea *man-machine* as a comprehensive framework for conceiving the human subject.

One way La Mettrie sought to demonstrate the causal relation between the physical and the mental by means of comparative anatomy.[42] In **L'homme machine** he argued that the significance of the relation between the size of the brain (relative to body mass) and the sophistication of psychological and cognitive processes is the same for man and animal. The larger the brain relative to body mass, the greater the sophistication. Man has the largest brain, and hence the greatest cognitive and social sophistication. He is followed closely by the ape, the beaver, the elephant, the dog and so on. This relation was also held to be true of different species. Thus the order of animal species begins with humanity in the highest position, followed by quadrupeds, birds, fish, and insects; the size the brain decreasing in proportion to the body weight as we descend the scale.[43] In La Mettrie's view, this correspondence is far too comprehensive to be explained as mere coincidence, and hence validates the assumed causal relation between the physical and the mental.

The materialist discourse had important implications for eighteenth century philosophical anthropology, because it relativized the conception of species. The assertion that the only criteria relevant for distinguishing between species were physical, implied that the boundaries between them were more open and flexible, and of course flew directly in the face of the Cartesian claim that humans were absolutely distinct from other species in virtue of their rational souls. Hence La Mettrie's famous claim: "Des animaux à l'homme, la transition n'est pas violente..."[44]

Perhaps the most important implication of this conception of man is that his nature must be understood in developmental terms, which is to say, as having evolved as a consequence of his body's interaction with its physical and social environment. The idea that man, like any animal, is a machine whose specific behavioral characteristics stem from his physiological make-up, necessitates an explanation of why, when his physical characteristics are in some cases nearly identical to certain animals, he seems to behave in such a radically different manner. To put this more succinctly, and recall our original point of departure, why are apes incapable of speech when our anatomies are so similar? The materialist answer to this is that language, like any other faculty related to consciousness, must be explained in terms of the species' experience of its environment. This involves reference to observable phenomena. First, that humans have a physiological structure which enables them to speak (vocal cords, brain size, etc.); and second, that their environment facilitates the development of language. The first is a necessary condition of speech, the second involves a process in which our neuro-physiology responds to our environment in a certain way. Both can be verified empirically, at least in principle, and hence conform to the foundational assumption that all human activity is the consequence of causal relations between material phenomena.

The assumption that human nature is the product of human experience poses a problem of origins, which is to say that it raises the question of what we are like prior to experience, and what sort of experience has caused us to develop as we have. The origins of language or rationality, of morality or society, all came to relevant problems on the materialist view, because it had ceased to be plausible that these phenomena were given us by God, or that they stemmed from some innate and unique capacity. La Mettrie was not himself particularly concerned to offer an account of this development, nor to describe the original nature of man. He simply assumed on the basis of comparative anatomy that originally, we were very like apes.[45] That there are now substantial differences between human and ape behaviour, is due to the different environments in which we have lived. The linguistic competence of humans results from their development in a social milieu, while the silence of apes is the consequence of their isolation in the forests. Thus the linguistic gulf between animals and humans which prompted the Cartesians to assert our substantial intellectual and moral superiority, is explained away in terms of different environments. This is well illustrated by La Mettrie's famous assertion that it must be possible to train an ape to speak, and so to make him a human being.[46]

Rousseau's debt to materialism is, as we noted above, a complicated one. As an extreme statement of the empiricist conviction that the human self is constituted by its sensory experience of a material world, it highlights both Rousseau's debt to the empiricist project and his strongest objections to it. His debt was to the general materialist approach of inquiry into the genealogy of human nature, which is to say, the view that the human subject could not be adequately understood in terms of innate, unchanging characteristics, and therefore had to be understood (at least partly) in terms of the contingent effects of its environment.

However, as we shall see below, materialists were not alone in asserting the need to understand human beings in terms of their evolution, nor indeed did Rousseau believe they provided the most coherent framework through which to investigate this evolution. There were two problems in the materialist paradigm that Rousseau's own philosophical anthropology was meant to solve. The first we alluded to above: the apparent implication that nature and freedom are incompatible. *L'homme machine* is wholly integrated into the natural world, but as such he is the product of the contingent relations between material bodies: in any given instance just one more phenomena in an infinitely complex and ultimately meaningless chain of cause and effect. This, as Rousseau points out in the *Discours sur l'inégalité*, cannot account for human agency: "car la Physique explique en quelque manière le mécanisme des sens et la formation des idées; mais dans la puissance de vouloir ou plutôt de choisir, et dans le sentiment de cette puissance on ne trouve que des actes purement spirituels, dont on n'explique rien par les Loix de la Mécanique."[47] A second problem Rousseau had with the materialist paradigm was its inability to explain the origins of language and society wholly in terms of the species experience of a material environment. The materialist could not, in Rousseau's view, offer an adequate explanation of why, given our common origin and nearly identical physiology, we should have developed language and society and apes should not. La Mettrie's assertion that we can explain this in terms of the apes' lack of social experience, or education, and thus that there are no reasons why apes cannot be taught to speak, is inadequate for Rousseau. In an apparent reference to La Mettrie in the *Essai sur l'origine des langues* Rousseau writes: "La langue de convention n'appartient qu'à l'homme. Voila pourquoi l'homme fait des progrès soit en bien soit en mal, et pourquoi les animaux n'en font point. Cette seule distinction paroit mener loin: on l'explique, dit-on, par la différence des organes. Je serois curieux de voir cette explication."[48] As the most extreme variant of the empiricist project, materialism exposed the limitations of empiricism itself. And while Rousseau found the less radical empiricism of Condillac more amenable, in the end he found it necessary to distance himself from it for substantially similar reasons.

1.6 Lockean Sensationalism

The influence of John Locke's philosophy on the French Enlightenment is well documented,[49] and Rousseau did not prove himself exceptional among his contemporaries by escaping this influence. However, the influence of Locke's epistemology on Rousseau's thought occurred largely because of Rousseau's knowledge of Locke's greatest French disciple, the Abbé de Condillac. Condillac's *Essai sur l'origine des connoissances humaines* (1746) was a systematic attempt to elaborate Locke's notion that all knowledge derives from our sensory experience. The work was in this respect both a supplement and a corrective to Locke's *An Essay Concerning Human Understanding*: a supplement in the sense that it tries to trace the human mind's acquisition of its distinctive faculties from their origin in sensation; and a corrective in that it attempts to purge Locke's epistemology of all ambiguity regarding the mind's innate powers to convert sensations into active thought. Condillac wanted to show that the mind needs no innate powers to acquire the capacity for the "higher", active faculties such as reflection and judgement.[50] The difficulty was of course how to explain the human mind's capacity to accomplish activities that are not obviously grounded in our sense perceptions, and yet nevertheless characteristic of normal human experience.

Condillac's importance for Rousseau is related to this issue. Condillac's conception of the subject demonstrated the necessity, and difficulty, of explaining the origin of language in human cognition. If, as Condillac claimed, all human knowledge can be traced to its origins in sensory experience, then some account of the origin of language was necessary. Language, as much for the sensationalists as for the Cartesians, was the *sine qua non* of those faculties that distinguish the human from the animal mind. Reflection, judgement, and imagination all distinguish us from animals, but none is possible without language. Yet because they reject the proposition that language is an innate human faculty, the sensationalists must explain how language arises in the human mind prior to its capacity to reflect or make abstract judgements. In this respect a solution to the problem of the origin of language represents a solution to the problem of how the mind's higher order operations can be acquired from the experience of sensations. Condillac, for his part, recognized this "... je suis convaincu que l'usage des signes est le principe qui développe le germe de toutes nos idées"[51], and he devoted the second half the his *Essai* to solving the problem.

From Rousseau's standpoint, the sensationalist account of the evolution of human cognition, and in particular their account of the origin of language, was extremely important. Like the sensationalists, Rousseau wanted to conceive human consciousness in developmental terms, as having evolved through its interactions with its environment. But more specifically, Rousseau did not think language could have been a natural human faculty, for to do so would have been to suppose that human beings were naturally social, and "... commettre la faute de ceux qui raisonnant sur l'État de Nature, y transportent les idées prises dans la Société..."[52] In fact, Condillac himself does not escape this charge, despite being given credit for making a substantial contribution to understanding the problem.

> Je pourrois me contenter de citer ou de repeter ici les recherches que Mr. l'Abbé de Condillac a faites sur cette matiére [the origin of languages]... Mais la maniére dont ce Philosophe résout les difficultés qu'il se fait à lui-même sur l'origine des signes institués, montrant qu'il a supposé ce que je mets en question, savoir une

sorte de société déjà établie entre les inventeurs du langage...⁵³

This highlights Rousseau's rather ambiguous indebtedness to the sensationalist project. On the one hand it directly addressed a number of the problems raised by his evolutionary account of the human species, including the problem of language origin; yet on the other it did so, on his view, in a largely unsatisfactory way. Rousseau's attempt to come to terms with what he perceived to be the limitations of sensationalism for his philosophical anthropology, provide us with a way of understanding the conception of subjectivity underlying his account of the species' evolution from nature to culture.

In the *Essai sur l'origine des connoissances humaines* Condillac traces the mind's development from its initial sensory experience to abstract reasoning which is not itself reducible to any sensation. The point of this, as we have seen, was to eliminate any vestiges of Cartesian dualism from the sensationalist project, by demonstrating the origins of all knowledge in sensation. Condillac identifies a number of stages through which consciousness passes, from simple sensation to abstract rationality. The most rudimentary level of consciousness is simple sense impressions, which constitute the mind's most basic experience and the source of all knowledge. At this level the mind is merely conscious of sensations occurring.⁵⁴ A more sophisticated level of consciousness occurs with the involuntary formation of *attention*, which Condillac defines as our greater awareness of some perceptions of objects over others. We focus our attention because some of the objects we perceive bear a more immediate relation to our well-being than others.⁵⁵ Because attention makes us aware of (at least some) of our perceptions, when these perceptions are repeated, we also become aware that they belong to us, that they are the perceptions of a self that exists over time. Condillac refers to this self-consciousness as reminiscence (réminiscence).⁵⁶ It is important to note here that unlike Descartes or his followers, Condillac finds the origins of self-consciousness in sensation - we have no intuitive awareness of the self as a unified subject that exists over time.

The first three stages of the mind's development occur, as it were, passively. The mind involuntarily acquires the consciousness it has of itself as a sense-perceiving subject, solely because it experiences sensations and possesses needs as a biological being. In Condillac's view, this is the level of animal consciousness.[57] In the next four chapters of the *Essai*, Condillac discusses the mind's acquisition of the faculties which allow it to direct its own mental processes: its attention, its memory, and most importantly its capacity for reflection. What becomes clear in this discussion is that the acquisition of language is the key to the mind's capacity for active thought. Language, which Condillac defines as the ability "à attacher des idées à des signes qu'il a lui-même choisis", gives us the ability to control and manipulate the faculties of memory, imagination, and contemplation[58]. These in turn make possible the development of the higher order mental processes associated with reflection: abstraction, comparison, and judgement.

In Condillac's view, language is a condition of our capacity to direct our own thought about the world, because the use of signs frees our consciousness from determination by our sensations. Without signs which can stand for our ideas, our attention is dominated by whatever object strikes it most forcefully, and our memory depends upon actual perceptions in order to recall past experiences. We cannot therefore voluntarily associate ideas with one another, which is to say, for Condillac, that we cannot reflect upon our experience. The substitution of signs for ideas allows us to recall ideas at will from our memory, or to isolate one idea in our attention so that we might concentrate upon it, analyze it, or combine it with others to construct a more complex idea. Language gives us control over our minds' experience. For Condillac then, the acquisition of language is absolutely crucial to the full development of our cognitive powers as human beings. Yet this very importance was itself problematic, in the sense that it is not clear how we might come to acquire the ability to substitute arbitrary signs for ideas, unless we had already some capacity for reason, which would seem, in turn, to presuppose some kind of language.

> ... Combien, par exemple, n'a-t-il pas fallu de réflexions pour former les langues, et de quel secours ces langues ne sont-elles pas à la réflexion! ...
> Il semble qu'on ne sauroit se servir des signes d'institution, si l'on n'étoit pas

Speaking Apes 39

déjà capable d'assez de réflexion pour les choisir et pour y attacher des idées: comment donc, m'objectera-t-on peut-être, l'exercice de la réflexion ne s'acquerroit-il que par l'usage de ces signes?"[59]

1.7 Conclusion

This question became the central problem in Rousseau's theory of language, and a problem of considerable importance for his philosophical anthropology as a whole. An inquiry into the origins of our social institutions (including inequality), entailed for Rousseau an inquiry into the origins of language. Language was the precondition of our species' capacity to live together socially. Without it, no notion of the social is conceiveable. But the problem of the origin of language is also important for Rousseau because, like the other philosophes of the mid-eighteenth century, he saw in its origin the key which had unlocked the human species' distinctive and unlimited potential for evolution.

Rousseau's answer to the problem of language origin drew upon both the Cartesian and sensationalist accounts of subjectivity. The significance of this is not that he provides a better answer to the problem than any of his contemporaries, nor even that his answer is interesting in and of itself, but rather that his attempt to solve this problem tells us a great deal about the conception of self underlying his philosophical anthropology and the moral theory he derives from it. Rousseau's preoccupation with language origin derives directly from the influence of Condillac's epistemology. But his attention to the problem led him to express some dissatisfaction with Condillac's solution to the problem. In the end, I shall argue, Rousseau invokes an number of essentially Cartesian assumptions to overcome what he took to be the limitations of the sensationalist account of the origin of language, and that his solution left him with an account of the self which had profound implications for his moral theory.

Endnotes

1. O.C. III, p. 122.

2. Ernst Cassirer, *The Question of Jean-Jacques Rousseau*, Peter Gay trans., (Bloomington: Indiana University Press, 1967), pp. 74-75.

3. O.C. III, p. 123.

4. Jean Starobinski, *La transparence et l'obstacle*, (Paris: Editions Gallimard, 1971), p. 361.

5. Jean Starobinski, "Introduction" in O.C. III, pp. LIII.-LIV.

6. It should be noted that this question is only problematic for those who could not have known, or do not accept, accounts of evolution basied on Darwin's *Origin of the Species*. Rousseau obviously falls into the former category. I will demonstrate below that although Rousseau did think of the human species as having evolved significantly over time, he did not think we had evolved from a non-human species into a human one. He retained a notion of the species as a fixed essence.

    This also helps to explain why force of circumstance alone cannot explain the unique evolution of the human species. In Rousseau's view environmental change was a necessary but not sufficient condition of our evolution from nature to culture. The same environmental changes could not produce a similarly dramatic evolution in animals, because they lack the requisite characteristics, free will and *perfectibilité*, necessary for this to occur.

7. O.C. III, p. 213-14.

8. O.C. III, p. 208.

9. Jean-Jacques Rousseau, *Essai sur l'origine des langues*, Charles Porset, ed., (Paris: A.G. Nizet, 1970), p. 89. (Hereafter cited as E.O.L.)

10. *Ibid.*, p. 87.

11. Claude Levi-Strauss, *Le Totémisme aujourd'hui*, (Paris: Presses Universitaires de France, 1965), p. 142.

12. Arthur O. Lovejoy, *The Great Chain of Being: A Study of the History of an Idea*, (Baltimore: The Johns Hopkins University Press, 1936), pp. 183-86.

13. *Ibid.*, pp. 185.

14. *Ibid.*, pp. 186-87. Lovejoy quotes Francis Bacon, not otherwise known for his committment to medieval cosmology, to the effect:

    Man, if we look to final causes, may be regarded as the centre of the world; insomuch that if man were taken away from the world, the rest would seem to be all astray, without aim or purpose, ... For the whole world works together in the service of man; and there is nothing from which he does not derive use and fruit... insomuch that all things seem to be going about man's business and not their own.

15. Rene Descartes, *The Principles of Philosophy*, in **The Philosophical Works of Descartes**, Elizabeth Haldane and G.T.R. Ross trans., (Cambridge: Cambridge University Press, 1931), p. 271.

16. Lovejoy, *Chain of Being*, p. 193-94.

17. Gottfried Wilhelm von Leibniz, **Monadology and Other Philosophical Essays**, trans. by Paul and Anne Martin Schrecker, (Indianapolis: Bobbs-Merrill, 1981), p. 86.

18. John Locke, *An Essay Concerning Human Understanding*, edited by Peter Nidditch, (Oxford: Clarendon Press, 1975), III, Chapter vi, §12.

19. Leibniz quoted in Lovejoy, *Chain of Being*, p. 145.

20. *Ibid.*, p. 195.

21. John Locke, **An Essay Concerning Human Understanding**, Bk.III. Chapter III, §15,16,17,18. It should be noted that Locke and Leibniz differed greatly over the limits of human knowledge. For Leibniz, essence could be known, his "Monadology" being an assertion of the principle that everything could be reduced to a "simple essence". The principle of continuity was nonetheless strengthened by scientific inquiry which rested on nominalist or empiricist foundations. The study of the physical properties of plants and animals supported the supposition of continuity in the Chain. The more natural history and biology progressed, the subtly graduated the Chain became.

22. Lovejoy, *Chain of Being*, pp. 233-35.

23. Robert Wokler, "Tyson and Buffon on the orang-utan," in **Studies on Voltaire and the Eighteenth Century**, 1976, pp. 2314-2316.

24. I use the term "empiricism" to refer to a range of epistemological positions, including La Mettrie's materialism and the more Lockean sensationalism of Condillac. What distinguishes these doctrines from the Cartesian positions with which I contrast them, is their rejection of the notion of innate ideas, and, with the exception of Locke, innate mental powers.

25. Edward Tyson, *Orang-outang, sive Homo Sylvestris, or the Anatomy of a Pygmie*, edited by Ashley Montague, (London: Dawsons of Pall Mall, 1966), pp. 55; see also Wokler, "Tyson and Buffon", pp. 2301-2319.

26. Jean Morel, "Récherches sur les sources du *Discours sur l'inégalité*" in *Annales de la Société J.J. Rousseau*, 1909, vol. 5, p. 179. Also Otis Fellows, "Buffon and Rousseau: Aspects of a Relationship" in *Proceedings from the Modern Languages Association*, June, 1960, pp. 184-96.

27. G.-L. L. comte de Buffon, *Histoire naturelle* in *Oeuvres philosophiques de Buffon*, edited by Jean Priveteau, (Paris: Presses Univeristaires de France, 1954), pp. 337B-338A.

28. *Ibid.*, pp. 327B-329B.

29. G.-L. L. comte de Buffon, *De l'homme*, (Paris: Francois Maspero, 1871), p. 44.

30. *Ibid.*, p. 45. Compare this passage with Rousseau in the *Discours sur l'inégalité*, where he claims that because it lacks the faculty of self-improvement "... un animal est, au bout de quelques mois, ce qu'il sera toute sa vie, et son espèce, au bout de mille ans, ce qu'elle étoit la première année de ces mille ans." (O.C. III, p. 142.)

31. Buffon, *Histoire naturelle*, pp. 356.

32. *Ibid.*, pp. 356A.

33. Buffon, *De l'homme*, pp. 320.

Tout concourt donc à prouver que le genre humain n'est pas composé d'espèces essentiellement différentes entre elles; qu'au contraire il n'y a eu originairement qu'une seule espèce d'hommes, qui, s'étant multipliée et répandue sur toute la surface de la terre, à subi différents changements par l'influence du climat, par la différence de la nourriture, par celle de la manière de vivre, par les maladies épidémiques, et aussi par le mélange varie à l'infini des individus plus ou moins ressemblants...

34. Buffon, *Histoire naturelle*, pp. 356B.

35. As we noted above, Descartes thought of animals as machines, which is to say as material beings incapable of rational thought. Humans on the otherhand have material bodies, but their bodies are animated by an innate soul capable of rational thought, language, and moral self-direction. The rational, or at least "thinking" nature of the self is the product of Descartes' methodology of radical doubt. Simply put, we can doubt everything except that we are doubting.

For Descartes language is crucial to the distinction between the human and the animal, because language is the medium through which thinking beings make their thoughts known to other thinking beings. In otherwords language presupposes what Descartes regarded as the definitive attribute of human beings. Descartes admitted that any animal with vocal cords could be trained to mimic speech, however he denied that any animal could speak human language. His denial was based on the view that human language was grounded in the ability to construct an infinite variety of sentences appropriate to an infinite variety of situations, and because of this must derive from a capacity that we have independent of our sense experience. Thus for Descartes, language was evidence of the unbounded nature of the human mind, and the essential difference between the animal and the human. In a letter to Henry More (1647) Descartes writes:

> [I]t has never yet been observed that any animal has arrived at such a degree of perfection as to make use of a true language... for the word is the sole sign and the only certain mark of the presence of thought hidden and wrapped up in the body; now all men, the most stupid and the most foolish, those even who are deprived of the organs of speech, make use of signs, whereas the brutes never do anything of the kind; which may be taken for the true distinction between man and brute. {Quoted in Naom Chomsky, *Cartesian Linguistics*, (New York: Harper & Row, 1966), p. 6.}

36. Rousseau, *Discours sur l'inégalité*, pp. 141-42.

37. O.C. III, p. 208-09.

38. *Ibid.*, p. 211. See also Buffon's chapter entitled "L'Ane" in *Histoire naturelle*.

39. Thomas L. Hankins, *Science and the Enlightenment*, (Cambridge: Cambridge University Press, 1985), p. 114-15.

Descartes had concluded in 1638 that with the exception of the human rational soul all natural objects were caused by inert particles of matter in motion. There was, for him, no basic difference between one's watch and one's pet dog.

40. Julien Offray de La Mettrie, *L'Homme machine*, edited by A. Vartanian, (Princeton: Princeton University Press, 1960), p. 158.

41. Ernst Cassirer, *The Philosophy of Enlightenment*, trans. Fritz C.A. Koelln and James P. Pettegrove, (Boston: Beacon Press, 1965), pp. 67-68.

42. Ann Thomson, *Materialism and Society in the Mid-eighteenth Century: La Mettrie's "Discours Préliminaire"*, (Genève-Paris: Libairie Droz, 1981), p. 41.

43. La Mettrie, *L'Homme machine*, p. 158.

44. *Ibid.*, p. 162.

45. *Ibid.*, p. 162.

> Qu'était l'homme, avant l'invention des mots et la connaissance des langues? Un animal de son espèce, qui avec beaucoup moins d'instinct naturel, que les autres, dont alors il ne se croioit pas Roi, n'était distingué du Singe et des autres animaux, que comme le singe l'est lui-même...

46. *Ibid.*, p. 160.

> mais la similitude de la structure et des opérations du singe est telle, que je ne doute presque point, si on exerçait parfaitement cet animal, qu'on ne vînt enfin à bout de lui apprendre à prononcer, et par conséquent à savoir une langue. Alors ce ne serait plus ni un homme sauvage, ni un homme manqué: ce serait un home parfait, un petit homme de ville, avec autant d'étoffe ou de muscles que nous-mêmes, pour penser et profiter de son éducation.

47. O.C. III., p. 142.

48. Rousseau, E.O.L., pp. 38-39.

49. The most notable recent account of this influence is Hans Aarsleff's, *From Locke to Saussure*, Princeton University Press, 1981, particularly pp. 101-120 and 146-210. See also, John Yolton, *John Locke and the Way of Ideas*, Oxford University Press, 1956, and Ernst Cassirer, *The Philosophy of Enlightenment*, notably chapter III.

50. Condillac, *Essai sur l'origine des connoissances humaines*, in *Oeuvres Philosophiques de Condillac*, edited by Georges Le Roy, (Paris: Press Universitaires de France, 1947) vol. I, p. 5. Condillac is critical of Locke because he simply assumes the powers necessary to explain how the mind converts the *data* of sensation into thought. "Il suppose, par exemple, qu'aussi-tôt que l'ame reçoit des idées par les

sens, elle peut, à son gré, les répéter, les composer, les unir ensemble avec une variété infinie, et en faire toutes sortes de notions complexes." Condillac believed he could show how the mind acquires these powers.

For Condillac the offending passages in Locke seem to be particularly *Essay* Bk.II. vii, §1,2, and Bk.III. vii. & ix. We might also consider Locke's statement in Bk.II. i, §4: "... the other fountain from which experience furnisheth the understanding with ideas is, -the perception of the operations of our own minds within us, as it is employed about the ideas it has got; - which operations, when the soul comes to reflect on and consider, do furnish the understanding with another set of ideas, which could not be had from without. And such are *perception, thinking doubting, believing, reasoning, knowing, willing,* and all the different actings of our own minds... This source of ideas every man has wholly in himself; and though it be not sense, as having nothing to do with external objects, yet it is very like it, and might properly enough be called *internal sense.*" This passage implies that the mind has powers or faculties internal to itself, which we can reflect upon (sense?) in order to create new ideas. For Condillac, awareness of one's innate cognitive powers carried more than a trivial trace of Descartes *Cogito*. He believed he could demonstrate how these powers were acquired in sensation.

51. *Ibid.*, p. 5.

52. O.C. III, p. 146.

53. *Ibid.*, p. 146.

54. Condillac, *Essai*, I. II.i. § 1, 2, 13.

55. *Ibid.*, §5,14,15.

56. *Ibid.*, §15.

57. *Ibid.*, §43.

58. *Ibid.*, §46.

59. *Ibid.*, I. II. v. §49.

2

The Problem of Language Origin

2.1 Introduction

Thus far I have argued that the importance of language in eighteenth-century intellectual life derived from the commonly held assumption that our possession of it helped to explain our unique characteristics as a species. Debate centred on the question of why, or in virtue of what we possess language; but there was little disagreement, among those who cared about such things, as to its tremendous significance for human consciousness and particularly for human knowledge. By the mid-eighteenth century, the identification of language, rationality and humanity had become commonplace to the extent that an inquiry into the origins of one entailed an inquiry into to the origins of the others. The philosophers, the anthropologists, and the natural historians of the Enlightenment saw language as the key to understanding the peculiar power and progress of the human mind.

That they should have done so was at least partly the consequence of a shift in the way European intellectuals understood the relation between language and knowledge, which occurred in the seventeenth and eighteenth centuries. At a general level, this shift involved a gradual abandoning of the pre-modern view of language as a something which

The Problem of Language Origin

bore a semblance or affinity to the world it described, for the view that language was a conventional tool or medium for representing the world.

The relation between language and knowledge is a crucial part of this shift. On the pre-modern view, knowing was in the most general sense about the discovery of a hierarchy of being already established by God. The universe was understood as a rational and harmonious cosmos, an order imbued with meaning because it was grounded in the will of a Divine Creator. Objects of knowledge were understood in relation to this order. The different elements of creation each had a place in the order of being in virtue of having been placed there by an omniscient and omnipotent God, and because of this were thought to embody or express a pre-established order of meanings.[1] On this view, the world could be understood as a text that required interpretation; and the acquisition of knowledge as the discovery and subsequent interpretation of already existing truths.

However, in the course of the scientific revolution, the world began to be described in terms of different metaphors, the most pervasive being the mechanical metaphor, the world as machine. As a machine, the world is composed of material objects, related to each other through contingent relations of cause and effect. The metaphor of world as machine, at least in its non-Deist forms, precluded knowledge of a Final Cause, and with it the view that relations between things in nature are imbued with Divine meaning. This is not of course to suggest that many people came to believe that God had no purposes for them or the world they lived in, nor that these purposes had no significance for their lives. However, the claim was increasingly made that God's purposes, and the meanings these might confer upon either human life or natural events, were beyond the scope of human knowledge. Cut adrift from the divine plan, the human mind was left to itself to determine its own meanings. Science, as the modern method of knowing par excellence, imposes its own order upon the natural world by gradually mapping out relations of cause and effect between discreet material entities. It imposes its own order upon nature, an order which is by definition conventional and open to revision. As such it cannot explain the essence of things, nor provide us with a framework for understanding the meaning and purpose of our own lives.

The shift from viewing knowledge as the discovery of a pre-established ontological order to the active imposition of a nomological order, is reflected in the view of language characteristic of each period. In the early modern period, language derived its meaning and significance from the relation it bore to the order of being. This relation can be understood in terms of the resemblance of affinity a sign bore to the hierarchy in which it was grounded. Signs were understood to have been placed on things by God, so that men could discover the hidden meaning that they embodied. The task of knowledge was thus to discover the resemblance of signs to a pre-established hierarchy of being; and the point to be emphasized is that signs were in no way constituted by the activity of knowing itself. It did not matter that they were unknown or undiscovered, for they were nevertheless present, waiting to be discovered. This is why the metaphor of the world as text is apposite to descriptions of the pre-modern conception of the relation between language and knowledge. For the pre-moderns knowledge presupposed a language prior to itself, a language invented and written by God into the fabric of creation, and thus grounded in this omniscience. The acquisition of knowledge involved learning a language of essences which revealed the truth because of its origin in the mind of God.[2]

The Enlightenment conception of the relation between language and reason moves decisively away from the pre-modern preoccupation with the discovery of affinity or resemblance. By the eighteenth century language had come to be understood as a means of representing the world, its function as representation established through the act of knowing. Another way of putting this is that signs ceased to be thought of as bearing a direct and divinely grounded resemblance to an already established order of meanings; rather, the sign came to be taken to represent our perception of a thing, and therefore constituted only insofar as we are engaged in the conscious experience of perceiving or knowing. Knowledge on the Enlightenment view is grounded in the relation of the sign to the signified. We come to understand the world by mapping out the connections between our distinct impressions. These impressions are represented and related to each other by means of a system of signs that is established and maintained by conventional agreement. Locke, whose epistemology had an important influence upon eighteenth century theories of language, expressed the new relations between words and things in this way.

> Thus we may conceive how words, which were by nature so well adapted to this purpose (i.e. communication), come to be made use of by Man, as Signs of their Ideas; not by natural connexion, that there is between particular articulate Sounds and certain Ideas, for then there would be but one Language amongst Men, but by voluntary Imposition, wherebye such a Word is made arbitrarily to the Mark of such an Idea. The use then of Words, is to be sensible Marks of Ideas; and the Ideas they stand for, as their proper and Immediate Signification.[3]

Locke's conception of language is typical of the Enlightenment because it regards words (signs) as the voluntary and conventional significations of ideas. The voluntary act of signification enables the subject to establish relations between the ideas he receives in perception, and thus to actively impose order upon his own experience. The act of signification is in this sense a process through which the agent exerts control over the contents of his consciousness. This is Condillac's point when he claims that language is the key to the mind's acquisition of its higher faculties. Prior to the invention of language the mind is aware of itself as a as the subject of sensory experience, but it is incapable of directing its own attention, of associating simple ideas into complex ones, of reflecting upon its own operation. With the acquisition of language, the subject becomes active in his thought: intentional, voluntary, and reflective. This is why language, for the philosophes of the Enlightenment, was the *sine qua non* of human progress, and thus why the explanation of its origin was so crucial.

2.2 Rousseau and Condillac on the Origin of Language

We have already noted that Rousseau was much impressed by Condillac's writings on the problem of language origin, but also that he believed Condillac's treatment of the problem begged a question of fundamental importance, which is how the rudimentary level of social relations necessary to explain the invention of language would have got going in the first place.[4] The problem here is a difficult one, because Rousseau shared with Condillac the Lockean view of language as a conventional code for representing the world. But as a convention, it must have, at some point, been agreed upon by its users, and this, as Rousseau says, is tantamount to asserting "... que la parole paroît avoir été fort nécessaire, pour établir l'usage de la parole."[5] Thus while Rousseau shared the standard Enlightenment view of language as a method of representing the world, and its corollary that language is a necessary condition of the development and progress of the human mind, he was less sanguine than his contemporaries about the prospect of explaining its actual origins.[6] Nevertheless, Rousseau believed the acquisition of language to be a crucial juncture in the species' history. It freed human consciousness from its effective determination by nature for the reasons Condillac had indicated. In the process it drew human beings into vastly more complicated relations with one another, and expedited the development of our rationality and our knowledge. Thus despite identifying the paradoxical nature of the problem of language origin, Rousseau could not escape the necessity of solving it.

In Rousseau's account of the species' evolution then, the greatest obstacle to our evolution from nature to society is the acquisition of language. On Rousseau's view, language could not have been a natural faculty, for if it were the distinction between natural and social man would be unsustainable. Language is a conventional, and therefore social institution; we cannot use it unless we are already engaged in social relations, and so in possessing it natural man would already be social. This, it should be noted, indicates

The Problem of Language Origin 51

an important difference between Rousseau and Condillac. For the latter, language had to have been acquired because otherwise it was evidence of the mind's innate rationality. For Rousseau, the assertion that humans were naturally asocial entailed an account of how they acquired language. In any case, if language is not natural, some account of its pre-history needs to be given to explain how it arose, as much for Condillac as for Rousseau. We need to know what developments made it possible for human beings to acquire their linguistic competence. It is in respect of these pre-histories that we can see most clearly the differences between them, and hence the extent to which Rousseau's account of our subjectivity departs from the sensationalist model.

Whereas Condillac's account of the subject's cognitive development prior to the acquisition of language relies wholly upon the mind's experience of sensation, and thus upon the self's experience of its environment, Rousseau's hinges on the species' innate faculty of *perfectibilité*. Rousseau did not accept the proposition that the origin of language could be explained wholly in terms of sensory experience, because his account of natural man depended upon natural man's full and stable integration into his environment. In this account there is nothing in natural man's environment or his way of life which could precipitate his development beyond the primitive condition, and consequently there can be nothing in either that would enable him to acquire language.[7] If human beings are naturally asocial, language cannot be the inevitable outcome of their natural experience.

Yet, as we shall see, this is precisely what Condillac's account of the origin of language implies. The internal logic of Rousseau's conception of natural man on the other hand demanded that he show how the species could have progressed both cognitively and socially to the level at which the acquisition of language was possible, while at the same time preserving its natural innocence. Furthermore, he needed to explain why this pre-linguistic development occurs at all, for if natural man is wholly integrated into the natural order, needing nothing beyond his own strength to satisfy his needs, it is not immediately evident why he would make even the smallest progress towards the intellectual sophistication necessary for the invention of language. Rousseau's solution to this problem hinges on his assertion that human beings are defined by an innate faculty of *perfectibilité*, a faculty of self-improvement.[8]

In the *Discours sur l'inégalité* Rousseau describes natural man's existence as independent and self-sufficient. Nature provides for the satisfaction of all his needs, which, with the exception of sexual desire, are anyway limited to those immediately relevant to his self-preservation.[9] As such, they could only have served as an obstacle to the invention of language, for as Rousseau notes in his *Essai sur l'origine des langues*:

> On prétend que les hommes inventèrent la parole pour exprimer leurs besoins; cette opinion me paroit insoutenable. L'effet naturel des prémiers besoins fut d'écarter les hommes et non de les rapprocher.[10]

If, further to this, we consider the extent to which language is a condition of any degree of social life, we are faced with the paradox to which we have already alluded. In Rousseau's words, how to determine "lequel à été le plus nécessaire, de la Société déjà liée, à l'institution des Langues, ou des Langues déjà inventée, à l'établissement de la Société".[11]

The second problem Rousseau identified with respect to the problem of explaining language origin also spoke directly to the limitations he found in Condillac's sensationalist epistemology. This stems from the apparent interdependence of language and reason in the species' evolution. The difficulty is that each seems to presuppose the other. For as Rousseau points out: "car si les hommes on eu besoin de la parole pur apprendre à penser; ils ont en bien plus besoin encore de savoir penser pour trouver l'art de la parole."[12] This remark identifies what is perhaps the fundamental problem in the empiricist account of how humans acquire language, and it marks Rousseau's point of departure from the sensationalist conception of the subject.

The primary problem on the empiricist account of the subject's development was to explain its transformation from a passive, sense determined consciousness to an active self-reflective one, capable of voluntarily associating and manipulating the ideas it receives in perception. It is language, as we have seen, that completes this transformation, hence

The Problem of Language Origin 53

the necessity of explaining its origin. Condillac's account of the origin of language in the second part of the *Essai sur l'origine des connoissances humaines* betrays the problem to which Rousseau alludes. On Condillac's view the pre-linguistic consciousness is dominated by the subject's involuntary association of the feelings arising from his needs, for example hunger or fear, with the sensations he has of the objects which satisfy them. Repeated experience of these associations establishes the subject's attention, and enables it to recognize itself as the subject of an ordered experience. However, at this stage consciousness and behaviour remain instinctual, determined in every case by needs or the sensations that give rise to them.[13] Condillac regards instinct as the operation of imagination (which evokes feelings associated with perception) without the aid of reflection.[14] The instinctual consciousness is characteristic of animals, precisely because they lack language, which would enable them to direct their own consciousness through the use of signs. But if, for Condillac, the pre-linguistic and animal consciousness can be equated, in virtue of what is it able to invent language and transform itself into an actively reasoning one?

Condillac's answer to this problem appears in the second part of the *Essai* in the form of a thought experiment, in which two children, both orphaned at birth by the great deluge,[15] are left to themselves in isolation from any form of human life. It is through the interaction of these two children that Condillac attempts to explain the genesis of language according to the principles of sensationalism.

Condillac assumes that original language must have arisen from spontaneous expressions of primal feelings, which is to say expressions of pleasure, pain, fear, anger, and so on. These initial expressions of feelings would have been grounded in the satisfaction or frustration of basic needs, which is consistent, as we indicated earlier, with Condillac's view that needs gave occasion for the invention of language. But such expressions were not of themselves language, because they were not *intended* to communicate anything. To use language the children must become aware that their cries convey meaning to one another, and that these meanings can be invoked at will.

This transformation occurs, language is invented, because of an innate feeling of sympathy the children have for one another, a feeling Condillac assumes is universal to the human species. The children are said to feel sympathy for each others' suffering, which would be signified by expressions of pain or frustration and actions directed at meeting some need. This feeling would inspire them to assist each other, each would identify immediately with the other, the need of the sufferer simply becoming the need of the other. The important point at this stage is that the children's identification with each other is unreflexive, and the associations one makes between the feelings and the expressions of the other are involuntary.[16] However, Condillac claims, as these experiences are repeated, their involuntary associations would gradually have become voluntary. Their expressions and actions would have become significations of feelings which they could recall at will and use to communicate those feelings to each other. Thus Condillac claims,

> Leur mémoire commença à avoir quelque exercice; ils purent disposer eux-mêmes de leur imagination, et ils parvinrent insensiblement à faire, avec réflexion, ce qu'ils n'avoient fait que par instinct.[17]

It is important to note what Condillac claims here. The children's ability to associate ideas, to connect expressions with things, passes from the involuntary to the voluntary wholly by means of repetitive experience, as he puts it, *insensiblement*. But this constitutes a transformation in human consciousness. The children are now able to consciously associate their gestures with their feelings, and this represents the beginning of a process by which their signifying activity becomes progressively more sophisticated. They gradually learn to replace the signification of gesture with signification by means of sounds, which were in turn supplemented by pictures or marks, and eventually became a phonetic alphabet. What is crucial to the development of language is the acquisition of the capacity for reflection, a conscious ability to establish an arbitrary relation between words and things. Yet this is not adequately explained. To say that we pass insensibly from a consciousness completely dominated by involuntary associations caused by our perceptions to one capable of directing its own associations, is equivalent to arguing that it happened because it happened. It is not, in other words, and explanation of anything.

From Rousseau's standpoint, Condillac's solution to the problem of language origin was both anthropologically and epistemologically suspect. To assume that these children had acquired some degree of social interaction, is to beg the question of how they might have done so. As we noted, Rousseau believed our original needs served to separate us, and so could not have been the source of our languages. But equally important, Rousseau also identified an intractable problem of circularity in Condillac's argument. Reason or reflection is required for us to choose arbitrary signs to stand for our perceptions and our ideas; yet language, insofar as it enables us to control the contents of our consciousness and reflect upon our experience, seems to be the condition of our capacity to reason.[18] When he comes to it, Condillac's explanation of the process through which language is invented does not really answer this objection, as he simply claims that we pass *insensibly* into the use of signs. Rousseau, as we shall see, has an account of the species pre-linguistic development, which he believed explained in broad outline how and why human beings would have evolved to the level of social and intellectual sophistication necessary to invent language. In this he differs markedly from Condillac.

It should be noted here that my claims that Rousseau was critical of Condillac's sensationalism, and that an opposition existed between empiricists and Cartesians on the question of language origin, are flatly denied by Hans Aarsleff, in his book **From Locke to Saussure**. In Aarsleff's view, Rousseau followed Condillac in all relevant respects on the question of language origin, accepting both the epistemological significance Condillac attached to the problem (which I don't deny), and his solution to the problem (which I do deny). Aarsleff argues that Rousseau's reference to the paradox of explaining the origin of language, and the criticism this entails for Condillac's explanation, only occurs because Rousseau assumes a state of nature in which human beings lead "an absolutely solitary life."[19] In Aarsleff's view, this is not a valid criticism of Condillac because he assumes a level of social interaction between the children, which in turn enables him to give a plausible account of the invention of speech.

Aarsleff goes on to argue that the extent of Rousseau's dependence on Condillac is evident from his second discussion of language origin in the second part of the *Discours sur l'inégalité*.[20] At this stage in the species' development, some level of social interaction has begun to take place, as it had for the children of Condillac's thought experiment, and so the origin of language poses no problem.[21] Aarsleff claims that Rousseau's two discussions are not contradictory because they rest on different assumptions. Furthermore, when Rousseau bases his discussion on assumptions identical to Condillac, he follows Condillac to the letter.[22] There is then no substantial disagreement between the two, and in fact, Aarsleff implies, Rousseau bases his solution to the problem of language origin on Condillac's philosophy.[23]

The agreement between Condillac and Rousseau on the origin of language Aarsleff posits is part of a larger claim in his essay *The Tradition of Condillac*, that there is in fact no distinction to be made between Cartesians and Lockean empiricists with respect to the origin of language. In Aarsleff's view, both Locke and Condillac believed, like Descartes, that human beings possessed an innate capacity for reflection, which allowed them to explain why humans alone invented language.[24] In support of this, Aarsleff quotes Condillac to the effect that: "De toutes les opérations que nous avons décrites, il en résulte une qui, pour ainsi dire, couronne l'entendement: c'est la raison...[la raison] n'est autre chose que la connoissance de la manière dont nous devons régler les opérations de notre ame."[25] And further: "On est capable de plus de réflexion à proportion qu'on a plus de raison. Cette dernière faculté produit donc la réflexion."[26] In Aarsleff's view Condillac regarded the power of *les liaisons des idées*, the voluntary association of ideas, as an innate reasoning power which explained our capacity for language. "Thus," he concludes, "in Condillac as in Locke, reflection is a powerful, active, creative, innate faculty, Professor Chomsky *non obstante*; and it is precisely for this reason that Condillac, building on Locke, could present a theory of the creation of human language."[27]

I want to make two observations about this interpretation of Condillac, and its implications for Rousseau's alleged agreement with his account of language origin. The first is that while Aarsleff is surely right that Locke took reflection to be an innate power of the mind,[28] Condillac is in fact critical of Locke on this very point, and states that he can show how the mind acquires this "operation".[29] Second, Condillac is also critical of Locke because he did not pay close enough attention to the role of language in the development of the human understanding. For Condillac, the invention of language marks the mind's shift from involuntary associations (*associations des idées*) to voluntary ones (*les liaisons des idées*). The basic operations of the mind are, in Condillac's view, developed from our initial sensory perceptions. *Perceptions, consciousness, attention*, and *reminiscence*, represent the mind's first operations, and none entails the voluntary association of ideas. The next three operations acquired are *imagination, contemplation*, and *memory*.[30] Of these, imagination and contemplation can occur without the voluntary association of ideas, but memory depends on the subject's capacity to connect ideas with arbitrary signs.

> Mais aussitôt qu'un homme commence à attacher des idées à des signes qu'il a lui-même choisis, on voit se former en lui la mémoire. Celle-ci acquise, il commence à disposer par lui-même de son imagination et à lui donner un nouvel exercice; car, par le secours des signes qu'il peut rappeler à son gré, il réveille, ou du moins il peut réveiller souvent les idées qui y sont liées.[31]

Once memory is formed by means of the voluntary association of signs with ideas, reflection follows, and the human mind is able to progress to its characteristic sophistication. If language is the condition of memory and reflection, the problem is to explain the origin of language. But, as Condillac himself notes, this poses another a problem: which comes first, reflection or language? "Combien, par exemple, n'a-t-il pas fallu de réflexions pour former les langues, et de quel secours ces langues ne sont-elles pas à la réflexion!" He promises to resolve this paradox in the second part. However, if he were, as Aarsleff claims, of the view that reflection or reason were an innate human faculties, he would not have conceived the problem of language origin in this way at all.

I would argue then that Aarsleff is wrong to assert that Locke and Condillac are in complete agreement about the origin of language, even though, in the end, Condillac does not succeed in demonstrating how language could have been acquired solely on the basis of sensation. I would also argue that Rousseau does not follow Condillac in all essentials on this question. Indeed, he was sensitive to both the circularity of Condillac's argument with respect to the relation between language and reason, as well as to its anthropological limitations of his demonstration of how language would arise between two isolated children. This is not to suggest that Condillac's treatment of the problem was either superficial or without influence on Rousseau. But it is to suggest that Condillac's sensationalist epistemology was inadequate to the task Rousseau set himself, of charting the species' evolution from its natural (pre-linguistic) state to its condition in society. Rousseau needed to explain the origin of language in terms of something other than a natural faculty of reflection, which is why he could accept neither the Cartesian account of language origin (which simply assumed it), nor Condillac's (which was unsuccessful in showing how we could have acquired language without it). He needed to do this because he saw language as the greatest obstacle to the species' transition from nature to society; and without an explanation of this transition he could not claim that mankind had acquired the corrupt characteristics which dominate its nature.

2.3 Conclusion

Rousseau's diagnosis of the circularity of developmental theories of language origin posed a difficult problem for his own account of the species' evolution. His philosophical anthropology entailed a developmental account of subjectivity in which human nature is constituted by the subject's experience, yet at the same time he recognized that experience alone could not adequately explain the species' evolution from nature to culture. His anthropology faced two contradictory requirements which the problem of language origin brings into sharp focus. On the one hand, it had to distinguish clearly between natural and social man; the two had to be conceived as radically different states of being. On the other hand he had to explain how these two states could be linked to each other on the continuum of human development. If language, and therefore rationality and sociability, are natural to the human species, the first distinction collapses because natural man ceases to be distinguishable from social man. The problem is that if these attributes need to be explained in developmental terms, nature and society appear to be two radically separate and irreconcilable forms of life, as unbridgeable, in eighteenth century terms, as the animal and the human. Rousseau's solution to this problem attempts to reconcile these two contradictory requirements, in effect to have it both ways. He asserts that the human species' evolution from nature to culture is achieved in virtue of its innately free and improvable nature. Yet at the same time this essential nature is meant to be understood merely as the potential to become a fully developed subjectivity. There is nothing about it which predestines the species to either its evolution beyond its natural condition, or the corrupt and dependent forms it takes in existing civil societies. In Rousseau's anthropology then, the human subject appears as a being defined in terms of an essential nature, which is nonetheless dependent on its interaction with specific forms of environmental condition for its fulfilment.

The theory of the subject that emerges in Rousseau's early works represents an attempt to meet the conflicting demands of his anthropology of human development. On their own, neither the Cartesian nor the sensationalist accounts of subjectivity provided a framework for explaining how a naturally free and perfectible being could be constituted as a corrupt and dependent one in civil society. By attempting to fuse these two models of the subject together, Rousseau was able to portray the species' development in a way more suited to his most fundamental argument in the *Discours sur l'inégalité*: that our species' progressive socialization has entailed the loss of our original nature. His assumption that we are defined by free will and *perfectibilité*, combined with the view that our consciousness and behaviour is constituted in and through our experience, gave him a way of explaining both why we had lost our original nature and what we might do to recover it. Yet at the same time the conception of the subject underlying his account of the species' evolution introduced a problematic tension into Rousseau's thought. His moral and political theory attempts to recover, in various ways, the original nature we have lost in society. The problem is that this recovery must be effected for a vastly more complex subjectivity; one which possesses both rationality and language, and whose consciousness is constituted in relation to other self-conscious, self-valuing being. The consciousness of social man, as well as the environment which forms it, is entirely different from the consciousness and condition of natural man. This raises the question of what, if anything, there remains to be recovered of our original nature, and following from this, whether such a recovery is at all plausible? In the following chapter I want to consider the question of what Rousseau meant by our original nature, and why he held it up as the foundation of the species' moral regeneration in society.

Endnotes

1. Charles Taylor, *Hegel*, (Cambridge: Cambridge University Press, 1976), pp. 4-5.

2. Michel Foucault, *The Order of Things*, Allan Sheridan trans., (London: Tavistock Institute, 1970), pp. 58-59.

3. Locke, *Essay*, Bk. II., Chapter 2, §1.

4. O.C. III, p. 146. (See above 1.6)

5. *Ibid.*, pp. 148-49.

6. *Ibid.*, p. 151.

7. *Ibid.*, p. 162.

8. E.O.L., p. 39.

    Rousseau claims here that the invention of language has less to do with the organization of our organs of speech, as La Mettrie had claimed, than it does with, "une faculté propre à l'homme, qui lui fait employer ses organes à cet usage..."

9. O.C. III, pp. 143, 214.

10. E.O.L., pp. 41-43.

    It is worth noting here that Rousseau may indeed be referring to Condillac, who argues in *Essai*, II., I., X., § 103. "Ce sont les besoins qui fournirent aux hommes les premières occasions de remarquer ce qui se passoit en eux-mêmes, et de l'exprimer par des actions, ensuite par des noms."

11. O.C. III, p. 151.

12. *Ibid.*, p. 147.

13. Condillac, *Essai*, I. II. i. § 15,16.

14. *Ibid.*, I. II. iv. §42, 43.

Language, Subjectivity, and Freedom

15. *Ibid.*, I. §1, p. 60.

    Condillac is careful to note here that Adam and Eve would not have had to acquire language because of the extraordinary intervention of God. However, it is at least conceivable, within the framework of the Biblical account of creation, that a male an a female child could have survived the flood without knowing language.

16. *Ibid.*, II. i. §2.

17. *Ibid.*, II. I. i. § 3.

18. See above, note #59.

19. O.C. III, p. 156.

20. *Ibid.*, pp. 165-66.

21. Aarsleff, *The Tradition of Condillac*, in **From Locke to Saussure**, pp. 156-57.

22. *Ibid.*, p. 157.

23. *Ibid.*, 156-57.

24. *Ibid.*, pp. 155, 164, 170.

25. Condillac, *Essai*, I. II. xi. §92.

26. *Ibid.*, I. II. xi. §107.

27. Aarsleff, *The Tradition of Condillac*, in **From Locke to Saussure**, p. 155.

28. See above note 50.

29. Condillac, *Essai*, "Introduction", p. 5, lines 5-25.
    Condillac is critical here of Locke because he simply assumes that the mind can exercise its power to reflect, while in his own view it must acquire the ability to exercise this power.

    Il [Locke] suppose, par exemple, qu'aussi-tôt que l'ame reçoit des idées par les sens, elle peut, à son gré, les répéter, les composer, les unir ensemble avec une variété infinie, et en faire toutes sortes de notions complexes. Mais il est constant que, dans l'enfance, nous avons éprouvé des sensations, long-temps avant d'en savoir tirer des idées. Ainsi, l'ame n'ayant pas, dés le premier instant, l'exercice de toutes ses opérations, il étoit essentiel, pour développer mieux l'origine de nos connoissances, de montrer comment elle acquiert cet exercice, et quel en est le progrès. Il ne paroît pas que Locke y ait pensé, ni que personne lui en ait fait le reproche, ou ait essayé de suppléer à cette partie de son ouvrage.

The clear implication here is that the mind acquires the capacity to reflect. This clearly distinguishes Condillac from Descartes, and it would seem in his own mind, if not Aarsleff's, to distinguish him from Locke.

30. *Ibid.*, I. II. i. §15; and I. II. ii. §17-26.

31. *Ibid.*, I. II. ii. §46.

3

Original Nature

3.1 Introduction

The problem of language origin reveals a problem in Rousseau's account of the species' evolution from nature to culture. Social life presupposes at least a minimal degree of language and rationality. Yet an explanation of the origins of any one of these seems to presuppose the acquisition of the others,[1] and thus to beg the question of whether it is at all possible to think of the species as having evolved from a natural to a social state. The paradox of language origin, as we have seen, posed difficulties for developmentalist accounts of subjectivity, pushing Condillac into an unsatisfactory resolution of the problem and La Mettrie to the seemingly untenable identification of apes and humans. Rousseau was among the first to recognize the limitations of the empiricist model of the subject in this respect. He projected the model onto an historical screen, and revealed an apparently intractable paradox at the very point at which humans must have been transformed from natural to social beings. A sense-bound, animal-like consciousness cannot become an actively thinking one on the basis of sense experience alone. Rousseau's solution to this paradox lies in his account of our nature in the original condition of humanity, which is

Original Nature

to say, in what he names as our distinctively human characteristics.

In the first part of the *Discours sur l'inégalité*, Rousseau asserts that we are distinguished from animals, and therefore defined as human, in virtue of two natural or innate characteristics: free will and the faculty of *perfectibilité*.[2] The latter is said to be a faculty possessed *en puissance* which, with the aid of circumstance, is the source of our unique development.[3] In Rousseau's view neither reason nor language could themselves have been natural attributes, as the Cartesians had argued. Such an assumption denies the opposition between nature and culture in the species' development, and therefore imputes to natural man an innate disposition towards corruption and dependence that Rousseau is at pains to deny. Humans are by nature isolated and good, while language and rationality are the acquired characteristics by which we are socialized and corrupted. Nevertheless, natural man must also be recognizably human, an observation that would be trivial were it not that there is so little in Rousseau's description of our original nature that distinguishes us from animals. Without some identifiably human traits, both Rousseau's account of natural man as essentially peaceful and good, as well as his account of the process through which this original goodness is lost, would lose their moral force. Insofar as original nature represents a standpoint from which to analyze and judge social life critically, it must entail some human characteristics. If not, there is no way of linking natural and social man, and what we were by nature is irrelevant to our existence in society.

The faculty of *perfectibilité* is an important part of Rousseau's solution to these problems. It allows him to distinguish humans from animals by offering an explanation of those attributes that obviously characterize humans (e.g. language and rationality), in terms of an innate potential to acquire them. As Rousseau conceives it, *perfectibilité* affords the species a potential to improve itself without at the same time implying anything determinate about what that improvement entails, nor even that it must occur. Rousseau did not think *perfectibilité* predetermined our moral development. It does not predestine us to a form of social life which denies our freedom and corrupts our virtue, whereas a natural capacity for reason and language, as we shall see presently, necessarily would.

The concept of *perfectibilité* also distinguishes his conception of the subject from the more fully empiricist projects of Condillac and La Mettrie. The former, as we have seen, invoked reflection to explain the acquisition of our capacity to reflect, while the latter believed he could educate apes to be human. Both regard the cognitive development of the species as a relatively uncomplicated process grounded in our essentially uniform sensual experience. As La Mettrie commented, "Des Animaux à l'Homme, la transition n'est pas violente."[4] But for Rousseau, this represents a kind of category mistake. He regarded the distinction between the animal and the human as a metaphysical one, borne out by the tremendous disparity, at the present stage of our evolution, between our cognitive capacities and theirs. Furthermore, while he regarded the epistemological paradigm employed to explain our cognitive development, at least by Condillac, as largely correct; he viewed the species' evolution as a much longer and more complex process than either the sensationalists or the materialists would seem to have allowed. In Rousseau's view it was true to say of both animals and humans that they accumulated knowledge through sensory experience of their environment, but their respective cognitive developments occur at entirely different levels. The accumulation of knowledge through experience does not itself explain how that knowledge comes to play a role in shaping the environment in which a species lives, nor why humans and not animals transcend the stable equilibrium of their natural state, to become progressively more rational in the process of their denaturation. The innate faculty of *perfectibilité* is part of Rousseau's explanation of this, and as such it plays a pivotal role in his philosophical anthropology.

The faculty of *perfectibilité* is also important to Rousseau's prescriptive moral and political theory. He regards the opposition between nature and culture as a deep antinomy in the moral and political life of civilized societies. What we are by nature is completely transformed by the psychological hegemony of *amour-propre* in developed social life. Rousseau's account of our evolution is one in which original freedom and goodness are lost as our social relations and our consciousness become more complex. Our history then, leaves us radically alienated from our natural potential. But it also, in Rousseau's view, imposes upon us the imperative need of recovering that potential. This does not mean recovering our original isolation and savagery. It means rather that we must recover, in a form appropriate to social life, the attributes that defined our species in its infancy. Our freedom certainly, but also the natural passions of self-love and pity. But we will leave the details of this recovery until later. For now what I want to claim is that the faculty of *perfectibilité* constitutes a unifying concept in the entire body of Rousseau's thought. It provides a conceptual link between his analysis of the social problem of alienation in the two *Discourses*, and the various attempts to overcome this problem found in his moral and political theory. For Rousseau, *perfectibilité* is the one natural attribute not transformed by the species' passage from nature to culture. The possibility of improvement remains a constant feature of human nature, and so provides the basis for a recovery of original nature within the context of social life. This is at least part of the reason why Rousseau's pessimism regarding the depth of our moral depravity did not deter him from seeking solutions to it.

If, as I claim, the faculty of *perfectibilité* is central to Rousseau's social critique and the prescriptive moral and political theory it implies, it would seem necessary to look more closely at what he means by the concept and what he takes its role in the species' development to be. It will be remembered that *perfectibilité* is introduced with free will as one of the two definitively human characteristics. These faculties, along with the natural passions of *amour de soi-même* and pity (both of which we do share with animals), represent the constituent features of original nature.[5] The connection between free will and *perfectibilité* is not incidental. The two are connected in Rousseau's mind because each represents a different aspect of the essential liberty of the human subject. I want now to consider each in turn.

3.2 Natural Liberty

Rousseau describes natural liberty as our freedom to resist or acquiesce in the impulsions of nature; a capacity of which, he claims, we are conscious.[6] The liberty we are said to possess in the natural state is purely negative in form: it is both freedom *from* determination by natural impulse, and freedom *from* the dependence, vanity and competition that characterizes life in civil society. It is important to distinguish Rousseau's wholly negative conception of natural liberty from the positive conception of moral freedom he outlines in **Du contrat social**. The latter is said to consist in living according to a law prescribed to oneself, and so in exerting a form of rational control over one's life.[7] Natural man's freedom involves no significant control over either his environment or his life. He is said to be conscious of himself as an agent, but he is at the same time fully integrated into his environment.[8] His behaviour is for all intents and purposes instinctual, which is to say he has neither the need nor the occasion to reflect upon his actions in the natural state. It is this lack of reflection which integrates him into his environment, and ensures that, all things being equal, he would have remained in that state indefinitely.[9]

Rousseau's account of natural liberty involves two contradictory notions. On the one hand, natural man is said to be free and conscious of his freedom; yet on the other, this freedom cannot have had the effect of disrupting the perfect equilibrium of his integration into nature. He must have been free in the natural state, but it appears that this freedom did not predetermine the species' evolution beyond that state. This raises the question of whether Rousseau's conception of natural liberty, and therefore his entire account of original nature, is at all plausible. For how can one be free and conscious of one's freedom, while at the same time an essentially instinctual being fully integrated into the natural order? And further to this, how can a self-conscious agent, even an extremely primitive one, remain wholly ignorant of other self-conscious agents, and so preserve his independence?

Original Nature 69

I raise this last question because Rousseau actually proposes two accounts of the self-consciousness in his discussion natural free agency in the *Discours sur l'inégalité*, and the fact they contradict each rather adds to the confusion surrounding his account of primitive man. In the first account, which we have noted, natural man is said to be immediately present to himself as an agent in the activity of choosing. "La Nature commande à tout animal, et la Bête obéït. L'homme éprouve la même impression, mais il se reconnoît libre d'acquiescer, ou de résister; et c'est surtout dans la conscience de cette liberté que se montre la spiritualité de son ame..."[10] In the second account of natural man's self-consciousness, elaborated in Note XV to the main text, he is described as having a self-consciousness very similar to social man's, though with the important qualification that he is not aware that others are self-conscious.[11] In this account natural man is said to be the sole observer himself and the sole judge of his own merit. Rousseau's point here is that as such, natural man would have been incapable of comparing himself with others, and hence free of the passions associated with *amour-propre*. But the self-consciousness he describes here implies two characteristics inconsistent with the first account of immediate self-presence.

First, it presupposes that natural man's conception of self involves a sense of duration, a sense of being a unified self over time. It presupposes this because Rousseau claims that natural man judges his own merit, and therefore values himself, something he can do only if his ends are grounded in a self-conscious will. He can only value himself if he is aware that he has ends which are his own and which he is concerned to realize. This requires a sense of the self persisting as a unity over time; the unity of self constituting the basis of the value of its successive parts. Without this sense of unity, the subject would have no way of valuing himself from one moment to the next, because he would have no way of regarding himself as the same being from one experience to the next. The sense of duration implied in the notion that natural man judged his own merit (accorded himself a value over time), is not required by the initial description of free will as an awareness of our ability to resist or acquiesce in the impulsions of nature. This kind of self-consciousness could simply be occasioned by sensations, and requires no enduring sense of self.[12]

A second aspect of the account of self-consciousness in Note XV which fits uneasily into Rousseau's first description of natural free agency, is an implied capacity to formulate desires into ends. If natural man values himself in the sense suggested in Note XV, he must presumably be able to distinguish between himself as a being with desires, and the desires he has at any given moment. This in turn implies that he has ends, which are acquired by reflecting upon oneself as a being with desires, some of which weigh more heavily than others, some of which one wishes to satisfy immediately, some later, and so on. An end thus implies a future state of affairs into which one can imaginatively project oneself, as well as some conception of the relation between that end and others. Unless one could project oneself into the future, and also measure one end against another, it is unclear how one could be in a position to judge one's own merit. Isolated from others, there would simply be nothing else upon which to evaluate ourselves.

The isolated self-consciousness described in Note XV is significant because it is quite impossible to square it with Rousseau's account of original nature in the main text of the *Discours sur l'inégalité*. As sole observer and judge of himself natural man must have possessed imagination, foresight, and memory, characteristics Rousseau otherwise denies him.[13] Furthermore, natural man could not possess a conception of himself as a unity existing over time without at the same time distinguishing himself from other such unities or unified selves. A self-conscious subject cannot therefore value itself without distinguishing itself from other self-conscious subjects, and thus without evaluating itself in relation to them. Rousseau's argument in Note XV therefore defeats its own purpose.[14]

The significance of this rather detailed discussion of natural man's self-consciousness arises from the important question of whether it is possible to be free without being conscious of oneself as a free agent. It is crucial to Rousseau's argument that natural man be free. The reconstitution of original nature in society must involve the reconstitution of freedom. Yet at the same time, as Rousseau's incoherence on this point indicates, freedom

Original Nature

implies self-consciousness, and self-consciousness implies an awareness of other self-conscious beings. From the standpoint of natural liberty then, Rousseau's account of original nature seems paradoxical. Natural man must have been free, but if freedom implies self-consciousness, he must also have been social.

What can be said in defence of Rousseau on this point, is that his initial account of natural man's consciousness of himself as a free being need not necessarily imply an awareness of other self-conscious persons. As a very primitive being motivated by what amounts to an instinctual drive for self-preservation, natural man would have experienced natural impulses for food, or sex, or whatever else this required. If we are to understand such a being as free, it must be in the very limited sense of undetermined responses to these impulses. This could involve choosing between two impulses experienced simultaneously, accompanied by an awareness of opting for one over the other. But this awareness would not have had implications beyond the moment in which the choice was made. He could not postpone the satisfaction of one desire in the hope of satisfying the other later, for this would require a sense of himself existing as a self over time, and would therefore entail distinguishing himself from other self-conscious beings. If he simply chose, and was aware of himself doing so in the moment the choice was made, his self-consciousness could be conceived as a private subjective experience.

Understood in this way, natural man's agency would have issued in behaviour very similar or even identical to the higher order animals. This relevant difference is that he would have been aware of himself in the moment of choice, and this characteristic could be said to constitute a part of his potential to develop into a rationally self-conscious agent capable of transforming desires into ends, of formulating moral principles, and acting according to them. What needs to be underlined is that in the original condition natural man's freedom could not, if Rousseau's distinction between nature and culture is to be maintained, have issued in any meaningful judgements regarding his experience of the natural order.

3.3 The Faculty of *Perfectibilité*

Natural man's other defining characteristic, the faculty of *perfectibilité*, is of no immediate relevance to Rousseau's account of natural self-consciousness. As a potential for self-improvement, this faculty's most obvious implications are for the future. It has been pointed out elsewhere that what cannot be denied, given Rousseau's premise of the species' origin in nature, is that it has some capacity for development beyond the natural state.[15] The question is, what does this tell us about natural man? In one sense of course, it does not tell us very much about him at all. It is simply circular to assert that natural man possessed a faculty of self-improvement, and then to substantiate this by noting how much the species has improved beyond its original condition. Nevertheless, Rousseau did believe that the faculty of *perfectibilité* had a determinate effect on the species' evolution, and therefore that it tells us something important about human nature. In possessing *perfectibilité*, Rousseau believed the species possessed a capacity to adapt to the conditions imposed on it by its environment in an undetermined way. Changes in this environment, and the *cumulative* effect of our adaptations to it, gradually issued in a transformation of human consciousness, and ultimately human nature.

Unlike animals, primitive man is said not to be subject to any set of determinate instincts. It is rather that he is capable of imitating the instinctual behaviour of other animals and, in this process, habituating himself to specific and relatively static modes of behaviour.[16] In effect, this behaviour is instinctual, and adequate to the satisfaction of his very limited needs. He does not reflect upon his behaviour because he lacks the capacity for communication,[17] and consequently the skills developed by any one primitive die with him.[18] The species as a whole makes no progress as a result of own activity or its reflection on that activity. In the primitive state then, we were for all intents and purposes integrated into nature without, either as individuals or as a species, possessing the capacity to intentionally upset the balance of that integration. What differentiated us from animals was

Original Nature 73

our capacity to acquire habitual modes of behaviour by means of imitation (rather than predetermined instinct). And while being in most cases determined by natural impulses triggered by sensations, we retained an immediate sense of self at specific moments, because we were capable on occasion of choosing between those our natural impulsions. At this stage, *perfectibilité* is significant wholly for the future. I did not affect our behaviour or our consciousness until it changes in our environmental circumstances forced us into new modes of life.[19]

We should at this point note that Rousseau's concept of *perfectibilité*, like his concept of nature, is used in different senses at different stages of the species' evolution. In the original state, *perfectibilité* affects the development of the species' nature only after changes have occurred in its environment. But once the species has evolved to the point at which it possesses language and rationality, the faculty begins to affect the development of our nature in a different way. In the earliest stages of our history, *perfectibilité* explains our development to the point at which language is acquired and intersubjective relations commence; in the second sense, the faculty explains our evolution as fully developed subjects. In both cases Rousseau regards it as a kind of open-ended potential for development, but the nature of that development differs radically according to the differences characteristic of the species at each stage.

Rousseau's account of the species evolution out of its original state illustrates the first sense in which he uses the concept of *perfectibilité*. A gradual increase in population causes the species to disperse over the face of the earth in search of the means to its subsistence. This produced a diversity of circumstances to which the species had to adapt itself. Different terrain, different climates, and conditions of relative scarcity, forced the primitives into new modes of living. They found it necessary, simply in the pursuit of subsistence, to adapt objects for use as tools. Those living by water invented tools for fishing, those inhabiting forests bows and arrows, and so on.[20] There are two important points to note here. The first is that the invention of tools appropriate to producing subsistence in specific environmental circumstances imposes a new diversity and specialization of activity on primitive man. Whereas before he had roamed the earth without constraint, subsistence always close at hand, he now became tied to specific environments and specific modes of life. The isolated and completely independent savages became "pêcheurs et Ichtyophages...Chasseurs et Guerriers".[21] These developments increased the incidence of contact the primitives had with one another, and eventually drew them into what we might term *proto*-social relations. The second point to note is that the activity of adapting tools for use, which developed as a consequence of changes in circumstances rather than conscious intention, gradually led the species towards an expansion of its self-consciousness. We gradually, as a consequence of our adaptations to uncontrollable changes in circumstance, began to recognize others as beings like ourselves: as self-conscious and self-valuing.[22]

Hitherto, natural man had only been aware of himself in the most immediate sense. However, Rousseau claims, with the repeated use of things in relation to himself, in particular the tools he had adapted for his own use, he is led to the insight that things can be understood in relation to one another. This new relation to natural objects "...produisirent enfin chez lui quelque sorte de réflexion, ou plutôt une prudence machinale qui lui indiquoit les précautions les plus nécessaires à sa sûreté."[23] His new capacity for prudential reasoning leads him to an awareness of his superiority over animals, and what follows is the epoch of the *first revolution*, which produced isolated families, romantic love, language, and finally a primitive form of society.[24]

In Rousseau's account of the species' initial passage from nature to society then, the faculty of *perfectibilité* begins as a mere potential for self-improvement, and through circumstances over which the species has no control, enables it to acquire the first glimmerings of reflection and the proto-society of the isolated family. In this sense *perfectibilité* is the cause of the species' transition from the pure state of nature to the *Golden Age*. However, it is in this first and very crucial sense that Rousseau's use of the concept is most ambiguous. *Perfectibilité* is crucial to his argument because he has to give a plausible explanation of why the species has evolved beyond its original condition.

Without this natural man cannot be conceived as good, and the fundamental antinomy between nature and culture in his account of our evolution would collapse. But the argument is ambiguous because his explanation of the process through which this occurs assumes on the one hand that natural man is inherently free and perfectible, but on the other that this issues neither in the desire nor the ability to control the environment in which he lives. We are therefore asked to conceive the species' evolution as one in which it makes very little, if any, positive contribution to its own development. Both sides of this somewhat paradoxical argument must be examined before we can conclude whether the faculty of *perfectibilité* serves as an adequate explanation of the species' initial development beyond its original state.

3.4 Perfectibilité and the Species' Evolution

Rousseau conceived the first stage of human evolution as pre-moral, which is to say that the advances achieved by the species prior to the invention of language are primarily cognitive, and do not involve the species in relations that could be called moral. During this first stage, *perfectibilité* involves both the capacity to adapt to environmental obstacles in the pursuit of subsistence, and the ability to accumulate knowledge on the basis of that experience. Both these capacities are somewhat problematic because they would seem to imply a degree of self-conscious intention inconsistent with Rousseau description of natural man. The capacity to adapt to environmental circumstance must be regarded as a kind of freedom, in Rousseau's terms, to the extent that while natural man was capable of spontaneously adapting his behaviour to meet his needs, animals are not.[25] However, this could not have been a fully self-conscious freedom, because according to Rousseau's description, primitive man would have had no idea of the significance of his innovations beyond their immediate effect upon his self-preservation. If beneficial to self-preservation, the innovation soon became habit. Each successful adaptation or innovation would have produced a new mode of behaviour, but this behaviour would have become habitual rather than one among many alternatives to be consciously chosen. This is to say that natural man may have been conscious of the choice involved while actually adapting his behaviour to cope with specific circumstances, but that he did not reflect upon the significance of either the choice or the innovation. The former would be forgotten and the latter would become habitual. It did not occur to him that he was possessed of a unique capacity to improve his overall condition, that he was superior to animals in this respect, or that he shared this capacity with other humans, until the process of adaptation had radically altered the circumstances in which he lived.

In Rousseau's description of the species' passage from nature to society then, there is a sense in which the species' development occurs in spite of itself. We are dependent upon the introduction of scarcity, or obstacles to the production of subsistence, for the realization of our potential as an improvable beings. This raises the question of whether or not Rousseau's argument is deterministic: does it imply that our present condition is the inevitable consequence of our existence in a material environment? Rousseau does in fact claim that were it not for a chance combination of several circumstances external to our nature (concours fortuit de plusieurs causes étrangeres), our potential faculties would have remained forever dormant, and the stable equilibrium of our natural state unbroken.[26] The species does not emerge from its isolated and severely limited consciousness until factors over which it has no control (population increase, scarcity) create the conditions necessary for its development to get going. Furthermore, Rousseau's account of its progress seems to lay decisive emphasis upon environmental factors: the production of tools, specialization in the production of subsistence, and changes in the mode of production. Each play a pivotal role in the species' evolution.[27]

However, an interpretation which places too much emphasis on these factors will entail implications that run counter to and indeed render incoherent Rousseau's account of the species' evolution.[28] Rousseau should not be read as an environmental determinist for two reasons. First, to claim that the species is socialized solely as a consequence of environmental factors, is to deny the stability of his integration into nature in the primitive condition, and by implication to suggest that our transformation into social beings is natural. On a strictly determinist reading, Rousseau would be arguing that our social condition, and all the corruption this entails, is grounded in nature. Obviously, if one holds, as Rousseau did, that the species is by nature good, such a reading is unacceptable. Second, the claim that environmental factors determine the species' evolution denies the innate freedom of natural man, and the role of *perfectibilité* in the species' history. This is in effect to deny that Rousseau regards these characteristics as distinctively human, and is therefore radically at odds with his account of natural man.[29]

Nevertheless, the question still remains as how or whether we can make sense of the role of *perfectibilité* in the species' pre-social development. Given that environmental factors play an integral, indeed in some sense causal role in human development, how are we to make sense of the claim that humans are innately free and capable of self-improvement, and that these faculties explain our unique evolution? One way of making sense of this is suggested by Robert Wokler, who reads Rousseau to be arguing that humans, as opposed to animals, play an active part in determining how they live, and therefore are in some degree at least responsible for their own development.

> It was, therefore, because our forebears would have been able to *select* and *organize* the mode of their unprogrammed response to natural drives rather than because they were endowed with any positive traits or virtues of their own that mankind alone enjoyed a prospect of development.[30]

Wokler's account of the role of *perfectibilité* stresses the importance of free will human development, and accurately notes the negative significance of free choice at this stage of the evolutionary process. In this respect, Wokler's reading offers an antidote to the determinist readings offered by Plattner and Durkheim. However, the extent that the verbs *select* and *organize* are compatible with Rousseau's description of our pre-social development is highly questionable. Wokler is right to stress the importance of free will to Rousseau's conception of natural man, but his reading implies that this liberty involved self-conscious intentions, whereas if any sense at all is to be made of Rousseau's account of natural man, this cannot be the case. Wokler goes on to claim that Rousseau judged our ancestors to have "...misapplied their freedom in the course of their development...[by]...adopting social relations which debased rather than improved their habits."[31] This accords primitive man too much responsibility for the species' present corruption. It implies that his freedom involved some conception of the implications his choices might have had for him beyond the moment they were made. But, as we have seen, Rousseau's primitive could not have had a conception of himself as a self existing over time, because such a conception of self presuppose an awareness of other selves. It therefore seems inaccurate to suggest that natural man progressed beyond his original condition because he was able to *select* and *organize* the manner of his unprogrammed responses to natural impulses, or that our freedom has been misapplied.

Wokler makes no distinction between Rousseau's account of the role of *perfectibilité* in the species' development prior to the invention of language, and its role after language is in use. Rousseau underlines this distinction in his initial discussion of language.

> les idées générales ne peuvent s'introduire dans l'Esprit qu'à l'aide des mots, et l'entendement ne les saisit que par des propositions. C'est une des raisons pourquoi les animaux ne sauroient se former de telles idées, ni jamais acquérir la perfectibilité qui en dépend.[32]

Three points are made here. First, that general ideas or abstractions, which Rousseau regards as characteristic of fully developed rationality, presuppose linguistic competence. Second, one form of *perfectibilité* depends on such ideas. And third, animals cannot acquire this *perfectibilité*, presumably because they lack language. This passage suggests a distinction between pre and post-linguistic capacities for self-improvement. Pre-linguistic *perfectibilité*, what we might term natural *perfectibilité*, does not require language to influence human development, indeed, Rousseau states elsewhere it is the reason we acquire language in the first place.[33] After language has been invented however, *perfectibilité* has a much more dramatic effect upon human development. It becomes the ground of the species progress towards morality and social life. In this sense, it is a double-edged sword. It is because we possess it that we have come to the sorry state in which we find ourselves in contemporary civil societies, but at the same time, for Rousseau, it holds out the possibility of improving that state, of realizing our natural potential for freedom and moral virtue.

The first sense in which Rousseau uses the concept of *perfectibilité* is, as I noted, somewhat obscure. He undoubtedly means to say that natural man possessed a potential faculty for self-improvement, for without this, it would be impossible to conceive the species' evolution as he does. But what does this tell us about the species' initial development? Given that it did not allow us to make any form of intentional contribution to our own development at this stage, what effect does this innate faculty have upon it? The most plausible answer seems to be that its effect was cumulative and unconscious, rather than immediate and intentional. This is to say that the species was able, because of *perfectibilité*, to adapt in an undetermined way to the changing circumstances of its environment. These adaptations gradually issued in new modes of behaviour, increased contact with others, and finally in the more sophisticated cognitive capability Rousseau refers to as "prudence machinale". The species' pursuit of subsistence is forced to take new forms under the press of environmental circumstance. These new forms of behaviour begin in turn to change the environment in which the species exists, and so to influence its development. Circumstances (e.g. floods, or earthquakes) force the primitives into more frequent and sustained contact, they begin rudimentary forms of co-operation in the production of subsistence, they gradually form into familial groups, and begin to recognize their common superiority over animals. None of this is intentional (at least in the sense of issuing from a conscious choice between ends), and so none of it can be said to constitute a choice for which natural man can be held responsible. Yet at the same time, without a faculty which enables the species to make undetermined responses to changing circumstances, no development would have occurred at all. Animals, after all, also experience changing circumstances such as scarcity and increased contact, yet they remain locked into their instinctual patterns of behaviour and consciousness.[34]

The two forms of *perfectibilité* then, can be distinguished in terms of the subject's capacity for intentionality. In the second sense Rousseau uses it, *perfectibilité* is transformed by the acquisition of language and rationality. With the acquisition of these two characteristics, it takes the form of intentional changes in behaviour and social organization which human beings choose on the basis of an accumulated store of knowledge. A this stage we can accurately speak of our forebears having "misapplied their freedom" in Wokler's sense, but we can do so only because the species has already undergone a pre-linguistic development which enables it to acquire the cognitive characteristics necessary for self-conscious intentionality. This is why language is central to Rousseau's account of the species' evolution, and why the origin of language is such an important problem for his anthropology. Without language, the primitives are dependent on environmental changes for circumstances which trigger changes in their natures. But once they possess language, they are able to impose their own self-consciously determined ends upon their environment, and thus to play an active role in their own development. Prior to the acquisition of language, the species cannot be in any sense responsible for its own development. Indeed, as I will argue below, the logic of Rousseau's argument leads us to the conclusion that the species' initial steps away from its primitive state occur naturally, and so cannot be regarded as having any necessarily detrimental implications at all.

None of this is to suggest however, that free will exercised as a capacity for adaptation and improvement plays an incidental role in Rousseau's account of the species' pre-linguistic evolution. If Wokler's libertarian interpretation of this development distorts the anthropological significance of natural man's capacity for free choice, the determinist thesis renders Rousseau's argument incomprehensible. For Rousseau, freedom and circumstance play equally fundamental roles in the species' initial steps beyond the pure state of nature. His anthropology assumes a compatibilist position on the question of free will and determinism, which stems from his attempt to graft together elements of both the Cartesian and sensationalist models of subjectivity. The first indubitable assumption of both

Original Nature 81

his anthropology and his moral philosophy is that human beings are inherently free. Yet this freedom of the subject does not entail any notion of a self which conceives itself or wills independent of its experience in the material world of nature. In our original state, Rousseau believed we exercised our freedom in response to our sensory experience of the material world, as unreflective choices between a very limited range of desires arising from our experience. Once our rationality and the variety of our needs becomes more sophisticated, the faculty of self-improvement is realized as an ability to control and manipulate our environment through self-consciously determined ends, however misconceived.

3.5 Conclusion

The apparent contradiction between the claim, on the one hand, that humans are innately free, and on the other, that this freedom is unreflective and as such has no directly determinate effect upon his evolution, stems from the impossibility of conceiving the species' history either as wholly the result of human nature, or wholly the consequence of environmental circumstances. Rousseau's account of the species' evolution regards each factor as a condition of the other. The first stages of the species' history occur within each individual subject's spontaneous response to the impulses induced in him by nature. But none of these responses have specific future implications for either the individual subject or the species as a whole.[15] They do not threaten the equilibrium of its natural state, nor predetermine the course of its moral development. It is not until circumstances beyond the species' control and quite independent of its actions have changed, that the undetermined responses of individual subjects begin to have a cumulative effect upon the species' evolution. Over centuries the environment slowly changes and forces very great numbers of individual primitives to adapt their behaviour. These responses produce new environmental obstacles to subsistence, new modes of behaviour and so on until the intersubjective relations of the *Golden Age* develop. Without these initial changes in the species' environment (i.e. the introduction of scarcity and the isolation of primitives in geographical areas), the entire process would never have got going.³⁶ But the point is also that without an innate or natural capacity to adapt to circumstances in an undetermined manner, it would be impossible to explain this process. The circumstances that bring the faculty of self-improvement to bear upon our evolution can clearly have no significance independent of our capacity to adapt our behaviour to meet them. The claim that humans are defined by their innate potential for self-improvement and free will allows Rousseau to assert that we need never have evolved to our present condition, while at the same time asserting that human beings are distinct in their essence from animals, and in virtue of this distinct essence possessed of potential moral attributes that should be realized. We are naturally free, and the moral problem is to recover this freedom in civil society.

The faculty of *perfectibilité* is invoked to explain the subject's transformation from a minimal human consciousness to a fully human one. Thus far we have only dealt with the initial stages of this transformation, but this is, I want to argue, crucial to the species' history. It is crucial because the entire nature/culture distinction hangs on the plausibility of his account of how the original primitives come to transcend their original integration into nature. If the initial movement away from nature is entirely the result of their free will, the moral significance of the natural state is drawn into question. Were this the case Rousseau would have to argue that natural man freely chose to leave the state of nature, the very point upon which he criticized Hobbes.³⁷ In Rousseau's terms a capacity for such self-conscious choice would entail an awareness of the intentions of others, and thus at minimum impute to the species a natural disposition towards dependence on them. Yet alternatively, the species' original integration cannot be so complete as to deny its humanity, or the very possibility of its evolution ever occurring. The faculty of *perfectibilité* is meant to reconcile the two sides of this paradox; it explains how the species can be natural and yet possess the potential to become social at the same time. However, it does this, it must be admitted, at the cost of a certain degree of ambiguity. It depends on our being able to conceive natural man's freedom, and his consciousness of that freedom, as issuing in choices that have no future significance for him, and which do not lead to an awareness of others as being self-conscious in the same way. Both are dubious propositions. They stem on the one hand from the view that consciousness originates in sensation, and so is immediately dependent upon the subject's experience of nature, and on the other that the human subject is defined by its capacity for free choice.

Rousseau's conception of subjectivity is therefore most problematic on the question of how the innate free will is given content. This problem is most acute in his account of natural man, who, lacking language and judgement, lacks the capacity to form his own ends, and therefore seems immediately dependent upon his environment. Unlike Kant, Rousseau did not conceive the self in transcendental terms, as unaffected by experience of the phenomenal world and capable of willing independent of its influence. In his view the self was grounded in nature, but at the same time he did not think human experience was conceivable without the attribute of freedom. This assumption has important implications for his thought as a whole. It is manifested as a powerful tension between nature and culture in his conception of our nature in civilized societies. The solution to the problem of dependence in civil societies requires that humans recover their original nature as free beings, yet this freedom is so limited and negative that it cannot serve as an adequate basis for prescribing how persons can be related to each other in civil society and at the same time retain their freedom. I shall argue in the following Chapter that Rousseau's conception of our natural liberty is in fact too limited to serve as the basis of our freedom in civil societies, and that his attempt to reconstitute our natural liberty in his prescriptive moral theory is better viewed as an attempt to recover the liberty of which the species has become capable during the *Golden Age*.

The philosophical anthropology of the ***Discours sur l'inégalité*** entails a conception of the self as inherently free, yet at the same time constituted by its experience. Projected onto an historical screen, it becomes Rousseau's answer to the opposing epistemological traditions informing the eighteenth century debate about the nature of man. Its originality consists in its insistence that the human subject cannot be adequately conceived without the natural freedom to determine itself, combined with the proposition that its nature must be realised in its experience. This way of conceiving the subject avoids the circularity of the more extreme empiricist paradigms because it admits as an initial premise the subject's ability to affect its own experience, and therefore provides us with an explanation of how it might have evolved from nature to culture.

Its plausibility rests on our being able to accept two kinds of development in the species' history. One in which its freedom and *perfectibilité* play a fundamental yet nevertheless reactive role; and another in which our faculty of self-improvement is transformed by the acquisition of language and reason into a capacity for self-conscious choice which becomes the determinate factor motivating our historical evolution. The two stages of this process correspond to the opposition between nature and culture I have argued is central to Rousseau's moral and political theory. In nature the species is integrated into its environment, and this integration makes it peaceful and good. The development it undergoes as a consequence of the changing conditions of its existence, a development which is completed with the establishment of nascent societies and the invention of rudimentary language, represents the realization of its natural potential. Our initial development is in other words entirely consistent with our nature, and therefore, in Rousseau's terms, has no necessarily detrimental moral implications for our future social existence.

The second stage of Rousseau's story represents the radical suppression of nature by the acquired characteristics of language, reason, and *amour-propre*. In this stage our development is dramatically accelerated, though not, it should be noted, until after the institution of private property, inequality, and a division of labour. This acceleration or "progress" moves the species away from the simple and relatively good order of nature towards the corrupt and artificial complexity of modern societies. The force of Rousseau's claim that we are alienated from nature only makes sense insofar as we understand nature to refer to our natural potential as human subjects. The problem is not, at least in the *Discours sur l'inégalité*, that as civilized beings we have rejected the barbarism and isolation our primitive state. It is rather that what began as the species' natural development away from its original condition ended up horribly wrong. The potential inherent in the natural freedom and *perfectibilité* characteristic of original nature has not been realized, and as a consequence our self-conscious attempts to "improve" our condition in society issue in increasingly artificial and corrupt institutions and practices. For Rousseau the nature/culture antinomy is felt most powerfully at the level of the individual subject's experience. As civilized beings we express our innate freedom and *perfectibilité* as an attempt to control and improve our environment, yet what this effort produces is an environment which is alien to our real natures, and which in turn constitutes us as corrupt and dependent social beings.

Endnotes

1. O.C. III, p. 147.

2. *Ibid.*, p. 142

3. *Ibid.*, p. 162.

4. La Mettrie, *L'Homme machine*, p. 162.

5. O.C. III, pp. 142-43, 153-54, 215-20.

6. *Ibid.*, p. 142.

7. *Ibid.*, p. 365.

8. *Ibid.*, pp. 142, 152.

9. *Ibid.*, p. 162.

10. *Ibid.*, pp. 141-42.

11. *Ibid.*, pp. 219-20.

12. Bronislaw Baczko, *Rousseau: Solitude et Communauté*, traduction par Claire Brendhel-Lamhout, (Paris: Mouton, 1974), p. 216.

    Baczko, in a discussion of the *Profession de foi du Savoyard Vicaire* argues that Rousseau rejected the materialist/sensationalist position that the self was reducible to sensations. He claims that for Rousseau, the sensations are the "cause occasionelle de la manifestation du sentiment du *moi*." The self of which we are conscious is always experienced in sensation, but it is not itself a sensation or a compilation of sensations. Baczko concludes that the sentiment of self is given pre-reflexively, which is to say possessed prior to our capacity to reason or judge actively. This suggests we should regard the first account of natural self-consciousness in the *Discours sur l'inégalité* as the one to which Rousseau most consistently adhered.

13. O.C. III. pp. 144; 217-18.

Original Nature 87

> Son imagination ne lui peint rien; son coeur ne lui demande rien. Ses modiques besoins se trouvent si aisément sous sa main, et il est si loin du degré de connoissances nécessaire pour désirer d'en acquérir de plus grandes, qu'il ne peut avoir ni prévoyance, ni curiosité...Son ame, que rien n'agite, le livre au seul sentiment de son existence actuelle, sans aucune idée de l'avenir, quelque prochain qu'il puisse être...

14. In suggesting that natural man could be the sole observer and judge of himself without at the same time comparing himself to others, Rousseau seems to be suggesting that it is possible to have an isolated (or private) experience of self-consciousness, which could preserve us from comparative evaluations and therefore *amour-propre*. I would argue that this cannot be maintained, but that Rousseau need not maintain it to provide a plausible account of natural man's self-consciousness and liberty. The impossibility of an isolated self-consciousness of the kind described in Note XV follows from Wittgenstein's argument in the *Philosophical Investigations* that a private language is impossible. {Ludvig Wittgenstein, *Philosophical Investigations*, Anscombe trans., (Oxford: Basil Blackwell, 1967), §201-07, 256-61ff.}

    In Wittgenstein's view it is possible to have a private subjective mental experience, for example a pain, but it is not possible to construct a language to describe the pain to oneself alone. The reason for this is that "when we speak of someone's having given a name to pain, what is presupposed is the existence of the grammar of the word pain." (§257) Meaning, as much for ourselves as for others, must be derived from a set of conventions about what is meaningful, a grammar or language game. (§261) Thus while the self-conscious savage may have the private experience of choosing between the impulsions of nature, he can have no language through which to understand this, and therefore no idea of its significance for him. This is consistent with Rousseau's first account of natural man's consciousness of his liberty, but not with the account of self-consciousness in Note XV. The latter account presupposes a considerable degree of abstraction from immediate experience (without this, there would be nothing to observe or to value), as well as a language in which to construct meaningful judgements regarding oneself. It may indeed be possible to abstract in some measure from one's experience without language, but it is very difficult to see how it would be possible to give meaning to those experiences without a language. If we accept Wittgenstein's claim that a private language is impossible, then a common language and thus intersubjective social relations are presupposed by Rousseau's second account of natural man's self-consciousness. We should also note that Rousseau himself claims that abstractions or general ideas cannot be conceived without the aid of language. (O.C. III., p. 149-59.) But a conception of the self independent of its experience, to which one accords value, surely involves just that: the use of an abstraction which can only be accomplished in language. It follows then that Rousseau's account of an isolated self-consciousness in Note XV is not consistent with his conception of original nature.

15. John Charvet, *The Social Problem in the Philosophy of Rousseau*, (London: Cambridge University Press, 1974), p. 10.

16. O.C. III, p. 135.

17. *Ibid.*, p. 147.

18. *Ibid.*, p. 199.

19. *Ibid.*, p. 143.

20. *Ibid.*, p. 165.

21. *Ibid.*, p. 165.

22. The character and significance of the first social relations, as well as Rousseau's explanation of their specific causes, will be examined in some detail in the following Chapter.

23. *Ibid.*, p. 165.

24. *Ibid.*, p. 167-69.   The very general account of this period given in the *Discours sur l'inégalité* is consistent with the more detailed accunt given in the *Essai sur l'origine des langues*, especially Chapter IX. The logical consistency between these two texts is discussed below, in Endnote 16, to Chapter 4.

25. O.C. III, p. 141.

26. *Ibid.*, p. 162.

27. *Ibid.*, pp. 164-66; E.O.L., pp. 105-07. See also Bazcko, *Rousseau: solitude et communauté*, p. 92.

28. For an interpretation of this kind see Emile Durkheim, *Montesquieu et Rousseau: precurseurs de la sociologie*, (Paris, 1953), pp. 134-40; and Marc Plattner, *Rousseau's State of Nature*, (New York, 1979).

29. O.C. III, pp. 141-42; E.O.L., pp. 38-39.

30. Robert Wokler, *Rousseau's Perfectibilian Libertarianism*, in *The Idea of Freedom*, Alan Ryan, ed., (London: Oxford University Press, 1979), p. 255. See also Robert

> Wokler, *Perfectible Apes in Decadent Cultures: Rousseau's Anthropology Re-visited*, in *Daedalus*, Summer, 1978, p. 127.

31. *Ibid.*, p. 238.

32. O.C. III, p. 149.

33. E.O.L., p. 39-40.

> L'invention de l'art de communiquer nos idées dépend moins des organes qui nous servent à cette communication, que d'une faculté propre à l'homme, qui lui fait employer ses organes à cet usage...La langue de convention n'appartient qu'à l'homme. Voila pourquoi l'homme fait des progrès, soit en bien, soit en mal, et pourquoi les animaux n'en font point.

34. O.C. III, p. 141.

35. Wokler makes this point. See Wokler, *Rousseau's Perfectibilian Libertarianism*, p. 238.

36. O.C. III, p. 160.

37. *Ibid.*, p. 153.

4

Rousseau's Arcadian Ideal

4.1 Introduction

In the last Chapter I argued that nature and culture constitute a basic antinomy in Rousseau's philosophical anthropology. To put the antinomy in its most extreme, and problematic form: nature and society are closed systems because their defining characteristics are fundamentally exclusive of one another. What humans are by nature they cannot be in society; and consequently Rousseau's attempt to link natural and social being on the continuum of human development constantly verges on paradox. Natural man is fundamentally good; there is nothing in either his nature or his environment that could precipitate his corruption. Social man is on the other hand corrupt, and the properties that define him as social: his recognition of others as self-conscious beings like himself, his language and his reason, are at the same time the basis of his corrupt nature. The problem Rousseau had, as I have noted, was to show how these two modes of being are related to one another. The characteristics defining our social nature cannot be present in the natural state, yet as the condition of our capacity to engage in social relations at all, they must have a cause external to the social state.

The problem is particularly evident in Rousseau's discussion of the origin of language. Language is an essential aspect of social life: our rationality, our awareness of others and our relations with them are inconceivable without it. As such it could not have been an attribute possessed by human beings in the state of nature. To attribute to the species a natural capacity for language would be to impute to it a natural propensity towards sociability and corruption.[1] Yet it is difficult, if not impossible to conceive of any form of society properly called, which does not presuppose some kind of language.[2] We therefore encounter a paradox. Language could not have been invented in the pure state of nature, so it must be a social phenomenon, that is, produced in society; yet society presupposes language as its condition, and so could not have produced it. As closed or mutually exclusive systems, nature and society appear as two autonomous and irreconcilable forms of life, not unlike the animal and the human in the Cartesian or *fixist* accounts of the order of being. Yet to be plausible, a philosophical anthropology that wishes to chart the evolution of the species' nature must establish a link between these two spheres. If we read Rousseau's account of the opposition between nature and culture in this extreme form, as between two autonomous and irreconcilable forms of life, we are left with the conclusion that his account of the subject's development is incoherent. This is well illustrated by Jacques Derrida's reading of Rousseau's linguistics, in which nature and culture are said to oppose each other across an unbridgeable gap, and so call for a solution in which the transition from one to the other is represented as simultaneously "absolutely natural and absolutely artificial".[3] Yet despite Derrida's perceptive interpretation of the tension between nature and society in Rousseau's thought, his conclusion hardly seems tenable. Rousseau does not argue that the species' transition from the natural to the social state was at once natural <u>and</u> artificial. To do so would, as we have seen, have drawn the stability and independence of man's natural state into question. Nevertheless, this very stability requires that there be a cause external to the natural state itself to explain the species' development away from it. One such cause might be Providence: that is, God's intervention might be invoked to explain what

Rousseau's account of our original nature cannot. Yet Rousseau explicitly rejects this position, claiming that he would prefer "former des conjectures tirées de la seule nature de l'homme et des Etres qui l'environnant, sur ce qu'auriot pur devenir le Genre-humain s'il fut reste abandonné a lui-même."[4] Another, and in Rousseau's terms more plausible alternative would be as Derrida suggests; simply to invoke a cause external to man's nature - a set of fortuitous but wholly arbitrary circumstances - which will then serve to supplement nature as an explanation of the species' transition from nature to society. In this sense the natural is supplemented by the artificial.[5] There are two good reasons for resisting this latter interpretation, which will in turn lead us to the conclusion I drew in the last section: i.e. that for Rousseau the first stages of the species' development are entirely natural; they represent the realization of the subject's natural potential, and as such have no necessarily detrimental effects on his nature, nor any significantly arbitrary or artificial component.

The first reason is that although Derrida accurately identifies the crucial tension in Rousseau's account of our development, he overstates the discontinuity or exclusivity of the two modes of life. For while it is the case that Rousseau views fully developed societies as the obverse of our existence according to nature, and as I have indicated, that he defines natural man solely in terms of his potential to acquire those characteristics that mark his social nature; there is nevertheless a period in human development when man is said to be a social being who lives according to nature. I refer here to the so-called *Golden Age*, what Rousseau describes as: "un juste milieu entre l'indolence de l'état primitif et la pétulante activité de notre amour-propre".[6] Rousseau regards this as the most stable and happy epoch of human evolution, and as such it blurs the lines between nature and culture conceived as "closed systems". I want to argue that this period represents the fulfilment of the species' natural potential, and so constitutes a bridge between the two seemingly distinct modes of life. The second reason for resisting Derrida's paradoxical conclusion is that there is no need, if my account of Rousseau's conception of the subject is correct, to regard "fortuitous circumstance" as either arbitrary or artificial in the sense of being external to nature. Rousseau regards the faculty of *perfectibilité* as our capacity to adapt to changes in our environmental circumstances in an undetermined way.[7] What is important in this respect is that some environmental change occurs as the condition of the species' development, of its realizing its natural potential. However the changes themselves need not take any specific form, because human nature is itself defined by its potential capacity for development. This is why Rousseau believes he can make accurate conjectures about this early period of the species' evolution. Our development begins with a change in material environment which undermines the perfect equilibrium of primitive man's relation to the natural order. Whatever the details of these changes, and Rousseau was well aware of the impossibility of verifying them empirically, their significance rests wholly on our nature as inherently free and improvable beings. They are not then, as Derrida suggests, external to nature and so arbitrary and artificial, except perhaps in the trivial sense that they occur independent of the species' will. They are rather entailed in the explanation of how a potentially social being realizes his social nature. For Rousseau, the subject's nature must be explained in relation to the environment in which he exists. The circumstances which influence his development only become artificial when they are themselves produced by self-conscious human intentions.[8]

The species' initial progress away from the pure state of nature occurs as a consequence of the interaction of the characteristics which define it as human (freedom and *perfectibilité*), with a physical environment marked by scarcity and the occurrence of occasional natural cataclysms.[9] These developments have the effect, as we saw above, of forcing the species into more specialized modes of producing subsistence and an increased frequency of contact with others. What might be termed proto-societies are formed: isolated, and for the most part self-sufficient families, which remain the basis of a very simple and limited form of social organization until the invention of metallurgy and the establishment of property.[10] There are two points to be made about this epoch. The first is that the development it facilitates in the species' nature is of a largely cognitive and psychological import, and second that Rousseau regards these developments as natural, and so advantageous to the species as a whole. The epoch of the first revolution brings about an important transformation in human cognitive capacities. We acquire rudimentary language and a limited capacity for rational calculation. But most importantly, we acquire a self-consciousness which entails a recognition of others as self-conscious, self-valuing beings like ourselves.[11]

The conclusion that these initial developments are natural derives from the considerations above. They represent the determinate realization of the species' natural potential, yet neither the process through which these characteristics are acquired, nor the implications of their being possessed, violates the limitations imposed on us by nature. Their acquisition is not the consequence of conscious intentions, and so is consistent with the undeveloped subjectivity of a natural being; and since what they issue in is a "juste milieu" which is both stable and happy, they cannot be regarded as the cause of our present corruption. They are however, and this is my second point, the necessary cognitive conditions of our subsequent progress into fully-fledged social beings. The acquisition of language is necessary for the species' progress beyond all but the most rudimentary social relations. It is indeed the most obvious means of distinguishing between man and animal, and as Rousseau points out, the reason we progress while animals do not.[12] With language, experience can be analyzed and shared, knowledge accumulated and progress achieved. The other, equally fundamental cognitive condition for our progress into fully social beings is that we must come to recognize others as self-conscious, self-valuing subjects like ourselves. In the most obvious sense, this is truism, because we cannot regard our relations with others a social unless they are to some extent intersubjective.[13] However, it would seem that Rousseau has something more than this truism in mind. Recognition of others as subjects like oneself gives rise to *amour-propre*, and so to man's competitive desire for the esteem of others. Ultimately, the desire for esteem in the eyes of others becomes a universal motive for the development of every attribute that might serve to distinguish one as superior to others.[14] In this sense, then, the recognition of others and the relative or comparative nature of the self-consciousness that depends on it, is a condition of our progress as corrupt social beings. However, it should be noted that Rousseau is not suggesting that intersubjective relations are themselves the cause of corruption. They give rise to *amour-propre*, but the infrequency and limited intensity of the individual's contact with other during the *Golden Age* severely restricts its influence on his nature. The species requires a further transformation in its environment, the institutionalization of inequality, for the moral hegemony of *amour-propre* to be established.[15]

In what follows I intend to examine Rousseau's account of the species' transition from nature to society. One contention I will make is that the *Golden Age* must be understood as an attempt to bridge two radically different modes of being: the natural and the social. It is therefore represented as the culmination of a natural process in which primitive man's potential humanity is realized, while at the same time as a quasi-social state in which the species' capacity for both progress and corruption have become manifest. The question this raises, given the deep tension between nature and culture in Rousseau's thought: is whether humans can be natural and social at the same time, or perhaps more fundamentally, can the subject possess the characteristics of humanity (as opposed to the mere potential to acquire these characteristics) without being corrupt? Rousseau clearly answers in the affirmative; and despite his extreme characterization of the differences between nature and society, I want to claim that he is not unjustified in his claim.

A second contention I wish to make is that there are three separate accounts of subjectivity in Rousseau's philosophical anthropology; each constituted by a different set of environmental circumstances; and each implying a different conception of freedom as its realization or fulfilment. In the *Essai sur l'origine des langues*, Rousseau delineates three possible modes of production ("manières de vivres"): hunting, pastoralism, and agriculture; to which correspond three types of man: savage, barbarian, and civilized man respectively.[16] These categories of the subject's relation to his environment correspond to the three stages of the species' evolution described in the *Discours sur l'inégalité*. Within each stage, the subject is constituted in a certain way: as pure potentiality, as the natural if as yet rudimentary realization of that potentiality, and finally as a social being whose conception of self is constantly influenced and distorted by his relations with others. In each of these stages Rousseau's account of the subject implies a specific conception of freedom: the savage man's freedom is purely negative or mechanical, barbaric man's freedom combines absence of constraint with authenticity of expression, while social man requires a positive or moral freedom conceived as self-legislating autonomy.

4.2 Sexuality and the Origins of Natural Society

I have argued that the period between the pure state of nature and the establishment of civil societies produces two important developments, which mark a radical change in the human subject. The recognition of others as self-conscious and self-valuing subjects like oneself, and the acquisition of language (with its consequent implications for our rationality), mark both the beginning of rudimentary social life and the acquisition of two cognitive attributes necessary for the subject's evolution into a fully social being. The acquisition of these characteristics occurs very slowly,[17] concurrently with a number of changes produced in the species' environment by its unintentional or unreflective adaptation to circumstances of scarcity and geographical isolation.[18] I want now to turn to a discussion of the process through which these new attributes are acquired, and to consider some of their implications for the subsequent development of the species' moral psychology.

There are two dimensions of human experience which Rousseau regards as crucial to our initial socialization: family life and sexuality.[19] Both have natural origins, yet both have an important role to play in the species' acquisition of its social nature. Unlike family life, sexuality, or sexual behaviour predates all forms of social life. In Rousseau's

Rousseau's Arcadian Ideal

view sexual desire is a natural biological fact about all species, and as such perfectly compatible with the isolated, non-social existence of natural man. It is he says, one of the three basic goods common to primitive human beings,[20] and though it may not be directly relevant to individual's self-preservation, it is a need which is satisfied without the consequence of socialization. Rousseau writes that: "Les males et les femelles s'unissoient fortuitement selon la rencontre, l'occasion, et le désir, sans que la parole fut un interprête fort nécessaire des choses qu'ils avoient à se dire: Ils se quittoient avec la même facilite."[21] He then goes on to claim, in Note XII, that Locke was mistaken to suppose that the sexual behaviour characteristic of human beings (notably the fact that females are capable of conceiving long before their progeny cease to be dependent on them) implies that males have a natural interest in providing for children, and thus that the family is natural to the human species.[22] Rousseau makes three specific points against Locke, but each simply highlights what he takes to be Locke's basic mistake, which is to assume that because it may be normally advantageous for the species to behave in a sexually monogamous fashion, it follows that they actually did so, and therefore that this was established by nature. "J'observerai d'abord que les preuves morales n'ont pas une grand force en matiére de Physique".[23] The point Rousseau wishes to make is that nothing social follows from the fact that we are sexual in the state of nature. It gives rise to no emotional ties and no need for communication. The reason for this is that we can distinguish between the moral and the physical in sexuality; and in the context of Rousseau's anthropology, it only makes sense to regard the former as social and the latter as natural.

> Commençons par distinguer le moral du Physique dans le sentiment de l'amour. Le Physique est ce désir générale que porte un sexe à s'unir à l'autre; Le moral est ce qui détermine se désir et le fixe sen un seul objet exclusivement...Or il est facile de voir que le moral de l'amour est un sentiment factice; ne de l'usage de la société, et célébré par les femmes, avec beaucoup d'habilété et soin pour, établir leur empire, et rendre dominant le sexe qui devroit obéir.[24]

This passage highlights a crucial distinction between natural and social man. The former's sexuality is purely physical: it is a general desire that is satisfied at random, literally, any man or woman will do. This is consistent with Rousseau's conception of natural man's self-consciousness, in that the intentions and evaluations of others form no part of his awareness.[25] Primitive man regards his sexual partners as instruments necessary for his immediate gratification; their needs have no bearing on his desire to use them, and as such he regards them as he would regard any animal, indeed any thing.[26] The importance of this distinction between the moral and the physical in love stems from the relation of sexual desire (and sexuality in general) to consciousness. Sexuality is made moral when the object of one's desire becomes a particular human being who is singled out from amongst others. The subject's awareness of the other in love ceases to be general or abstract, and places him in a relation of comparative evaluation with the other. The needs and desires of the beloved take on importance for the lover because he now wants his love to be reciprocated, he wants not only the beloved, but also the beloved's desire and preference. He is thus dependent on the other's preference or esteem, a phenomena he cannot control, and this comes to be a source of deep anxiety in the moral psychology of social man. However, at this stage, that is during the initial transformation of sexuality and emotional ties in general, Rousseau is not primarily concerned with the anxiety latent in love relations. He is, rather, concerned to show that what had previously been an unreflective and general desire, now becomes a complex moral passion which draws human beings into intersubjective relations with each other. As physical desire is particularized, the subject's awareness expands to include the other as identical to himself, which is to say as a self-conscious, self-valuing person, who is in a position to evaluate him, and whose favourable valuation he needs.

The transformation of sexual desire from physical to moral is therefore a crucial stage in the species' socialization. It is also, as we can see, intimately tied to the rise in importance of *amour-propre* in the moral psychology of human relations. For not only does it give rise to the recognition of others as beings like ourselves, but it also involves us in consideration of merit and beauty, and ultimately in feelings of preference which produce in us anxiety about the esteem of others.[27] However, this is not to suggest, as Schwartz does, that the moralization of sexuality "brings about the total socialization of the human species".[28] For Rousseau, sexuality and family life have important implications for the other dimensions of human experience, but they cannot be analyzed independently of them, nor accorded a primary causal role in human development. Furthermore, while the connection between sexuality and *amour-propre* is important, especially as a means of explaining how the isolated self-consciousness of natural man is broadened to include others, it does not establish a direct link between the non-moral independence of primitive man and the corrupt interdependence of civilized man. The question that needs to be asked, given the internal link between sexuality and interdependence, is why it does not disrupt the stability of the *Golden Age*; bringing about, to use Schwartz's phrase: "the total socialization of the human species"?

In answer to this, the first point to be considered is the natural origin of the sentiment of love. After the process of adaptive innovation outlined in the previous chapter produces more settled modes of life, and the formation of isolated families, the species begins to experience the new sentiment of conjugal love. "Les prémiers développemens de coeur furent l'effet d'une situation nouvelle qui reunissoit dans une habitation commune les maris et les Femmes, les Pères et les Enfans: l'habitude de vivre ensemble fit naître des plus doux sentimens qui soient connus des hommes, l'amour conjugal et l'amour paternel".[29] The new families are represented as isolated and unified little societies, held together by mutual affection of primitive conjugal and paternal love. As long, Rousseau claims, as these rudimentary and isolated family societies were preserved, as long as they remained self sufficient economic units; the species would have remained free, happy and good to the extend allowed us by our relatively undeveloped nature.[30] In this respect conjugal love, which preserves the unity of the family and thus its independence, is crucial to the stability of the *Golden Age*. It serves as a constraint upon the development of more complex social relations, while at the same time establishing emotional ties between people. It must therefore be assumed to deepen their understanding of one another, at least to the extent of enabling them to distinguish between those they loved and those they did not. The emotional unity of the first families also appears, in the chronology of Rousseau's account in both the *Discours sur l'inégalité*, and the *Essai*, to be the natural precursor of romantic love.

Rousseau clearly regards romantic love as a more complex psychological phenomena than primitive conjugal love. It also has more profound moral and social implications. The moral implications, as I noted above, stem from the particularization of the subject's desire. In fixing his desire upon one out of many, he accepts that person as another subject who needs and desires have a value for him. He enters into a moral relation with his beloved. But at the same time, in forming this new attachment, he discovers in himself a persistent anxiety about his standing in his beloved's esteem, because he now desires her emotional commitment as well as her physical being. From the standpoint of socialization, romantic love is seen to draw the hitherto isolated families into more frequent and complex relations with one another, eventually producing a form of primitive society - which Rousseau represents as "la fête primitive".[31] In both the *Discours sur l'inégalité* and the *Essai* Rousseau claims that the sexuality of the young family members draws the various families into more frequent contact with one another.

> Un voisinage permanent ne peut manquer d'engendrer enfin quelque liaison entre diverses familles. De jeune gens de differens sexes habitent des Cabanes voisines, le commerce passages que demande la Nature en amene bientôt un autre, non moins doux et plus permanent par la fréquentation mutuelle.[32]

Ultimately, this issues in the relatively more complex social milieu characterized by "la fête primitive". Evaluative judgments: considerations of merit and beauty and preference are extended beyond the lovers to embrace everyone. Public esteem becomes a need, though it would seem reasonable to conclude that it remains less compelling at this stage than the subject's need for his beloved's esteem.

Rousseau's account of the origin of language and society in the *Essai* develops the same theme. The original families are described as self-sufficient groups with their own modes of communication, which sustain themselves by inbreeding.[33] Presumably these families, like the isolated primitives who preceded them, would have been able to persist in their isolation and self-sufficiency indefinitely. However, as in the *Discours sur l'inégalité*, the environments in which some of these families find themselves force them to adapt their behaviour. The need for water leads them into more frequent contact and some degree of co-operation: "dans les lieux arides où l'on ne pouvoit avoir de l'eau que par des puits, il fallut bien se réunir pour les creuser ou du moins s'accorder pour leur usage. Telle dut être l'origine des sociétés et des langues dans les pays chauds.[34] Rousseau goes on to claim that these new areas of proximity occasion the first ties *between* families. The young people of different families begin to frequent on another's company; the sexual drive that has hitherto been satisfied instinctually and habitually with family members, now takes on an emotional or passionate character which draws the lovers into a recognition of each other's subjectivity.[35] Their relations thus take on a moral dimension. These new relations are subsequently generalized, as in the *Discours sur l'inégalité*, into public festivals ("La se firent les prémiéres fêtes")[36] which indicates that the status of self-conscious, self-valuing subject is eventually accorded to all, and so a relatively more complex social structure is born.

Sexual desire is the most important human need during the species' transition from nature to primitive society, because it draws the subject into what we can identify as social or moral relations. Previous to the advent of romantic love, our needs (and this includes our sexual needs) had served to separate us and to reinforce our isolation. The establishment of families which follows the process of adaptation imposed on the species by nature, produces an expansion of human needs. As life becomes more sedentary and the species' relatively more enlightened; what might be termed rustic comforts were acquired, and with habitual use became needs.[37] However these new needs did not undermine the independence of the original families, nor initiate the spiral expansion of wants and needs that comes to characterize social life after the establishment of property and inequality. In this stage the species' needs act as a limiting condition upon its development, because they remain simple enough to be satisfied by independent effort. No individual is as yet in need of another.[38] However, the needs arising out of the new human sexuality also characteristic of this period fit uneasily into Rousseau's claim that man's independence is preserved in the *Golden Age*. They are neither wholly related to physical desires, as they were for natural man, nor completely satisfiable by independent effort. For as we have seen, the lover's need for his beloved is as much psychological as physical. He needs her desire and her esteem to feel secure in his love, and this places him in a position of dependence on her. His need to be singled out from amongst others by her remains constant and insatiable. He can never in principle completely understand or control her feelings, and thus can never feel completely secure.

Sexuality is crucial to the transition from nature to culture because it links the species to both levels of existence. The needs arising out of the subject's sexual life have both a natural and a social aspect. The physical need for sexual gratification, which is met independently in the pure state of nature, remains a constant and natural impulsion in the species' nature once the first families are established. It provides the subject with a natural need for others; a need which is not of itself enough to establish any significant forms of dependence, but which nevertheless ensures his frequent contact with them. When combined with the cumulative effect of environmental changes and adopted modes of meeting subsistence, natural sexual desire gives rise to the sentiment of love. This new sentiment has a double character. As the product of a natural process it is described as: "sentiment tendre et doux", as a new and pleasurable feeling that draws the primitives together and dampens their ferocity. It gives rise to unreflective and spontaneous feelings of pleasure, to joyous festivals, to moral (and thus social) relations of an innocent kind.[39] In this sense the first "stirrings of the heart" produce a kind of natural society; relations between subjects based primarily upon a feeling that arises in the natural course of the species' development. Yet at the same time the sentiment of love has a strictly social character. It introduces an intersubjective dimension into the individual's relations with others, and so dramatically deepens their complexity. Whereas prior to the advent of romantic love the other had appeared merely as an instrument of satisfaction, she now appears as a subject in her own right, as a being whose consciousness has a bearing, indeed a value for oneself. Love entails this heightened awareness of the other and as a consequence *amour-propre*. It is therefore social, and its implications are profoundly dangerous to morals. By quoting in full the passage cited above, we can see Rousseau alluding to the dual character of this feeling.

> Un sentiment tendre et doux s'insinue dan l'âme, et par la moindre opposition devient une fureur impétueuse: la jalousie s'éveille avec l'amour, la Discorde triomphe, et la plus douce passions reçoit des sacrifices de sang humaine.[40]

We can see then that the needs arising from romantic love fit uneasily into Rousseau's account of primitive society. They are not wholly satisfiable by independent effort, and they do establish relations of dependence. In fact they involve the subject in a new and much more complex consciousness of self. In the pure state of nature man's self-consciousness had precluded any awareness of others as self-conscious subjects like himself. When combined with his natural instinct for self-preservation, this isolated self-consciousness issued in a benign but non-moral self-love, *amour de soi-même*. Natural man valued himself above all others, but his conception of his superior value was achieved independently, without reference to anyone else. The advent of love places the subject in a new relation to others. The beloved takes on a distinguishable value for the lover; she becomes a self-conscious, self-valuing subject in her own right, whose consciousness of him comes to have a bearing on his own self-evaluation. The subject must now reconstitute his conception of self, and particularly his conception of his value, in relation to how he is valued or esteemed by his beloved. This immediate relation between lovers is then generalized so that the need for esteem becomes a central concern in the subject's relations with all others. For Rousseau, the crucial change initiated by this new self-consciousness occurs in the character of our self-love: the independent and benign *amour de soi-même* becomes a relative and factitious *amour-propre*.[41] Awareness of others as self-valuing subjects like ourselves immediately draws the priority of our own value into question. Thus what each individual had assumed instinctively in nature (i.e. the priority of his own value over all others), could now only be maintained *relative* to others, through their recognition of it. The problem is that because everyone needs this recognition, it is not forthcoming. There is as a consequence much potential for both anxiety and dependence in the new psychology of human relations. *Amour-propre* demands that the value one accords to oneself be substantiated by others' recognition of it; yet one can never be sure that recognition is given sincerely, nor ever cease in one's efforts to secure it.

The new self-consciousness fostered by romantic love is entailed in the role Rousseau believes this sentiment plays in the species' evolution, which is that of final bridge between the pure state of nature and primitive society. Romantic love enables natural man to achieve the cognitive progress necessary to engage in social relations with others. The species is portrayed as having made some cognitive progress beyond its instinctual isolation in the pure state of nature by the time the original families are established. It has some conception of relations between things, described as a mechanical prudence; and an awareness of its common superiority over other animals. These developments are said to have prepared man for his later claim to priority as an individual.[42] Yet while preparing him for this claim of priority, or even inclining him towards it, they do not draw him into intersubjective relations with others. As yet the self-consciousness of others forms no part of his experience, and he cannot make the claim to priority Rousseau refers to until it does. The final cognitive leap necessary to explain our capacity for social relations remains to be made, and the sentiment of love is invoked to explain it.

Rousseau refers to the moral aspect of love as something that only arises in society, and in this respect it is like language and rationality -- a characteristic definitive of man in his social state. However, there is a sense in which love is unlike both language and rationality, which makes it a more suitable explanation of the origin of identifiably social relations. Given the radical cognitive break that defines Rousseau's opposition between natural and social life, both language and rationality prove intractably paradoxical as explanations of the origin of society. The origin of each presupposes a degree of cognitive development (and thus social life), which makes nonsense of Rousseau's account of natural man. However, as a passion, love can be seen to arise without presupposing the same degree of cognitive or social development. The lover's interest in his beloved stems first from an unreflective feeling, and it is only as a consequence of this unreflective feeling that he makes the cognitive leap to a recognition of her subjectivity. His previous development has, to a certain extent, prepared him for this recognition, but it is the new feeling that serves to focus his interest and motivate the development of his understanding.[43] Romantic love can be seen as the source of the species' first social relations, because the process which produces it is natural.

Romantic love ties the species to its origin in nature and its fully human existence in society. It has a dual character, in that it is the product of a natural process, which has nevertheless entirely social implications. The society it founds reflects this dual character; it is at once natural and social, what we referred to at the beginning as "natural society". The epoch of what Rousseau calls in the *Essai*, *le siècle d'or*, represents the period in which man's natural potentiality is fulfilled. The species' natural potential has evolved into an identifiably human form of subjectivity; man has become rational, linguistically competent, and most importantly self-conscious in such a way as to enable him to engage in moral relations with others. The social life of this period is natural because it involves relations between fully human subjects who are as yet neither corrupt nor alienated from their true nature. Yet these relations, *qua* social relations, entail at very least a propensity towards dependence; so the question must arise as to whether Rousseau's account of romantic love, and more importantly the *natural society* it founds, is not hopelessly paradoxical given the implications for corruption both entail? If it is, the opposition between nature and society must remain unresolved, because no account of how the subject realizes his natural potential, and thus his inherent value as human being, can be given.

4.3 The Problem of *Amour-Propre* in the *Golden Age*

Rousseau portrays the nascent society formed out of the original families as a Arcadian ideal; and though the *amour-propre* that arises with the new self-consciousness has produced a diminution of natural pity, and perhaps even instances of revenge and cruelty, morality has been introduced into human relations and the species has entered upon the happiest, best, and most stable period of its evolution.

> Ainsi quoique les hommes fussent devenus moins endurans, et que la pitié naturelle eut déjà souffert quelque altération, se période du développement des facultés humaines, tenant un juste milieu entre l'indolence de l'état primitif et la pétulante activité de notre amour-propre, dut être l'époque la plus heureuse, et la plus durable. Plus on y réflechit, plus on trouve que cet état etoit le moins sujet aux révolutions, le meilleur à l'homme, et qu'il n'en a du sortir que par quelque funeste hazard qui pour l'utilité commun eut du ne jamais arriver. L'exemple des Sauvages qu'on a presque tous trouvés à ce point semble confirmer que le Genre-humaine étoit fait pour y rester toujours, que cet état est la véritable jeunesse du Monde et que tous les progrès ultérieurs ont été en apparence autant de pas vers la perfection de l'individu, et en effet ver la décrépitude de l'espèce.[44]

The potential which defined the species as human in the state of nature has come to be realized: the subject is in some degree self-conscious, rational, and linguistically competent, but he has yet to experience the radical dependence and self-estrangement characteristic of his civilized counterparts. This period of uncorrupted social relations, of *natural society* is, I have argued, a necessary stage in Rousseau's account of the species' evolution. The claim that man is by nature good cannot be sustained by the account of primitive man in the pure state of nature, because there is no morality in his actions. The claim can only be substantiated if Rousseau can show that man is good once his natural potential as a human subject has come to fruition, and he is engaged in social relations with others. The problem is of course that the self-consciousness characteristic of the fully developed subject, and presupposed by social relations of any kind, entails a certain degree of psychological dependence. The question therefore arises as to what keeps this dependence and its attendant passion, *amour-propre*, from dominating the moral psychology of the species' relations at this stage?

Rousseau's answer is apparently straightforward. The mode of producing subsistence in nascent society remains primitive; each person's labour is aimed at self-sufficiency and as a consequence there is not division of labour. The organizational principle of *natural society* ensures that each person's independence is in all significant respects preserved. Rousseau writes:

> En un mot tant qu'ils s'appliquérent qu'a des ouvrages qu'un seul pouvoit faire, et qu'à des arts qui n'avoient pas besoin des concours de plusieurs mains, ils vécurent libres, sains, bons et heureux autant qu'ils pouvoient l'être par leur Nature, et continuérent a jour entre eux des douceurs d'un commerce indépendant.[45]

The claim is that although the new environment is social, it nevertheless imposes itself as a limiting condition upon the subject's development. The self-sufficient mode of production ensures that no individual stands in need of another for his livelihood, and therefore that there are no relations of domination and subservience. Each subject knows every other as his equal, and as a consequence no relations of dependence significant enough to corrupt him can arise. Thus just as nature had providentially constrained the development of natural man, the primitive anarchism of natural society limits the moral degeneration of early social man.

Yet for this to be a plausible explanation of how early social man's *amour-propre* is restrained, it must be borne out at the level of the individual's moral psychology. The self-sufficient pastoralism characteristic of this period explains why people have relatively little contact with one another, but Rousseau does not fully explain why the psychological interdependence already established between people would not of itself lead them into more frequent, complex, and ultimately corrupt relations. He has after all identified *amour-propre* as the source of our corruption in society, and *amour-propre* is already aroused. The need for others' esteem is manifest in the particular relations between lovers, and in the more general relations of "la fête primitif".

> Chacun commenca a regarder les autres et a vouloir être regarde soi-même, et l'estime publique eut un prix. Celui qui chantoit ou dansoit le mieux; le

plus beau, le plus fort, le plus adroit ou le plus éloquent devint le plus
consideré, et ce fut la le premier pas ver l'inégalité, et ver vice en même
tems.⁴⁶

The new self-consciousness requires the subject to re-constitute his self-consciousness in relation to others; and this requirement has two, apparently contradictory implications. On the one hand it makes possible moral relations: that is, relations in which the inherent value of the other as a self-conscious, self-determining being, can be recognized and respected. Yet on the other hand it has the consequence of relativizing the subject's self-love, thus making him both competitive and dependent at the same time. The primary value the individual had hitherto accorded himself as a natural consequence of his isolated self-consciousness, is now drawn into question by his recognizing that others value themselves in the same way. The value each accords himself gives rise to the universal and equal claim for the right to consideration.

> Sitôt que les hommes eurent commencé à s'apprecier mutuellement et que
> l'idée de la considération fut formée dans leur esprit, chacun prétendit y
> avoir droit; et il ne fut plus possible d'en manquer impunément pour
> personne. De la sortirent les premiers devoirs de la civilité, même parmi les
> sauvages, et delà tour tort volontaire devient un outrage, parce qu'avec le
> mal qui résultoit de l'injure, l'offensé y voyoit le mépris de sa personne
> souvent plus insuportable que le mal même.⁴⁷

An element of corruption and even self-estrangement has entered the psychology of the subject's relations with others. He now finds it necessary to be civil in lieu of the right to consideration claimed by others, both because he wishes to avoid conflict and because he is expecting civility from them. Nevertheless, the respect he shows them necessarily diminishes his own value, which he cannot but regard as greater. This contradiction is then reconciled by the pretence of civility: each pretends to value those others whose good opinion he desires, as a means of securing their recognition of his value. The severity of Rousseau's critique of the psychology of social relations is in this case extreme: he seems to be arguing that our vanity as social beings denies the very possibility of sincere respect for others. Such respect draws our own value into question, it undermines the basis for our self-love and so leaves us in an intolerable state of anxiety and envy. Yet at the same time each person must crave, and seek, this respect from others as acknowledgement of his superior value.[48] It would seem then that even in the festive and rustic simplicity of natural society, the subject has reason to appear to be what he is not. Undoubtedly, Rousseau intends this bleak picture of our moral psychology to explain the corruption and alienation characteristic of fully developed civil societies; he cannot avoid the implication that some degree of corruption and self-estrangement is entailed in the self-consciousness necessary for social relations themselves. In nature the subject's conception of self is so limited that it is unmediated by his concern for others. But this is replaced with a conception of self in which one's value is determined relative to the status and opinions of others. The subject no longer know himself as an independent unity, but rather as a complex personality in which being and appearance are two separate things: in which what one *is* can be separated from what one is valued for; and what one feels or thinks can be different from what one says and does. The point is that the impetus for competition, manipulation, and for self-estrangement in the form of dependence on the opinions of others, is present from the beginning in the moral psychology of social relations. Is it, one might fairly ask, plausible that the limitations imposed by the lack of economic development could serve to restrain this impetus, and thus the wholesale socialization and corruption of the human species?

4.4 Natural Language and Authenticity

The short answer to this is yes, however the argument of the *Discours sur l'inégalité* does not explain in any degree of detail how the lack of economic development works as a limiting condition at the level of the individual's moral psychology. As a consequence, the impetus towards corruption and self-estrangement entailed in self-consciousness seems far more powerful than the effect of the socio-economic structure meant to restrain it. However, Rousseau's philosophy of language, and in particular his account of the history of the species' linguistic development, offers a more detailed and convincing account of the subject's moral psychology during the pastoral anarchism of *le siècle d'or*. In the *Essai*, Rousseau links three different forms of social life with three different modes of production:

> A la division précendente se reportent les trois états de l'homme considéré par raport à la société. Le sauvage est chasseur, le barbare est berger, l'homme civil est laboureur.[49]

These three forms of social life are also linked with three separate stages in the species' linguistic development.[50] The link between linguistic and socio-economic progress is made, as I argued in the previous chapter, because language is the most concrete manifestation of the species' cognitive development. Its origin presupposes both an other-regarding self-consciousness and some degree of rationality; and its development tracks the species' cognitive and social progress. We thus find original languages to be figurative, passionate and expressive; reflecting their origins in the passions and the limited development of the subject's needs and rationality.[51] The language of civilized peoples on the other hand reflects the complexity of civilized life and the highly developed subjectivity of civilized man: the radical expansion of needs, the increased importance of rationality, and the corrupt intensity of our social relations, all come to be reflected in the nature of our language. Rousseau writes:

> il devient plus juste et moins passionné; il substitue aux sentimens les idées, il ne parle plus coeur mais a la raison...la langue devient plus exacte plus claire, mais plus traînante plus sourde et plus froide.[52]

At any given stage of the species' social development then, language reveals much about the level of its cognitive, psychological and moral development. The language of natural society gives us some insight into Rousseau's conception of the species' subjectivity just following its emergence from the pure state of nature: both of how it is constituted by the new social environment, and why its independence and innocence is preserved.

In the *Essai*, Rousseau argues that language and society (i.e. intersubjective, social relations) arise in the first instance from the passions, from romantic live.[53] However implausible this argument may be in detail, it is based on the more fundamental premise alluded to above: that it is by the force of their passions, rather than their needs, that human beings are first drawn into society and communication.

> On ne commença pas par raisoner mais par sentir. On prétend que les hommes inventèrent la parole pour exprimer leurs besoins; cette opinion me paroit insoutenable. L'effet naturel des premiers besoins fut d'écarter les hommes et non de les rapprocher...De cela seul il suit avec evidence que l'origine des langues n'est point due aux prémiers besoins des hommes; il seroit absurde que la cause qui les écart vint le moyen qui les unit. D'où peut donc venir cette origine? Des besoins moraux, des passions.[54]

The origins of human language in passions leads to an important distinction in Rousseau's philosophy of language: the distinction between languages of passion or feeling and languages of need. The former arise first, in southern regions, and reflect the feelings on which they are based. They are figurative and musical because they arose as spontaneous expressions of natural feeling, and they speak directly to the heart of the other.[55] The languages of need arise much later in human history, in northern regions where the hostile environment forces people to struggle for subsistence. In these areas work replaces idleness, and need replaces passion as the motive force behind communication. The languages that develop in these areas are as a consequence more suited to the satisfaction of needs: they are more suited to the analysis of experience than the expression of feeling, they speak to reason rather than the heart. Rousseau puts it cryptically: in northern languages "le premier mot ne fut pas chez eux, aimez-moi, (as it was in languages of feeling), mais, aidez-moi".[56]

The need/passion, north/south distinction between languages Rousseau makes in the *Essai*, has important implications for his account of the subject's moral life in primitive society. First, the original languages were passionate in character. It therefore follows, given both the general structural consistency of argument between the *Essai* and the *Discours sur l'inégalité*, and their nearly identical accounts of the emotional origins of language and society, that the languages of primitive societies (i.e. those prior to the establishment of agriculture) were passionate in character. The second implication, which follows on from this, is that the languages of passion characteristic of primitive societies were more natural, and as such we shall see, more authentic than the languages of need characteristic of civil societies. For Rousseau, the original languages of feeling were the medium through which early social man developed in relation to others. They were therefore necessary for the realization of his natural potential, without at the same time contributing to his further development, and the corruption that would inevitably follow in its train. Original language allows the self to be constituted in relation to another. But at the same time, it minimizes the degree of dependence, as well as anxiety over relative status, that the subject necessarily experiences when faced with other self-conscious individuals.

Rousseau's argument for the more natural and authentic character of passionate language is mainly historical, but is has nevertheless important implications for his conception of the subjects' moral psychology at this stage of the species' development. We noted above that Rousseau saw the history of linguistic development as the progress of language from passion to reason; from the figurative and poetic expression of primal feelings to the rational and conventional representation of ideas in conventional discourse.[57] Yet the term "progress" must be used advisedly here, because Rousseau is ambivalent about the actual gains achieved with the species' acquisition of conventional, grammatical language. His ambivalence stems from the fact that linguistic development cannot be dissociated from intellectual and social development. As the species' needs become more extensive, its social relations more complicated, and its reason more developed, language loses its passionate character and becomes more logical: more suited to the exact analysis and representation of experience; but less suited to the expression and communication of feeling.

The invention of alphabet-based, grammatical language, provides humans with a conventional method of analyzing and representing the world of their experience.[58] This has undoubted gains attached to it; expanding our knowledge of the natural world and increasing our control over it. However, it becomes at the same time an instrument through which we can control, manipulate, and even suppress other people. Conventional language speaks to reason, and so allows the speaker to manipulate the consciousness of others in a way he could not speaking a language of passion.[59] Rousseau's account of the founding of civil society in the *Discours sur l'inégalité* offers an example of how language can be used as an instrument of manipulation and oppression. The contract which founds civil society is described as a seduction of the poor by the rich. The rich man, realizing that he is insecure in the possession of his wealth, proposes political society and the rule of law as a means of providing universal peace and prosperity.[60] Yet the proposed contract is bogus, for its simply has the effect of legitimizing the inequality already established; and in the name of justice and freedom subjects the majority to injustice and servitude: "pour le profit quelque ambitieux assujétirent désormais tout le Genre-humain au travail, à la servitude, et à la misére."[61] The point is that this fateful seduction of the poor presupposes a well established conventional language, in which people's experience, their values, and their needs, can be represented and communicated. As seducer, the rich man speaks to the needs (and therefore the reason) of the multitude, which he knows to be easier to deceive than their hearts. Indeed, as Rousseau describes it, the poor are already corrupt: their wants have already outstripped what they naturally need; their minds are ready to be deceived. The multitude already had:

> trop d'avarice et d'ambition, pour pouvoir longtems se passer de Maîtres. Tous coururent au devant de leurs fers croyant assurer leur liberté; car avec assés de raison pour sentir les avantages d'un établissement politique, ils n'avoient pas assés d'expérience pour en prévoir les dangers.[62]

It is only by speaking the languages of need that the rich can deceive the poor, because this is the only discourse complex enough to misrepresent their true needs in a convincing way, and so deceive them into accepting misery and servitude under the guise of justice and liberty.

The language of feeling on the other hand, is suited neither to the misrepresentation of true needs nor the deception of pretended intentions. It is based on primal feelings such as pity, love, anger and fear; and it develops as a discourse suited to the spontaneous and direct expression of these feelings. Whereas developed language subjects what it wishes to represent to analysis, by dividing it into its component parts, and then re-ordering those parts according to the logic of conventional grammar; the passionate language of early social man expresses feelings directly, without the mediation of analysis or reflection. Thus Rousseau writes:

> Non seulement tous les tours de cette langue devroient être en images, en sentiments, en figures; mais dans sa partie mécanique elle devroit répondre à son premier objet, et présenter au sens ainsi qu'à l'entendement les impressions presque inévitables de la passion qui cherche à se communiquer.[63]

For this reason, early language was musical and poetic. It attempted to articulate in sound what is present in the emotions, and in Rousseau's view the most natural way to accomplish this is by imitation. Thus: "Avec les prémiéres voix se formérent les prémiéres articulations ou les prémiers sons, selon le genre de la passion qui dictoit les un ou les autres."[64] We go on to learn that music, poetry, and language each had a common origin in the passions ignited by the first love relations. Thus, the first languages are said to be fusions of poetry and music. Sounds were used to imitate feelings, rather than represent ideas, and this produced a simple but melodic language which, though unsuited to the articulation of ideas, was far superior to our own for the expression of passion.[65] In Rousseau's view, passion-based language is a more authentic mode of communication than conventional, grammatical language. Its authenticity stemmed from two characteristics: first, that it expressed passions, which are our original and most natural moral experience; second, that it was imitative and melodic, and therefore represented its object in the most direct and transparent way possible.

To illustrate this Rousseau develops the outline of a moral aesthetic in the latter half of the ***Essai sur l'origine des langues***. He argues here that the power of art as a medium of expression lies in its capacity to move us morally, and that this moral power derives from its imitative character. Thus in painting, it is the representation of figure and form by drawing, rather than the configuration or balance of colour, that moves us as moral beings to identify with and feel some interest in the subject of a work of art.[66] Similarly, in music we are drawn to and moved by melodies; sounds which naturally imitate human feelings. Harmony on the other hand, has a merely conventional beauty, which while pleasing to the ear as colours are pleasing to the eye, cannot speak to our essence or nature as moral beings.

> La mélodie en imitant les inflexions de la voix exprime les plaintes les cris de douleur ou joye, les menaces, les gémissemens; tous les signes vocaux des passions sont de son ressort. Elle imite les accens des langues, et les tours affectés dans chaque idiome á certains mouvement de l'ame; elle n'imite pas seulement, elle parle, et son langage inarticulé mais vif ardent passionné a cent fois plus d'énergie qui la parole même. Voila d'où naît la force des imitations musicales; voila d'où naît l'empire du chant sur les coeurs sensibles. L'harmonie y peut concourir en certain sistêmes en liant la succession des sons pas quelque loix de modulation, en rendant les intonations plus justes, en pourtant à l'oreille un témoignage assuré de cette justesse, en rapprochant et fixant à des intervalles consonans et lies des inflexions inappréciables. Mais en donnant aussi des entraves à la mélodie elle lui ôte l'énergie et l'expression, elle efface l'accent passionné pour y substituer l'intervalle harmonique...en un mot, elle sépare tellement le chant et la parole que ces deux langages se combatent se contrarient s'ôtent mutuellement tout caractére de vérité...[67]

In original language melody and speech are combined to form a passionate, expressive, and authentic medium of communication. This first melodic language not only imitates natural human feelings; unencumbered by conventional techniques of representation, it speaks them purely and directly. The stress on musicality, on the melodic character of early speech reflects Rousseau's concern with the moral effects of language. Like figurative representation in painting, melody speaks to our natural essence as moral beings; it evokes an emotional (and in Rousseau's view) moral response in the listener, which elevates music to the status of art.[68] Harmony on the other hand, is seen to be the technique of arranging or ordering sounds; as such akin to science: a purely intellectual activity which aims at conventional (i.e. socially produced) conceptions of beauty and order. It "shackles" and "enervates" melody precisely because it turns music away from its imitative character as a transparent medium for the communication of feeling, to a technique for the representation of ideas. The parallel between the degeneration of music and the development of language is very close in Rousseau's mind. Harmony is seen to have destroyed the original unity of music and speech to the mutual detriment of both modes of expression. He claims that northern peoples, whose language arose later and in response to their needs, cannot express strong passions in song without sounding ridiculous. The point being that their languages are unsuited to passionate expression because they arose as a method of analyzing and controlling the world of their experience. Northern languages are products of more complex societies; as such they are instrumental rather than expressive, logical rather than imitative, intellectual and rational rather than passionate. In this respect writing is to linguistic development what harmony is to the development of music. It imposes a conventional order upon speech, subjecting its melodic spontaneity to grammatical structure.

> L'écriture, qui semble devoir fixer la langue est précisément ce qui l'altére; elle n'en change par les mots mais le génie; elle substitue l'exactitude à l'expression. L'on rend ses sentimens quand on parle et ses idées quand on écrit.[69]

The histories of language and music are both marked by the improvement of conventional technique of representation, and a consequent decline in expressiveness and moral force. In Rousseau's view, this progress in techniques of communication produces an unintended and unwelcome consequence; it interposes arbitrary rules of meaning and grammatical structure between communicating subjects. Where once their relations had been marked by the uninhibited and transparent communication of natural feelings; they are now marked by masked intentions and complex rivalries, by a language which enables them to manipulate meanings and deceive others, but not to express what they naturally or authentically feel.

We can see then the extent to which original language manifests the ideal social life of *le siècle d'or*, while at the same time posing itself as a limiting condition on the subject's development and subsequent corruption. The language of feeling allows for unmediated communication between subjects. The passions which arise in them as a consequence of their increased contact with others (whom they now recognize as self-conscious), give rise to an imitative and melodic language suited only to the pure expression of feeling. They cannot, in speaking such language, mask their motives or deceive others about what they feel. Their relations must necessarily be innocent and transparent as a result; they would not admit of the discrepancy between being and appearance characteristic of advanced social relations, because they are based entirely on the immediate expression of feeling. Equally, from the standpoint of self-consciousness, the self must be seen to be present to itself in the most immediate and direct way. In being dominated psychologically by what he feels, the subject would have found it virtually impossible to experience any sense of discrepancy between what he was and what he wanted to be. He is simply, in any given moment, what he feels himself to be, and he re-affirms it to himself and those around him by expressing himself in vital, passionate language. Early social man, to use an old cliché, wears his heart, indeed his whole being, on his sleeve. As Rousseau writes:

> Les prémiéres langues, filles du plaisir et non du besoin porterent longtems l'enseigne de leur père; leur accent séducteur ne s'effaça qu'avec les sentimens qui les avoient fait naître, lorsque de nouveaux besoins introduits parmi les hommes forcérent chacun de ne songer qu'à lui-même et de retirer son coeur au dedans de lui.[70]

Such language then, admits of little, if any possibility of self-estrangement or psychological interdependence. When combined with the rustic simplicity of early social life, the relatively limited development of man's needs and the independent production of subsistence, it makes plausible Rousseau's claim that the period of the *Golden Age* was the best and happiest for the human species. The plausibility of this ideal of natural society is crucial to his philosophical anthropology. It represents the fulfilment of our natural potential as human beings, and so bridges the yawning gap between nature and culture. The subject is represented as fully human: as self-conscious, linguistically competent, and capable of moral relations; yet this realization of what was held in nature as mere potential does not establish psychological interdependence of an extent necessary to corrupt him. The subject is opened to the possibility of dependence, indeed some degree of dependence is always entailed in Rousseau's conception of intersubjective relations; but his language and the limited nature of his social life preserve him from the radical dependence and self-estrangement he will experience in civil society. In natural society man is good, not as a potentially human natural man, but as a social being whose interdependence and authentic self-expression have moral significance. He is now a moral being whose independence is preserved in social relations.

It is in this sense that Rousseau's portrait of *le siècle d'or* is of an Arcadian ideal. Humans have reached the limit of their natural potential as a moral beings in social relations which preserve their independence and allow for authentic self-expression. Our moral nature, which for Rousseau constitutes our essential value, remains to be developed under the auspices of a civil society characterized by property, inequality and ever-increasing sophistication. Like a newly erected statue of Glaucus, the species faces a future of disfigurement.

4.5 The Decline of Arcadia and the Possibility of Freedom

The ideal social life of *le siècle d'or* comes to an end with the accidental invention of metallurgy, and the subsequent development of agriculture.[71] The species' evolution changes fundamentally at this point. What had hitherto been the development of man's natural or innate potential, now becomes rapid progress under the auspices of civil society: towards greater knowledge and the increasing sophistication and complexity of social relations, but also towards inequality, corruption, and self-estrangement. Environment comes to play a radically different role in human development: for whereas before man's environment had been natural, and as such limited his development to the realization of his natural potential, it has now become social to an extent that encourages, indeed motivates, the species' progress away from nature. The invention of these two technologies is portrayed as accidental, because there can be nothing about natural society itself, as the product of a natural process, that would give rise to this second great "revolution". Rousseau needs to explain the breakdown of natural society in terms of a cause external to it, because to do otherwise would be to contradict his basic assertion that the species is naturally good. The chance invention of metallurgy is claimed to be a necessary condition for the development of agriculture, which Rousseau regards as the mode of production characteristic of the first civil societies. The cultivation of land leads to the institution of property, trade, and the specialization or division of labour follows. Gradually, natural inequalities of strength and skill come to be embodied in more permanent and significant inequalities of wealth and power.[72] The most important moral implication of this new development towards inequality is an increase in physical and psychological dependence between people. A division of labour builds up around the new industries such that people begin to need each other: first for the production of subsistence, but eventually for the satisfaction of a plethora of new, artificial needs arising out of the competition for relative status. Physical dependence is the immediate consequence of property. Natural inequalities give some a disproportionate control over material resources, and this makes others dependent on them. These new and visible inequalities of wealth produce even more damaging effects in the moral psychology of the subject's relations. The capacity for psychological dependence is already, it must be remembered, an aspect of the subject's experience. But with the increased social inequalities produced by private property, this largely dormant capacity becomes the dominant theme in the psychology of our moral and social relations. Our cognitive faculties (reason, imagination, etc.), our language and our knowledge all undergo rapid development; but at the same time we become deeply dependent on others. Our *amour-propre* is interested, being and appearance become two entirely different things.

D'un autre côté, de libre et indépendant qu'étoit auparavant l'homme, le voilà par une multitude de nouveaux besoins assujéti, pour ainsi dire, à toute la Nature, et surtout à ses semblables dont il devient l'esclave en un sens, même en devenant leur maître; riche, il a besoin de leurs services; pauvre, il a besoin de leurs secours, et la médiocrité ne le met point en état de se passer d'eux. Il faut donc qu'il cherche sans cesse à les intéresser la son sort, à leur faire trouver en effet on en apparence leur profit à travailler pour le sien: ce qui le rend fourbe et artificieux avec les uns, impérieux et dur avec les autres, et la met dans la nécessité d'abuser tous ceux dont il a besoin quand il ne peut s'en faire craindre, et qu'il ne trouve pas son intérêt à les servir utilement. Enfin l'ambition dévorante, l'ardeur d'élever sa fortune relative, moins par un véritable besoin que pour se mettre au-dessus des autres, inspire à tous les hommes un noir penchant à se nuire mutuellement, un jalousie secrete d'autant plus dangereuse que, pour faire son coup plus en sûreté, elle prend souvent le masque de la bienveillance, en un mot, concurrence et rivalité d'une part, de l'autre opposition d'intérêt, et toujours le désir cache de faire son profit aux depends d'autrui.[73]

The species' rapidly accelerating development, on the one hand towards civilization and political society, on the other towards dependence and rivalry, is caused in the immediate sense by a transformation in the mode of production. The evils Rousseau outlines above are: "le premier effet de la propriété et la cortège inséparable de l'inégalité naissante". But at the same time it must be noted that the species had to undergo an equally important pre-history before property was introduced and wreaked its disastrous effects. Property would be inconceivable without the development of self-consciousness which proceeds it. Another point we can reiterate, is that for Rousseau property marks a fundamental break in the species' evolution. Prior to its introduction, the species' development is natural to the extend that man only acquires characteristics which he has the natural potential to acquire; while afterwards, he acquires characteristics as a direct result of his social existence, characteristics which are artificial and invariably destructive of his natural potential for freedom.

The effect of property and inequality on the subject's moral psychology is, as we see from Rousseau's prose, disastrous. His relations with others can no longer be maintained, or even understood independent of a social structure which places him in conflict with all others: conflict for material resources but even more importantly for esteem or relative status. The manifest social inequalities that result from property remove all natural constraints upon the subject's *amour-propre*; and the effect of this is to further expand his self-consciousness. He has been transformed from a natural to a social being. As a natural being, he is dominated by primal passions (i.e. *amour de soi-même*, pity, anger, love etc.), and as long as *amour-propre* is restrained these remain the dominant motivations in the subject's moral life. In being dominated by these passions, the subject experiences no asymmetry nor contradiction between what he is for himself, and what he wants to be for others. He expresses himself as he is, authentically, and as a consequence his relations with others do not threaten the independence of his conception of self. But as *amour-propre* comes to dominate the subject's moral psychology, he is socialized and placed under the yoke of a "multitude of new needs". These new needs are artificial, i.e. they are neither derived from nor bear any relation to the natural self, because they arise from the subject's perception that others possess something he lacks. The new needs are a manifestation of these subject's insecurity or anxiety over his status relative to others; of a love of self which is contingent upon the perception of how one is perceived by others. The subject's conception of self is thus alienated to the opinions of others. Social man loses his natural autonomy. The opposition between nature and culture surfaces at the level of moral psychology as an opposition between natural autonomy and social dependence; or in a more extreme, Rousseauiste formulation, between freedom and slavery.

I have argued that the philosophical anthropology of the ***Discours sur l'inégalité*** and the ***Essai sur l'origine des langues*** can be read as an account of the subject's development from nature to culture. In such a reading it is assumed that the conception of the subject characteristic of any of the three stages Rousseau outlines in our evolution, will have an important bearing on the nature and extent of the subject's moral life at that stage. Subjectivity assumes a distinct and identifiable form in each stage; and each of these forms implies a specific conception of freedom as its highest moral value. I want now to briefly discuss each of these forms of subjectivity in relation to the conception of freedom they imply.

In the pure state of nature the subject is constituted almost entirely by his environment. He is defined by two natural or innate characteristics: free-will and *perfectibilité*, but while these characteristics set him apart from complete determination by the material forces of nature, they do not distinguish him behaviourally from animals. They indicate two important things about the human subject: first that he is possessed of an awareness of himself as an agent, and second that he has the natural potential to become a moral being. But while Rousseau clearly regards natural man as good, and even free,[74] he does not regard him as moral, because the self-consciousness of others forms no part of his experience, and so has no bearing on his own conception of self. In what sense then, can such a subject be free? Rousseau's answer can only be that natural man is free in a purely negative. In the pure state of nature the self is absolutely independent and unified. Its powers are equal to its needs, and it is therefore physically independent. The subject's awareness of itself is also free from all external psychological influences; the intention and opinions of others simply have no significance for him, and he is thus free from the dependence, vanity, and competition that characterizes the experience of civilized man. The freedom of the underdeveloped subject is thus in no sense a positive faculty. He is valued primarily for what he is not, i.e. dependent and corrupt, and what he has the potential to become, i.e. a moral being who retains his freedom. The kind of freedom available to primitive man is of merely tangential moral significance. The fact that he has free will and *perfectibilité* only indicates a natural potential for freedom in the context of moral or social relations. It is in other words significant purely for its future implications, but of itself of no moral import whatsoever. Given that the subject's self-consciousness must undergo a radical change before he can enter moral relations, we can conclude that the negative freedom available to him in his most primitive state will no longer suffice as an expression of his natural essence when he enters society. The freedom of the social subject, who is defined by his capacity to engage in intersubjective (and hence moral)

Rousseau's Arcadian Ideal 123

relations with others, must take on a positive, moral dimension.

Once the subject has entered nascent society, his natural potential as a free and improvable being has been realized. His self-consciousness has been expanded to include recognition of self-conscious others, he has a certain degree of rationality and the use of language. It is thus at this stage necessary to understand the subject as constituted in his relations with other subjects. On the one hand, his cognitive faculties have progressed far beyond those he possessed in the pure state of nature; but on the other his natural independence is now threatened by the birth of *amour-propre* in a self-consciousness necessarily informed by comparisons with others. With this new self-consciousness the subject can no longer be regarded as he was in nature, as an entirely independent unity. His relations with others introduce new, psychological constraints upon his freedom; he can now become dependent on others for his conception of self, and so in a fundamental sense cease to embody and express his true nature. The freedom of the subject at this stage cannot be purely negative, because what threatens his independence is not external physical restraints of the kind that could deny natural man his freedom, but rather the kind of internal, psychological constraints natural man had been too limited to experience. The freedom of early social man must therefore involve a positive, moral dimension, which Rousseau attempts to give it by insisting on the authentic nature of self-expression in early forms of language. In fact, the freedom of early social man involves a combination of negative and positive elements. It is negative to the extent that the mode of production is characterized by self-subsistent labour. The subject is as a consequence preserved from any form of economic dependence on others, and in general from very frequent or complex relations of any kind. But this relative physical independence from others does not preclude the possibility of moral relations, and these as we have seen entail the possibility of psychological interdependence. The subject is preserved from this by the fact that his relations with others arise out of primal or natural passions; the medium through which he expresses himself (passionate language), serves as a means of preserving the passionate and natural character of these relations, by ensuring that each subject authentically expresses what he feels. The self's independence is preserved, because the medium through which it is related to others does not admit of deception or manipulation. The positive or moral element of early social man's freedom is therefore the authenticity of his self-expression. The self is present to itself and to others exactly as it is, thus avoiding the dependence and conflict characteristic of social life in its more developed forms.

The final stage of the species' evolution is marked by the loss of both physical and psychological independence. The division of labour and inequality of wealth characteristic of civil societies puts each individual in need of others: the poor need the rich for their survival, and the rich need the poor to preserve their wealth and to re-affirm their sense of superiority. The unity and independence of the self has been lost with the alienation of each individual's conception of self and sense of value to the opinions of others. *Amour-propre* has become the motive force behind the development of each subject's identity, and as in consequence each ceases to embody his original nature. This, in Rousseau's view, is the central problem in social existence, and the great tragedy of the species' evolution.

> Telle est, en effet, la véritable cause de toutes ces différences: le Sauvage vit en lui-même; l'homme sociable toûjours hors de lui ne sait vivre que dans l'opinions des autres, et c'est, pour ainsi dire, de leur seul jugement qu'il tire le sentiment de sa propre éxistence.[75]

The species' transition to civil society has meant the loss of its physical and psychological independence. We have lost our freedom, and with it the innocence and authenticity Rousseau associated with our original nature. Furthermore, the degree of our cognitive, moral, and social development denies the possibility of ever returning to nature, or of recovering our natural freedom as primitive but authentically self-expressive savages. If we are ever to recover our natural freedom it must be in a re-constituted form, appropriate to our consciousness and the degree of interdependence characteristic of civil societies. This is clearly no small task. Our natural passions silenced by the hegemony of *amour-propre*, our capacity to determine ourselves independent of the opinions of others forfeited, we are caught, as Rousseau would have it, in a vicious circle of dependence and corruption. How then are we to recover our original nature from the inauthentic, socially induced contingency in which it is mired? For Rousseau, the answer to this lay in our potential for moral freedom. He believed we could recover our original nature in a form of autonomy which combined our newly acquired capacity for rational self-legislation, with a recovery of the natural passions we had lost with the advent of corrupt civil societies. For Rousseau then, the recovery of our original nature as free beings meant moral and social renewal. In what remains, I want to consider Rousseau's most important treatment of the problem of moral renewal. For this, we must turn to *Emile*, Rousseau's most important work of moral theory.

Endnotes

1. O.C. III, p. 146 Rousseau claims here:

   "La prémiére (difficulté) qui se présente est d'imaginer comme elles (les langues) purent devenir nécessaires; car les Hommes n'ayant nulle correspondance entre eux, ni aucun besoin d'en avoir, on ne conçoit ni la nécessité de cette invention, ni sa possibilité, se elle ne fut par indispensable".

2. *Ibid*., p. 151.

3. Jacques Derrida, "La linguistique de Rousseau" in *Revue international de philosophie*, 1967/74, no. 82, pp. 452-54. Derrida proposes that we view Rousseau's account of the relation between nature and society as a relation between two closed systems, or discontinuous orders, marked off from one another by an "epistemic break". He goes on to claim that Rousseau's solution to the problem of man's evolution from nature to society is simultaneously "absolument naturelle et absolument artificielle". It is artificial in that Rousseau invokes arbitrary circumstance, a "concours fortuit de plusieurs causes étrangères" (O.C., III, p. 162) to explain how man's *perfectibilité* comes to have a bearing on the species' development, and so initiate its movement away from nature. However Derrida claims, it is at the same time natural in the sense that what is developed as a consequence of these fortuitous circumstances is man's natural potentiality (virtualité). The species' natural potential is thus nature's link with it opposite, society. "La notion de virtualité assure donc une fonction de cohésion et de soudre entre les deux ordres discontinus, comme entre les deux temporalités - progression insensible et rupture tranchant -qui rythment le passage de la nature à la société".

4. O.C. III, p. 133.

5. Derrida, "La linguistique de Rousseau", p. 453. Derrida elaborates his notion of *supplémentarité* as it applies to Rousseau in *De la grammatologie*, (Paris: Miniut, 1967), pp. 360 ff.

6. O.C. III, p. 171.

7. *Ibid*., pp. 141-43, 165-66. The point to be reiterated here is that the effect of these adaptations is cumulative rather than immediate. Without language, it is difficult, if not impossible, for individual innovations to be passed on to others and so generalized. As a consequence Rousseau assumes that the species' adaptations

gradually transform its environment into one in which human beings are forced into more sustained contact with one another.

8. The possible exception to this is the invention of metallurgy, which for Rousseau marks the beginning of truly interdependent and corrupt social life, and which he represents as a specific and quite fantastic accident. (See O.C. III, pp. 171-72.) However, the revolution initiated by metallurgy constitutes a special case which I will take up below. The basic point here is that the species has already entered a rudimentary form of social life in which his natural capacities have received full expression. Metallurgy thus initiates the transformation from one form of social life to another. It should also be noted that like all the "accidents" which precede it, the invention of metallurgy depends on the species' nature (at this stage its awareness of others, its language and reason) for its significance.

9. *Ibid.*, p. 168. See also Starobinski's note, pp. 1343, where he suggests that Rousseau followed Buffon's theory of the transformations of the planet.

10. *Ibid.*, p. 171.

11. *Ibid.*, pp. 167-70, 219-20.

12. Jean-Jacques Rousseau, *Essai sur l'origine des langues*, edited by Charles Porset, (Paris: A.G. Nizet, 1970). p. 39; also O.C. III, p. 149.

13. Thus we do not regard our relations with plants as social. Some people regard their relations with (some) animals as social or moral; but I take it that they presume that the animals in question share with us the morally relevant characteristics of selfhood: some degree of self-consciousness, emotions, and perhaps some intentions. It is because natural man does not recognize these characteristics in his fellows (except the capacity to suffer), that his relations with them are neither social nor moral.

14. O.C. III, pp. 174-75.

15. *Ibid.*, pp. 172-74.

16. E.O.L., pp. 105-6, 57.

I assume in what follows that there is a general conceptual consistency between the *Essai* and the *Discour sur l'inégalité*. In doing so I have no desire (nor need) to enter the debate over their respective dates of composition. Both are works of philosophical anthropology in that they treat the species' evolution, though the *Essai* has a more specific emphasis (linguistic and musical development). Their general conceptual consistency arises from two shared assumptions: one, that language is acquired during the period between the first and second revolutions; and two, that human nature is constituted by its relation to the environment in which it exists. The evolution of language therefore fits the more general historical framework of the species' evolution sketched in the *Discours sur l'inégalité*, and as well corresponds to the central theoretical premise of Rousseau's account of this evolution. We can therefore see the *Essai* as a useful supplement to the more general exposition of the species' evolution found in the *Discours*.

An argument supporting my claim for conceptual consistency is made in Michel Duchet et Michel Launay, Sychronie et Diachronie: *L'Essai sur l'origine des langues et le second discours* in **Revue international de philosophie**, 1967, LXXXII, pp. 421-42; see also Robert Wokler, *L'Essai sur l'origine des langues en tant que fragment des Discours sur l'inégalité* in **Rousseau et Voltaire: Acts du Colloques international de Nice**, 1978. Also the introduction by Charles Porset to his edition (cited above) of the *Essai*.

17. O.C. III, p. 167.

18. See above Chapter 3.

19. I use the term *sexuality* here in a broad sense, to include both sexual and romantic experience, though it will be seen that sexuality means something different for Rousseau at each stage of the species' development.

20. *Ibid.*, p. 143.

21. *Ibid.*, p. 147

22. *Ibid.*, pp. 214-215.

23. *Ibid.*, p. 215.

24. *Ibid.*, p. 157-58.

25. See above Chapter 3.

26. Their desire makes them dependent upon others, but these others have no more significance for them than any object or thing. In *Emile* Rousseau argues that dependence on things, as opposed to dependence on others, is natural and non-moral. Such dependence engenders no vices. (O.C. IV, p. 311.)

27. O.C. III, p. 169. At the end of the paragraph Rousseau claims that: "la jalousie s'éveille avec l'amour; la Discorde triomphe, et la plus douce des passions reçoit des sacrifices de sang humaine". Thus what seems to have a natural origin ends up producing bloody sacrifice. However, I do not take Rousseau to be claiming that bloody sacrifice is the immediate product of love. Rather, he is attempting to underline both the intensity of the passion and its ultimate consequence. It does indeed give rise to anxiety about how we rank in the esteem of the beloved, but this does not of itself issue in widespread competition and corruption. The ultimate consequence of bloody sacrifices depends upon more frequent and complex social relations for its realization.

28. This point of view is argued, to my mind unconvincingly, by Joel Schwartz in *The Sexual Politics of Jean-Jacques Rousseau*, (The University of Chicago Press, 1984); pp. 27ff.

29. O.C. III, p. 168.

30. *Ibid.*, p. 171.

31. The term is Starobinski's, not Rousseau's. See Note 4, O.C. III, p. 1344, where he contrasts it with "la fête civique".

32. *Ibid.*, p. 169.

33. E.O.L., ed Porset, pp. 125.

    Rousseau expands upon the nature of the bonds that held original families together in an interesting way here. He suggests that incest was characteristic of the sexuality of these primitive families, presumably because he wants to explain how isolated family units could sustain themselves. He also suggests that they had their own "langues domestiques", that their sexual contact was largely instinctual, and that habit took the place of preference. The picture differs slightly from the account given in the *Discours sur l'inégalité*, where conjugal love is stressed as the unifying force. Here there seems a distinct absence of emotional bonding: "il y avoit des mariages, mais il n'y avoit point d'amour".

34. *Ibid.*, p. 123.

35. *Ibid.*, p. 123.

36. E.O.L., pp. 123-25; O.C. III, pp. 214, 143.

37. O.C. III, p. 168.

38. *Ibid.*, p. 171.

39. *Ibid.*, p. 169; E.O.L., p. 125.

40. O.C. III, p. 169.

41. *Ibid.*, pp. 219-220.

42. *Ibid.*, pp. 165-66.

43. *Ibid.*, p. 143.

   Rousseau here asserts that the passions and the understanding effect each other in the species' development. He claims of the passions: "C'est par leur activité, que notre raison se perfectionne...Les Passions, a leur tour, tirent leur origine de nos besoins, et leur progrès de nos connoissances". The relation between love and social self-consciousness would seem to fit this framework. The passion itself focuses attention and improves the subject's understanding of the other. It is seen to arise from the frequentation inspired by sexual need, and once society becomes more complicated (which entails a parallel advance in the subject's understanding), the passion becomes much more complex.

44. *Ibid.*, p. 171.

45. *Ibid.*, p. 171.

46. *Ibid.*, p. 169.

47. *Ibid.*, p. 170.

48. Rousseau's view of love between two people does to some extent form an exception to the severity of his moral psychology in the *Discours sur l'inégalité*. He certainly believes that love involves a degree of sincere mutual respect. However, he also sees relations between men and women as involving a struggle for domination, in which men naturally want to see their superiority reflected. See J. Schwartz, op.cit., chapters 3,4. Women must thus conspire to allow men the appearance of mastery, while all the time making them dependent. See *Emile*, O.C. IV, pp. 696-97.

49. E.O.L., p. 107.

50. *Ibid.*, p. 57.

51. *Ibid.*, p. 41.

52. *Ibid.*, p. 55.

53. See above, §4.2; also *Ibid.*, pp. 123-27.

54. *Ibid.*, pp. 41-43.

55. *Ibid.*, pp. 41-43, 45, 51, 55.

56. *Ibid.*, p. 131.

57. *Ibid.*, pp. 43, 57.

58. O.C. III, pp. 148-51. Rousseau here discusses the relation between language and cognition, and makes the point that conventional language is a necessary condition for the development of the human understanding.

59. See Robert Wokler, "Rousseau's Anthropology Revisited: *Perfectible Apes in Decadent Cultures* in *Daedalus*, Summer, 1978, pp. 119-22.

60. O.C. III, p. 177.

61. *Ibid.*, p. 178.

62. *Ibid.*, p. 177-78.

63. E.O.L., p. 51.

64. *Ibid.*, p. 139.

65. *Ibid.*, p. 141-42.

66. *Ibid.*, p. 147.

67. *Ibid.*, p. 159.

68. *Ibid.*, p. 153.

69. *Ibid.*, p. 67.

70. *Ibid.*, p. 127.

71. O.C. III, pp. 172-73.

72. *Ibid.*, pp. 173-74.

73. *Ibid.*, pp. 174-75.

74. *Ibid.*, pp. 193.

75. *Ibid.*, pp. 193.

5

The Metaphysics of Freedom

5.1 Introduction

We turn now to a discussion of **Emile**, Rousseau's most substantial and important work of moral theory. In the last chapter I argued that the central problem in Rousseau's anthropology was his account of the species transition from nature to society; two modes of existence which seemed mutually exclusive and irreconcilable. Natural man is good because he is not involved in social relations with others. He is isolated, and therefore independent for two reasons: first, he is aware of himself as an agent but unaware that other such agents exist; and second, he is perfectly self-sufficient in the production of his subsistence, his capacities are equal to his needs and so he stands in no need of anyone else.[1] Social man, on the other hand, is corrupt and dependent precisely because he is involved in relations with others whom he recognizes as being like himself: self-valuing and self-interested. These relations occur within a social structure characterized by private property and inequality. This structure gives rise to, and continually reinforces the subject's economic and psychological dependence, thus rendering social man alienated and corrupt. Rousseau's anthropology traces man's evolution from the natural to the social condition; but insofar as the defining features of these two modes of life are mutually exclusive, both his account of this evolution and the moral imperative of reconstituting man's original nature in society are fraught with ambiguity and incoherence.

In one way or another this tension has been identified by many of Rousseau's commentators. One response to it has been to conclude nature and society are in fact irreconcilable in the way Rousseau conceives them, and therefore that his account of the species' development and his solution to the problem of man's corruption in society must fail. I want now to look briefly at two ostensibly very different readings of Rousseau, by Jacques Derrida and John Charvet, both of which draw this general conclusion. I also want to suggest, subsequently, that this conclusion about Rousseau's anthropological and moral theory can be avoided.

According to Derrida nature and society constitute two discontinuous orders for Rousseau; and as such they render his accounts of the origin of language and society at best paradoxical, and at worst incoherent.[2] He claims that Rousseau is concerned, albeit innocently, to defend the central myth in the history of western philosophy: viz. the epistemological and moral priority of the subject's presence to itself. Both the idealized consciousness of natural man, (its isolation and the perfect symmetry between need and desire), and the authenticity of the voice of conscience proposed by the Savoyard Vicar as the basis of man's moral freedom, manifest a desire to recover the unity of man's being through what Derrida views as a completely unfounded doctrine of self-presence. For Derrida, what is important about Rousseau is that while his intention is to recover this unity in a moral consciousness in which the subject's awareness of itself is unmediated by written language and corrupt social relations; his arguments show precisely that such an ideal is impossible. Each time Rousseau attempts to articulate the origin of something, whether it be of man, of language, or of society, his argument dissolves into paradox. He is unable to show the origin or essence of anything, without showing that this origin or essence simply cannot be grasped.[3] In respect of the subject, whose evolution from nature to its present condition Rousseau wishes to describe, his argument defeats itself. Original man is an ideal that can only be grasped through the medium of written language, yet the

The Metaphysics of Freedom 135

absence of written language as a factor which mediates self-consciousness is the condition of natural man's being an ideal in the first place. Self-presence, and this entails both authenticity and freedom, is a false ideal because it condemns written language as a medium through which to know oneself, and yet it has written language as its very condition. In this respect Rousseau's project of recovering original nature was doomed from the outset, and his solution to the social problem constitutes a kind of logocentric chimera.

Charvet's critique of Rousseau is more straightforward, and moves with more economy to the central problem of reconciling nature and society. He notes that the *Discours sur l'inégalité* leaves Rousseau with a "radical opposition between nature and society", and further,

> The problem with which this opposition presents Rousseau is how, if we can neither return to nature in its original form, nor be content with our present corrupt social existence, we can reform man in such away as to bring about a reconciliation between nature and society.[4]

In Charvet's view this reconciliation simply cannot take place on Rousseau's assumptions. The principle reason for this is that what defines man in nature, his natural self-sufficiency, "existing absolutely for himself alone and needing no relation to another', cannot be reproduced in the context of society without denying man the possibility of satisfactory social relations. To retain the natural principle of absolute self-sufficiency in society, the individual can only relate to others as abstract and undifferentiated extensions of himself.[5]

This fundamental point is borne out in a number of Charvet's arguments, of which we will note only two. He observes that the new social consciousness retains man's natural self-sufficiency, but in doing so it fails to explain why any person possessed of it would want to engage in social relations of any kind. By definition, a self-sufficient being needs no one. To overcome this problem, Rousseau proposed a modified, and indeed contradictory principle of nature in which man is said to be in need of others because of his generic weakness. This weakness is common to all, and it enables men to identify and sympathize with each other in light of their common capacity for suffering.⁶ Thus, Charvet claims, there is an ambiguity in Rousseau's argument. It stems from the original principle of nature, self-sufficiency, which cannot be given adequate expression in society, and so requires modification when Rousseau finds it necessary to explain how and why Emile will be related to others. A second and equally critical point is made in respect of the two ways Emile is meant to be related to others: through pity, and by the universalization of self-interest into a conception of the common good. In Charvet's view, both parody the actual nature of our moral and political relations. The conception of pity which draws Emile towards others denies the subjective character of their suffering. He identifies with the other, but he is drawn to him because of their common capacity for suffering and not because of any particular characteristics that person may possess. As a consequence it is irrelevant to Emile who the specific person suffering is, or in what consists the nature of his suffering. The sufferer is de-personalized be being made into an extension of Emile, and as such he can expect little in the way of personal concern for his specific needs.⁷

Similarly, Rousseau's account of the proper pursuit of the common good precludes the individual's acceptance of another person's particular ends or interests as a value for himself. To do so is to become dependent on a being who is differentiated from others, and for Rousseau this kind of dependence corrupts. The common interest is that interest all can be said to share (i.e. the equal right to pursue one's own good); in seeking it I pursue my own good as well as the good of others. This allows one's will to be constituted in relation to the will of others, yet at the same time it preserves one's independence because it recognizes no differentiation between one's own interest and the interest of others. Again, the individual is related to other persons as abstract extensions of himself. This conception of the common good suppresses all conflicting interests into one unifying common interest. It precludes any compromise between conflicting wills, because compromise requires that one seek a state of affairs amenable to oneself and one's opponent. To do this the opponent must be differentiated from everyone else as a value for one, and as a consequence one must be dependent upon him it a way that will lead to the corruption of both.[8]

In re-counting these two very different renderings of Rousseau my intention is to highlight what I have been claiming is a central point of tension in his thought: the opposition between and consequent aspiration to, a reconciliation of nature and society. Both have identified these two states as being as radically opposed to one another, and consequently both are highly critical of Rousseau's attempt to give expression to his ideal of human nature in society. It the two orders are radically discontinuous, then the attempt to found a new social consciousness upon nature will, as Charvet shows convincingly, break down into absurdity. In what follows I want to present an alternative interpretation of Rousseau's attempt to re-constitute the subject's natural character in society, based on a rather different view of the opposition between nature and society in his thought.

In the previous Chapter I argued that Rousseau's account of the species' transition from the pure state of nature to the primitive society of *le siècle d'or* was based upon natural causes. The interaction of man's original nature as a free and improvable being with a physical environment which gradually encouraged more frequent contact amongst natural men, and imposed the necessity of more specialized modes of producing subsistence, produces the transition to what I have called "natural society". The limited social relations the species' has at this stage of its development, and the passions these relations spawn, have no morally detrimental effects on man because they are products of nature. The subject is presented as having improved himself: he is self-conscious, linguistically competent and engaged in relations with others which are intersubjective and therefore potentially moral. The primitive love relation is in this respect paradigmatic. The primitive lover accepts his beloved as a value for himself, but in the process he comes to recognize that she values herself as he does. This produces a desire for his love to be reciprocated, and hence a certain degree of anxiety about what she feels. However, this anxiety does not produce the radical dependence typical of the full play of *amour-propre*. Two factors limit its insidious effect: first, man's language at this stage is based wholly upon the direct expression of primal or natural feeling; and second, the mode of production is characterized by self-sufficient families, ensuring a minimum degree of economic dependence. These factors preserve the subject's independence by ensuring that his relations with others are infrequent, and when they do occur, immediate and fully transparent.

For Rousseau, the Golden Age constitutes a primitive or rustic ideal, a half way point, or "golden mean" between the pure isolation of nature and the complete other dependence of civil society.[9] The subject has realized his natural potential to the extent necessary for him to engage in relations which are recognizably social, but he is not corrupted in these relations, nor is his natural freedom compromised. The epoch recalls a time when man's original nature as an independent being was reconciled to a minimal degree of social life. As such it is important for Rousseau's moral theory. It serves as a more adequate basis on which to found a new social consciousness than the absolute isolation of natural man. Rousseau's professed intention in *Emile* is to found a new social consciousness upon nature,[10] but as we have seen there are great difficulties with this when nature is understood to mean the complete self-sufficiency of natural man. As a self-sufficient and isolated unity, natural man is an unlikely basis for this new consciousness; for while he is free, his freedom is purely negative and can only be retained in the absence of what must be integral to any definition of society, that is, intersubjective relations.[11] Yet in nascent society man retains his freedom even though he is aware of others as valuers of themselves. And it is because of this that his freedom at this stage has a positive moral and social component to it, which makes it relevant to man's existence in society in a way that the negative freedom (or isolation) of the pure state of nature cannot be.

The relevance of nascent man's freedom for Rousseau's attempt to reconstitute human nature in society derives primarily from the authentic character of primitive social man's self-understanding and self-expression. He is present to himself and to others in a transparent and unmediated way, as pure feeling. The language which mediates his relations with them is suited only to the expression of primal passions such as love and pity, or jealousy and fear. It denies him the capacity to deceive others about himself or his desires, and so preserves the unity of being and appearance which Rousseau saw as crucial to the subject's freedom in society.[12]

While Rousseau does seem to argue that the moral passions of love and pity would be dominant in the Golden Age, he also implies that love must have given rise to corrupt feelings such as jealousy and envy. This in turn implies that being and appearance must have come apart, because both entail a desire to be something other than what one is, a desire which is both unauthentic and other-dependent. It follows then that the natural passions which arose in the Golden Age could not serve as the basis of man's freedom in society, because there was no original unity to reconstitute except the irredeemable unity of natural man. However, while it is the case on Rousseau's argument that the early primitive relations could have given rise to feelings of jealousy and envy, it does not follow that these feelings must have produced the rupture between being and appearance typical of corrupt social relations; Rousseau's primitive social man had emotions similar to those of a child. He may have been jealous of a rival, or envious of a better dancer, but if this led him to desire to be something other than what he was, this desire did not persist, and nor did it have any significance for him beyond the moment in which it was felt. His feelings of jealousy or envy, like all his other passions, would have been felt immediately and powerfully, but they would have been expressed just as immediately, most likely as anger or frustration. These expressions of anger and frustration led, as Rousseau indicates, to conflict and even violence; but what they did not lead to was anxiety about one's standing with others, and thus the desire to present an unauthentic version of oneself, as a means of gaining their esteem. The childlike character of primitive social man's emotions, their immediate and transparent character, preserves him from the distinction between being and appearance, and the psychological dependence which arises from it. I will argue below that Rousseau's educational project is intended to produce a person who retains the unity of being possessed by primitive social man, rather than the absolute self-sufficiency of the natural savage. This is not to deny that Rousseau was concerned to recover man's original nature in his moral theory, but rather to suggest that we understand his conception of original nature in broader, more developmental terms. He saw the characteristics this being had acquired as products of his natural development, and in this sense primitive social man can be said to embody original nature. The new social consciousness upon which Rousseau based his conception of moral freedom entailed to a certain degree both the productive self-sufficiency and authentic self-expressiveness of primitive social man. It is meant of course to account for the self-realization of an immensely more complex subject, whose social relations are conditioned by private property and inequality, and therefore stand as a much greater obstacle to his freedom. Nevertheless, Emile will be for others what he is for himself, and Rousseau saw this as the basis of his moral freedom.

The discussion of Rousseau's moral theory in *Emile* involves four sections, which are discussed in the following three chapters. The first section, covered in this chapter, examines his metaphysic of the self as it is propounded in the *Profession de foi du Vicaire Savoyard*. I treat this first in order to underline the consistency of Rousseau's epistemological assumptions in the *Discours sur l'inégalité*, the *Essai sur l'origine des langues*, and *Emile*. In each work the subject's development is governed by assumptions drawn from Rousseau's attempted synthesis Cartesian and sensationalist epistemology These assumptions receive their most explicit exposition in the *Profession de foi*. In light of their consistency, I contend that we should view *Emile* as an attempt to re-think the species' history in a manner which overcomes the radical corruption of original nature. Like natural man, Emile undergoes the transition from nature to culture; however, his education is meant to preserve him from the dependence and corruption engendered by *amour-propre* and so is offered as a solution to the social problem identified in the *Discours sur l'inégalité*. The conception of the subject which underlies his education has an important influence upon its method and the goal to which it aspires. The nature of Emile's freedom and the obstacles to its realization both have their roots in Rousseau's conception of the self.

The second section, covered in the next chapter, will examine the pre-moral or natural stage in Emile's education, which mirrors the development of natural man from the pure state of nature to the primitive social life of the "Golden Age." Emile's physical and cognitive attributes undergo substantial development during this stage, but this development is said to be in accordance with nature, and so issues in no morally detrimental effects. Emile's character as a 'natural' subject will be examined, and this character will be shown to be an inadequate basis upon which to develop a moral consciousness, identical in this respect to the isolated consciousness of natural man.

The third section, covered in the last chapter, will be a discussion of Emile's transition into the realm of social life, and the various ways in which it is possible for him to be related to others without falling prey to corruption and dependence. The effect of sexuality upon Emile's moral development is in this respect crucial, and it will be examined in relation to the role sexuality plays in the socialization of the species. Sexuality raises the same fundamental moral problem in both *Emile* and the *Discours sur l'inégalité*: namely, how it is possible to be related to another human being who constitutes a value for one without succumbing to the corrupt passion of *amour-propre*. This section will examine two of these solutions: one based on pity, and one based on romantic love.

The final section will attempt to integrate the discussions in the previous three into an overall view and assessment of Rousseau's intention in *Emile*. It will centre specifically on his conception of autonomy, which represents for Rousseau man's return to himself -- the re-constitution of original nature in society. Keeping in mind the broader conception of man's original nature suggested above, I will argue that Rousseau's conception of autonomy can be understood as an attempt to reconcile two, only apparently contradictory principles. On the one hand it entails a proto-expressivist concern for the subject's need to express his authentic feelings in an unmediated and transparent way. On the other it involves a conception of self-mastery achieved through obedience to principles determined by autonomous reason. Freedom is thus seen to involve the synthesis of natural passion and autonomous reason within the self.

5.2 The Vicar's Metaphysic of the Self

The *Profession de foi du Vicaire Savoyard* contains Rousseau's most explicitly philosophical account of his conception of the self. The metaphysical argument in the *Profession de foi* has often been read as an adjunct to Rousseau's more primary moral concern there, which is to discover the source of moral truth in the nature of the self.[13] The Vicar is presented as a man, not unlike Rousseau himself, who can find neither certainty nor comfort in the philosophical, moral, and religious dogmas of his day.[14] He faces what Baczko terms "une crise morale"; an experience of deep conflict between his nature as a human being and the moral and political relations characteristic of the world he inhabits.[15] This crisis turns the Vicar inward, to search for what is true and essential about himself, and so establish some degree of certainty about his moral experience.

> j'étois dans ces disposition d'incertitude et de doute que Descartes éxige pour la recherche de la vérité. Cet état est peu fait durer, il est inquiétant et pénible, il n'y a que l'intérest du vice ou la paresse de l'ame qui nous y laisse. Je n'avois point la coeur assés corrompu pour m'y plaire...[16]

What follows is the Vicar's attempt to discover his essential nature, so that he might find some footing upon which to resolve the moral crisis he faces as a consequence of living in a corrupt society. In this sense it is clear that Rousseau's interest in the nature of the subject is not primarily metaphysical. However, as in the *Discours sur l'inégalité*, and we might add, the work of which the *Profession de foi* forms only a part, the moral problem of man's existence in society begs the question of what he is naturally or essentially, stripped of the artificial and corrupt characteristics he acquires in social life. It raises, in otherwords, the metaphysical problem of what defines us as human beings, and the Vicar finds it necessary to establish this definition before he can proceed to resolve the moral crisis he faces.

The moral argument of the *Profession de foi* is firmly within the modern individualist tradition. It is also, as we shall see, consistent with Rousseau's moral theory in the rest of

Emile. Rousseau claims in the *Profession de foi* that the essential features of social man are his innate freedom of the will, his moral conscience, and his active judgement; and that these give him sovereignty over his moral and political experience. Each individual can, and indeed must become the legislative source of his own code of moral conduct. The Vicar's profession offers a metaphysical argument for what Charles Taylor has called the self-defining subject;[17] a conception of the individual whose basic right and fullest self-realization is the autonomy to determine the laws according to which he lives. The Vicar's intention, as he expresses it, is to return to himself.[18] In this respect his profession bears a close affinity to Rousseau's search for the species' origin in the **Discours sur l'inégalité**. Both texts begin with an attempt to uncover the nature or essence of the subject stripped of the corrupt characteristics he has acquired in society. The Vicar's analysis of himself reveals the three apparently definitive attributes noted above (free-will, moral conscience, and active judgement.)[19] Natural man, on the other hand, is said to be defined by the two innate principles of freedom and *perfectibilité*.[20] The two accounts of the subject are not identical, however they are consistent in terms of the epistemological principles upon which they are based. In both cases the subject is said to be immediately present to himself as a free being, and yet in both the subject's consciousness is dominated by its sensory perceptions. This apparent paradox derives, as I have argued above, from Rousseau's attempt to define the self by fusing two, traditionally opposed, philosophical discourses of the period: Cartesian rationalism and Lockean empiricism (especially as it was espoused by Condillac). The differences between the two accounts stem largely from the fact that they refer to the subject at different stages in his evolution. Natural man lacks active reason and a moral conscience, but only because his nature is undeveloped. He holds these attributes in potential, and given the proper circumstances his *perfectibilité* will enable him to develop them. What the Vicar discovers when he returns to himself is Rousseau's idea of what defines a human being. These principles link him conceptually with natural man and Emile. They govern the evolution of the species' nature in the **Discours sur l'inégalité**, they govern the child's development in **Emile**, and they determine the nature of the Vicar's solution to his moral crisis.

The Vicar begins his self-examination from a standpoint which is meant to recall Descartes' principle of methodical doubt. It is not knowledge alone that the Vicar doubts, but also all religious and moral systems according to which people are meant to order their lives. He finds this condition insupportable, and turns to an examination of himself to bring it to an end. The most certain observation he can make is that: "J'existe et j'ai des sens par lesquelles je suis affecté. Voila la première vérité qui me frape, et a laquelle je suis force d'acquiescer."[21] This is meant to be a factual observation of indubitable certainty; for one cannot doubt that one exists, and one is never exempt from sensations. However, the observation raises a question about the self: "Ai-je un sentiment propre mon existence, ou ne la sens-je que par mes sensations?"[22] The problem is whether we have a conception of ourselves independent of our sensations, and if we do, how this can be articulated when our consciousness is always affected by them. Rousseau's answer is rather less than convincing, but more important for what it asserts than for its coherence. His problem puts in mind of Hume's famous dilemma: we cannot conceive the self because we are always affected by our sense perceptions, yet not to conceive it denies us any sense of identity, which is equally absurd.[23] Rousseau's answer however, puts us in mind of Descartes, whose proof of the existence of corporal bodies outside the self seems to be the source of Rousseau's position on this issue.[24] The Vicar notes that his sensations take place inside him because they make him sense his existence; yet at the same time their cause is external to him, because he can do nothing to effect their occurrence. It follows from this that there are bodies outside him that are the cause of his sensations, and he concludes: "Ainsi non seulement j'existe, mais il existe d'autres êtres, savoir les objets des mes sensations, et quand ces objets ne seroient que des idées, toujours est-il vrai que ces idées ne sont par moi."[25] Finally, he adds that these bodies must be material.

We find then that the self is something other than the sensations which constantly affect it, and thus that it is distinct from the material world which causes us to have sensations. The Vicar has not yet made a direct assertion about the nature of the self, but

The Metaphysics of Freedom

two things might be inferred. One, that the self is a unified or *simple* entity immediately present to itself over time, and two, that this self cannot be reduced to material substance. The term *simple* is introduced to describe Rousseau's conception of the self as an undifferentiated unity throughout a succession of different experiences. As subject of experience, the self is unchanged throughout its existence, and does not, in its essential attributes of free will and *perfectibilité*, differ from other selves. It is unified or simple because its sensations have no effect upon its character as the subject of experience. Rousseau argues that this simple self can be discovered in the mere experience of sensation. He claims in a note that "l'être sensitif est indivisible et un". This is a response to the radical empiricism of La Mettrie, Helvétius and Condillac, for whom the self is the product of its sensory experience, rather than the presupposition of experience itself.

It would be instructive at this point to compare Rousseau's account of the self as an simple, undifferentiated unity over time and circumstance, with the empiricist-based view of the self as the continuity of a person's experiences. This distinction is made by Derek Parfit in his essay "Later Selves and Moral Principles" in Alan Montefiore ed., **Philosophy and Personal Relations**. Parfit opposes a "complex" view of the self to the "simple" view, a version of which I have ascribed to Rousseau. The complex view is more compatible with, and indeed has its origins in the classic empiricist accounts of the self developed in the eighteenth century: notably those of Condillac, Helvétius and Hume. According to Parfit, the simple view takes personhood, or personal identity to be a special kind of "deep" fact about persons. In every case in which there is a question of whether something is a person, or whether someone is identical to a future or past person, these facts must hold completely or not at all. On the simple view there are no degrees of personhood or personal identity: one either is a person or is not a person; one either is that person with whom one has connections in memory, or one is not. The "simple" view therefore entails a notion of the self as a distinct or unchanging entity. This is not of course to say that a self's personal identity remains unchanged through the course of its experience, but rather, that "whatever happens, any future experience must be either wholly mine, or not mine at all."²⁶

In proposing the complex view Parfit suggests that we think of personal identity in a manner comparable to the way we think of a nation's survival. A nation's survival involves certain continuities: its political system, its language, ethnic groupings and so on. These continuities may be disrupted, for instance by an invasion, and this will weaken them, but once we know what these disruptions were (or are), it no longer makes sense to ask if the nation ceased to exist during them. The reason being that the nation's survival simply is these continuities. One could perhaps say that it ceased to be itself for a time, but in the long term preserved its continuity and therefore survived.

Parfit claims the self can be viewed in the same way, that is, as bodily and psychological continuities. These continuities are in their logic "all or nothing", in the sense that an entity which has them is a self, while one that lacks them cannot be. Similarly, to say of a self at one time that it is identical to a self at another time, it must be true that such continuity exists between them. However, continuity arises out of *connectedness*, which is a matter of degree. By connectedness Parfit means a sense of strong identity with an experience in the past, or a future intention. Obviously, with respect to our past experiences, connectedness is achieved through memory. Thus we are most strongly connected with those experiences we remember most vividly. However, it should be noted that it is not necessary that we remember all our past experiences to have a sense of our continuity as selves. For instance it is possible to have forgotten an experience in the past without ceasing to be the person who had that experience. This is possible if one is able to remember each day between this event and the present (and presumably some events prior to the forgotten one). This suggests continuity of memory, and therefore a self or personal identity which entails a forgotten experience. The point being that the forgotten experience does not destroy the continuity which constitutes one's sense of self. The important point about connectedness for Parfit's argument is that it admits of degrees. We are more or less strongly connected with different experiences in our past, and because continuity is based on strong connections, our sense of what we are is contingent upon those experiences with which we have the strongest connections in memory. Thus Parfit writes: "We can use the word 'I' and other pronouns, so that they cover only the part of our lives to which, when speaking, we have the strongest psychological connections. We assign the rest of our lives to what we call "other selves".[27] The simple view, on the other hand, takes it as "deeply true that all parts of a person's life are as much parts of his life."[28] The advantages for Rousseau's moral theory of a conception of the self as a simple, undifferentiated unity are considered below.

5.3 The Vicar's Dualism

The Vicar's next indubitable observation is: "je réfléchis sur les objets de mes sensations, et trouvant en moi la faculté de les compares, je ne sens doué d'une force active que je ne savois pas avoir auparavant."[29] This active force is apparent from his analysis of sensation. Objects appear to the senses as separate, discrete entities. By comparison and analysis the mind imposes a conventional order, (and ultimately meaning), upon the endlessly disparate sensations one experiences. The Vicar claims that no purely passive being can do this,[30] because sensations in themselves have no intrinsic order or meaning, and a purely passive being has no capacity for discovering relations, and hence order, among them. The Vicar thus discovers in himself the distinctive faculty of an intelligent being: the capacity for active (ie. undetermined) judgment, or put slightly different, the capacity to bestow meaning upon an intrinsically meaningless series of events.[31] As he claims: "Selon moi la faculté distinctive de l'être actif ou intelligent est de pouvoir donner un sens à mot est."[32] We know that we possess active judgement because we have ideas of relation which cannot be produced by sensations themselves, and so must be produced in us. These judgements are said to be the source of our errors, and only to occur on the occasion of our experiencing sensation. Thus as intelligent beings humans

148   *Language, Subjectivity, and Freedom*

have some control over their experience and understanding of the world.

> Qu'on donne tel ou tel nom a cette force de mon esprit qui rapproche et compare mes sensations; qu'on l'appelle attention, méditation, réflexion ou comme on voudra; toujours est-il vrai qu'elle est en moi et non dans les choses, que c'est moi seul qui la produis, quoique je ne la produise qu'a l'occasion de l'impression que font sur moi les objets.[33]

To this point Rousseau has made three basic claims about the self, each of which is said to be discoverable by anyone, simply in the exercise of self-reflection. First, the subject is always (at least when conscious) affected by sensations; second, it nevertheless has a direct and immediate "sentiment" of itself as an entity distinct from those sensations; and third, it is aware of itself as a being possessed of active judgement. Rousseau goes on to add another basic feature to his account of the self, which is its capacity for spontaneous or voluntary action. The Vicar claims to have a powerful and immediate sense of his own free-will; so strong that it overrides any evidence to the contrary. To deny it is as much to deny that he exists.[34] Finally, he derives his first article of faith through a version of the ontological argument. He claims that because matter cannot produce motion, the action and reaction of material bodies in nature must lead us back to a First Cause which itself cannot be material. This Cause must be a will, hence: "Je crois donc qu'une volonté meut l'univers et anime la nature. Voila mon prémier dogme, ou mon prémier article de foi"[35]

The initial stages of the Vicar's profession of faith indicate again Rousseau's consistent attempt to define the subject in terms of two, traditionally opposed epistemologies. This links the account of the self in the *Profession de foi* with the conception of the subject underlying his philosophical anthropology in the ***Discours sur l'inégalité***. The statement: "j'existe et j'ai des sens par lesquelles je suis affecté", refers to the reader to the central insights of both the Cartesian and sensationalist theories of subjectivity. For the Cartesians, the subject is present to itself in reflection, and this self-presence is unmediated by emotion. Their most fundamental intuition is of their existence as thinking beings, independent of sensation. We find this cryptically expressed in the famous inference: "Cogito ergo sum". Rousseau is only in partial agreement with the Cartesian intuition, for while he believes he has a special and direct access in reflection to his essential nature, he finds it very difficult to deny the sensationalist claim that all knowledge, including self-knowledge, is conditioned by our sensory perceptions.[36] The Vicar's paradoxical starting point derives from his desire to regard man as naturally or inherently free, which he can only do if he adheres to a conception of the subject as independent of and prior to its sensory experience. Yet at the same time he wants to describe the subject (and the species) in developmental terms, as products of their economic and social history, and he can only do this if he regards the subject as acquiring at least some constituent elements of his nature in experience. Thus, the Vicar's immediate intuition is of himself as both independent of his sensory experience, and radically situated within it.[37]

The Vicar's initial observations are in all important aspects identical to Rousseau's metaphysic of natural man in the *Discours sur l'inégalité*. He claims first that animals and human beings can be compared in terms of their understanding, because both acquire ideas through sensory perception. In this respect they differ only in degree. Where they differ in kind however, is in respect of the will. The animal will is wholly determined by its sensory perception of the environment, and we can infer from this that the animal's subjectivity is, at least for Rousseau, radically situated. The human will on the other hand is said to be free to resist or acquiesce in the impulsions of nature, and he argues further that human beings are conscious of their capacity for free will.[38] Rousseau is not specific about what this self-consciousness involves, but it is clear that he regards it as crucial to his account of natural man. He reiterates it, however unconvincingly, in Note X. where he claims that natural man is the sole spectator and judge of himself.[39] In both arguments Rousseau attempts to reach a compromise between the subject's natural autonomy and the developmental psychology of the sensationalists. The circularity of the Vicar's argument arises from Rousseau's rather schematic attempt to derive his "sentiment de l'existence" from the nature of his sensory experience. But Hume's dilemma is rather more profound than the simplicity of Rousseau's solution might suggest. Rousseau's problem was that he believed both the Cartesian and sensationalist theories of the self to be true in some degree. That is, he believed human beings to be distinguished from animals in virtue of their natural freedom and their awareness of it, and yet he could not reject the insight of sensationalist psychology, which told him that the subject acquires his faculties and dispositions through his (largely) sensory experience of the world. At this most basic level then, Rousseau's attempted compromise implies a dualistic account of the self, in which man is divided between the essential and active spiritual substance of his soul, and the contingent and determined corporal substance of his body.[40] This dualism is, I want to stress, derived from his attempt to define the self in terms of these two traditions, and it is central for understanding Rousseau's moral project. The problem for natural man, and for Emile who represents him in the guise of a child, is to retain their essential autonomy as their natures begin to be constituted by their social experience. The Vicar's problem, as fully developed adult in civil society, is to rediscover and remain in touch with the essentially human aspects of his nature: his moral conscience and active reason.

I have claimed that the epistemological assumptions Rousseau makes in the *Discours sur l'inégalité* and *Emile* are consistent, and that this consistence indicates that the two texts form a continuous and, in terms of each other, consistent argument. This is further evidenced by Rousseau's discussion of reason. It might be objected that his account of reason in the two works is inconsistent, for while he argues in the *Profession de foi* that active reason is an essential attribute of the self, one which puts man first in the chain of being, he claims in the *Discours sur l'inégalité*, that reason is an acquired characteristic in respect of which men differ from animals only in degree.[41] But as I noted in the second chapter, the difference is merely one of context. The Vicar differs from natural man in virtue of living in society, and so like the rest of his species at this stage of its development, he has acquired active reason. It seems to the Vicar that reason is an essential aspect of his subjectivity, because he is aware of himself making comparisons and judgements, and imposing meaning upon his experience: j'oserai prétendre à l'honneur de

The Metaphysics of Freedom 151

penser."[42] Natural man possesses this attribute in potential, in the form of an innate faculty of *perfectibilité*, which with the aid of circumstance enables him to acquire active reason and language.[43] The conceptual link between natural man and the Vicar must be made in terms of what defines them as subjects. Reason is natural to man in the sense that he alone has the (innate) potential to acquire it, and once he does, he alone is capable of moral freedom.

The analysis of how humans reason is consistent in both texts. In both Rousseau stresses the active or autonomous character of judgement; and in both its importance derives from its relation to the moral dimension of human life. The Vicar claims of himself:

> Par la sensation, les objets s'offrent à moi séparés, isolés, tels qu'ils sont dans la nature; par la comparaison, je les remue, je les transporte, pour ainsi dire, je les pose l'un sur l'autre pour prononcer sur leur différence ou sur leur similitude, et généralement sur tous leurs reports.[44]

By enabling us to impose a conventional order of meaning upon our experience, judgement gives us a kind of sovereignty over it. It equates understanding with the active imposition of control over ourselves and the world we experience. It enables us to determine ourselves and so creates a corresponding responsibility for our actions, ideas, and so on. Here we see the connexion between active reason and morality. The former is the necessary, though as we shall see not sufficient condition for the latter. In the *Discours sur l'inégalité*, Rousseau discusses reason in relation to language and comes to the paradoxical conclusion that each is the condition of the other. Language is said to be crucial to thought in the sense that it enables us to employ generic concepts or abstractions to order and analyze our experience. Again, this marks the difference between man and animal, as well as the distinction between natural and social man. The monkey that moves from nut to nut has no archetype idea of fruit in his mind. He simply reacts to a visual sensation which recalls a tactile sensation. He does not compare the particular nuts he encounters to each other, and hence cannot categorize the experience he has of them. He is unable to subject his own experience to analysis, and so unable to free himself from determination by his sensations.[45] Because they lack active reason, neither animals nor natural men are moral, yet it is because natural men have an innate potential to acquire this faculty that they have a history, and a chance to achieve moral freedom.

Rousseau concludes this section of the Vicar's profession with the first two articles of his faith: he believes that a Will moves the universe and animates nature, and secondly that this Will is intelligent.[46] Both suggest a Deistic conception of the universe as a providential order created by God, and this underlies Rousseau's view of nature as fundamentally good. The Vicar simply infers from the awesome complexity and apparent harmony of the natural world that it must be governed by a Divine Will, and in doing so it he seems to reject the materialist conception of nature as an amalgam of blind forces and inherently meaningless events. As he exclaims polemically: "Que d'absurdes suppositions pour déduire tout cette harmonie d'aveugle mécanisme de la matière mue fortuitement!"[47] Rousseau's deism is central to his argument in the *Profession de foi* because he wants to show that man's freedom can be consistent with nature, or part of God's plan for the world. We will see below that the innate sentiment conscience, which the Vicar regards as the "voice of nature", mediates between man's freedom (to do either good or evil) and the natural order which is only a source of goodness and virtue.[48] For now it is important to note that Rousseau sees the subject as part of nature, but at the same time independent of it in virtue of his free-will and active reason. It is therefore quite consistent that he should develop a dualistic conception of the self in which man is divided between a material and a spiritual substance. This will be his third article of faith that man is free and that his actions are animated by an immaterial substance.[49] Rousseau's argument for this entails a critique of philosophical materialism, a doctrine which denies both his dualistic conception of the self and the view of nature as a providential order. In short, the denunciation of materialism is crucial to the coherence of his conception of man's freedom.

After establishing the existence and attributes of the Deity, the Vicar measures

The Metaphysics of Freedom 153

himself against the other species, and finds himself, as we have noted, to be incontestably of the first rank in virtue of his will and his intelligence. He repeats again the various attributes which distinguish humans from animals (reason, taste, morality), and then asserts that materialism denies this distinction and so cannot be true. In a reference to Helvétius,[50] (which could apply equally to La Mettrie) he claims:

> Ame abjecte, c'est ta triste philosophie qui te rend semblable à elles; ou plutôt tu veux en vain t'avilir; ton génie dépose contre tes principes, ton coeur bienfaisant dément ta doctrine, et l'abus même de tes facultés prouve leur excellence en depit de toi.[51]

Materialism denies God, but equally important it denies man's freedom because it recognizes only one substance: matter. In recognizing only matter, it subjects man, beast, and mineral alike to the laws of mechanism and the banal homogeneity of a world without active intelligence, creativity or morality.

Rousseau attempts to counter the monism of the materialists with an argument for two distinct substances, matter and spirit, which is distinctly Cartesian in lineage.[52] His first intimation of these two substances comes from himself. He feels himself to be divided in his nature between two principles: one which raises him up to the love of justice, beauty and truth, his so to speak, higher nature; and one which draws him into the empire of mere sensation and desire, his baser or lower self. From this he concludes, with Saint Paul:

> non, l'homme n'est point un; je veux et je ne veux pas, je me sens a la foi esclave et libre; je vois le bien, je l'aime, et je fais le mal: je suis actif quand j'écoute la raison, passif quand mes passions m'entraînant.[53]

We can see then that his freedom is dependent upon an active spiritual substance which allows him mastery over senses and his passions, at least those which originate in his experience of the social world. The Vicar begins by claiming that matter must lack the power to think because it is extended and divisible. In a long note to the main text he then castigates "philosophie moderne", for attempting to reduce everything to matter. His basic point is that the logic of materialism leads us to the view that all things are sensitive, because it refuses to distinguish between humans, who obviously are sensitive, and rocks or trees or any other material object. In Rousseau's view this is absurd, because such an assumption cannot possibly account for the unity of the individual *I* that must characterize a human, or indeed any sensitive being. The problem is that matter is extended and divisible, and so can be reduced to the most minute particles: e.g. a stone is a collection of atoms which compose the lattice structure of the minerals which in turn compose the rock. If such a being is sensitive, where do we locate the 'I' which experiences sensation? We cannot, and thus it follows a sensible being, like man, is one and indivisible. The Vicar thus claims: "Les parties sensibles sont étendues mais l'être sensitif est indivisible et un; il ne se partage pas, il est tout entier ou nul: 1 sensitif n'est donc pas un corps."[54] The same, he adds, applies to a reasoning being.

Rousseau's point here is that both sensation and intelligence presuppose a simple self, which is the subject of experience. This recalls Parfit's distinction, noted above, between "simple" and "complex" views of the self. The radical empiricist or complex view of the self relies upon the "prima facie" assumption that the self is unified, or to be more precise, able to conceive of itself as a unity, because of its memory. This, as we saw, is crucial to Parfit's conception of the self as a continuity arising out of strong connections. Rousseau does not to my knowledge attack the role of memory in the empiricist account of the self, but his position lends itself to such an attack. On Rousseau's view memory, like sensation itself, presupposes a self which is not itself the product of either memory or sensation. However plausible it may be to characterize a person's identity as the continuity he feels with his past experiences and future intentions, it must be the case that the faculties which give rise to these continuities, the memory and the imagination, are not themselves the product of the experiences they unify. Another way of posing this problem is to ask the question, what is it that does the remembering, or the imagining? Rousseau, makes the same point in respect of the sensationalist account of the species' development, in which all faculties traditionally understood to be definitively human (language, self-consciousness, and rationality), are said to be the product of the brain's reaction to its material environment.[55] The problem is again that any account of how the

The Metaphysics of Freedom   155

subject acquires these faculties presupposes an innate or essential characteristic in virtue of which they could be acquired. This characteristic must be a characteristic of something, and in Rousseau's view it is of a simple, undifferentiated self, which is the subject of experience. In the *Discours sur l'inégalité* the species' passage from nature to culture presupposes *perfectibilité*; while the Vicar claims that an active spiritual essence is the condition of his having the kind of experience he has. Both arguments entail a conception of self as a simple, undifferentiated unity which is the subject of experience.

The materialists are compared to a deaf man who refuses to listen to the inner voice of the self, which must cry out against the conclusions of their philosophy. Rousseau's rhetorical point implies a conundrum for which he has no entirely satisfactory explanation. The materialists deny that the self is prior to and thus independent of its experience, and as a consequence they deny the idea of free-will. As Helvétius writes in *De l'Esprit:*

> Que seroit-ce alors que la liberté? on ne pourroit entendre, par ce mot, que le pouvoir libre de vouloir ou de ne pas vouloir une chose; mais ce pouvoir supposeroit qu'il peut y avoir des volontés sans motifs, et par conséquent des effets sans cause. Il faudroit donc que nous pussions également nous vouloir du bien ou du mal; supposition absolument impossible.[56]

Their denial of the subject's autonomy is based on the assumption that all knowledge begins in sensation. A self conceived prior to its experience cannot be perceived in sensation, and so cannot be the object of knowledge. Helvétius' claim that there can be no will without motive is based on the belief that all action has its source in, and is therefore contingent upon sensory experience. Rousseau's dilemma stems from his acceptance of the tenet that all knowledge begins in sensation.[57] This is why the Vicar at no point claims knowledge of the self in the strict sense. What he does claim is a "sentiment" of the self which accompanies his sensations, and which the metaphor of the inner voice is meant to express. His argument that the attributes of thought and free-will define the self must proceed as a critique of the materialist position, because he cannot invoke direct evidence for them beyond what he feels to be true. "Nul être matériel n'est actif par lui-même, et moi je le suis. On a beau me disputer cela, je le sens, et ce sentiment qui me parle est plus fort que la raison qui le combat."[58] Rousseau's strategy is to show that an actively thinking self is the condition of our having the kind of experience we have, by showing that we simply cannot attribute the sense of self-mastery implicit in our experience to a material being. The materialists, for all their logical rigor, offend against reason and feeling, and so must be wrong. The proof that no material being can be the subject of sensory experience verifies the feeling of freedom implicit in human action, and leads the Vicar to his third article of faith: "L'homme est donc libre dans ses actions et comme animé d'une substance immatérielle."[59]

The Vicar and natural man represent two different stages in the species' development. However, in both metaphysical and moral terms, they stand in a similar and apparently paradoxical relationship to nature. Both are part of nature: they are physically subject to their environment, and their consciousness is always affected by their sensory perceptions of it. Yet at the same time they are said to be free and so capable of determining themselves independent of the causal nexus to which they are necessarily subject as physical beings. This, as we noted, is the problematic implication of the view that the self is a simple, unchanging entity, which exists independent of its sensory experience. If we accept the proposition that the "simple" self is the subject of experience and therefore its condition, how then can it be related to the experience it is said to be independent of? How can we be free, as Rousseau's argument demands, to cause actions in the phenomenal world? There is no obvious answer to this question. The Vicar's answer is to return to himself, and claim an indubitable sentiment of his own freedom, but he has no explanation of how, or why he possesses it.

In moral terms natural man has no sense of his existence as a contradiction because he is, for all intents and purposes, wholly integrated into the natural order.[60] His active, spiritual nature has as yet only a potential form; his consciousness remains unified (by which we mean wholly concerned with himself), and he is independent, peaceful, and good. The important thing to keep in mind is that natural man retains his original unity as a subject even after his spiritual essence has become determinate (i.e. actual as opposed to potential). In *le siècle d'or* he has begun to have desires and feelings which derive from his relations with others (and are therefore not wholly physical), but he remains unified and independent as a subject because he is dominated by natural or primal passions which ensure a symmetry between what he is (what he feels himself to be), and how he appears to others. The Vicar, on the other hand, feels himself to be divided between his higher and lower self: that is, between his active reason and will combined with his natural passions, and his artificial, *amour-propre* induced desires.[61] The desires and passions that derive from his lower or artificial self are felt to corrupt and enslave, while the principles which derive from his active spiritual self give him a sense of his autonomy. The Vicar longs to overcome this self-division. He longs for the original unity represented by natural man, but can only achieve it as a being whose development has taken him far beyond the stage where the independent production of subsistence, or the expressive, childlike relations with others typical of the "Golden Age" are possible. As such, he cannot recover his original nature, yet he must in some way re-constitute it. In the *Profession de foi* this re-constitution is accomplished by opposing an innate (or natural) moral sentiment which the Vicar refers to as the conscience, to the artificial and corrupt passion of *amour-propre*. Reason is not of itself enough to motivate the subject to choose the good and so remain free from the dependence engendered by *amour-propre*. It requires a grounding in something else, a feeling which will reconcile our freely determined actions to nature, and thus restore the original unity of our being.

5.4 The Voice of Nature

Having established the metaphysical basis of his doctrine, the Vicar turns to a discussion of the principles of conduct consistent with them. He wishes to discover what moral precepts he ought to prescribe for himself so that he might fulfil his destiny in accordance with God's intention. The possession of free will implies a moral end for man; he must determine for himself the proper principles of virtuous conduct. The Vicar therefore reflects upon himself, and discovers the natural source or ground of his virtue. This source is not, as it turns out, active reason, which has to this point been treated as characteristic of man's "higher" self; but rather a "sentiment" referred to as the conscience: an innate feeling for the right and the good which everyone possesses in some measure.

> Il est donc au fond des ames un principe inné de justice et de vertu, sur lequel, malgré nos propre maximes, nous jugeons nos actions et celles d'autrui comme bonnes ou mauvaises, et c'est à ce principe que je donne le nom de conscience.[62]

The conscience is innate and therefore natural, and because of this said to be part of the "higher", active self. Rousseau wants in this way to link it to man's freedom.[63] Yet at the same time it is linked to nature in the sense that nature is said to direct us through the voice of conscience: he "qui la suit obéit à la nature et ne craint point de s'égarer."[64] By invoking this innate feeling Rousseau returns to the central premise of his moral and political thought; i.e. that man is naturally or essentially good, and his corruption only acquired in society. The claim that we possess an innate conscience is an expression of this premise in the sense that it is said to be an inclination to do good which every person, regardless of how depraved, possesses in some measure.[65] It speaks for the original goodness of our nature amid the clamour of our corrupt and artificial passions.

The assertion that the conscience is the innate source of our moral precepts involves a distinction between natural and artificial "sentiments." The former are those we have prior to the acquisition of *amour-propre*, and the powerful passions which derive from the subject's desire for relative status. In the *Discours sur l'inégalité*, Rousseau suggests that two natural passions: self-love (*amour de soi-même*) and pity, are characteristic of original nature, but these are eventually suppressed by the artificial passions deriving from *amour-propre*. The conscience, it would seem, can be understood as an extension or social form of these natural passions, one which becomes a source of morality in social life. The claim that people possess this sentiment is of course impossible to confirm or deny in an objective sense, and Rousseau simply instructs us to consult our feelings. His point is that the "voice of nature," or the moral precepts which derive from nature, are universal in the sense that they speak to each person in the form of a profound feeling about what is right and good. People have wide varieties of experience and live in very different physical and cultural circumstances; yet their judgements, what they think is right or wrong in their experience, is everywhere the same. There is a natural similitude among moral judgements because their basis is the natural human feeling of conscience.[66] It remains the case however that most, if not all people, are deaf to the dictates of conscience, but for Rousseau this just testifies to the degree of alienation in modern civil societies. Yet he does not seem, at least in the *Profession de foi*, to regard this as irreparable. The fact that one's nature has been distorted by social development imposes an obligation to rediscover one's natural or authentic self. The Vicar embraces this obligation and finds in his essential nature a "voice" which can serve as the universal basis of justice and morality.

I noted at the end of the last section that Rousseau's strategy in the *Profession de foi* is to elaborate the natural ground of our capacity for moral freedom, and in so doing, overcome the opposition between nature and society implicit in the moral life of each person in civil society. This was said to be possible if our freedom to make active moral judgements was grounded in innate or natural sentiments. However, one might object to this formulation of Rousseau's strategy on the grounds that Rousseau cannot be attempting to ground his solution to the social problem in natural sentiments. The reason for this being that natural sentiments, at least insofar as they appear in natural man, are entirely amoral. The dominant natural sentiment is *amour de soi-même*, a wholly self-referential impulse which leads natural man to give preference to himself over others in any situation of competition or conflict. Morality on the other hand, demands that we give preference to equality over self-interest, and therefore morality cannot be based on the natural order of the passions. On the contrary, it requires a radical re-ordering of the natural passions.

In answering such an objection, it is impossible to deny that Rousseau's solution to the social problem involves a radical re-ordering of the passions, in which natural self-love is subordinated to the other-regarding passions of pity, love, and patriotism. This involves a de-naturing of man, as Rousseau remarks at the beginning of *Emile*. He argues there that the best social institutions are those that de-nature man, those which take his absolute existence from him to give him a relative one, transporting the "I" into the common unity of the civil society. The argument is that ancient republics such as Rome de-natured men by suppressing their natural, self-regarding sentiments and replacing them with love of the fatherland. This subsumes the individual into "la patrie" by means of the emotional power of patriotism. "Un Citoyen de Rome n'étoit ni Caius ni Lucius; C'étoit un Romain: même il aimoit la patrie exclusivement à lui." Further on in the passage Rousseau claims:

> Celui qui dans l'ordre civil veut conserver la primauté des sentimens de la nature, ne sait ce qu'il veut. Toujours en contradiction avec lui-même, toujours flotant entre ses penchans et ses devoirs il ne sera jamais ni homme ni citoyen; il ne sera bon ni pour lui ni pour les autres.[67]

In Rousseau's view the great strength of Roman institutions lay in their capacity to re-order the passions such that love of country replaced love of self. This type of education is impossible in the modern world, because the public and the private have been sundered. Man in civil society is no longer either good for himself or good for others, and as a consequence there are now two contradictory forms of education: one that is public and common, another that is domestic and private. The public education is hopeless because neither fatherlands nor citizens in the ancient sense exist anymore. There are no

The Metaphysics of Freedom 161

states worthy of the type of patriotism necessary to subordinate natural self-love to civil allegiance. Modern colleges train "hommes double" who are "paroissant toujours rapporter tout aux autres, et ne rapportant jamais rien qu'à eux seuls."[68] Rousseau's point is that the de-naturing possible in the social education of the ancient republics can no longer be accomplished. What is left to us is the domestic or natural education, which involves raising man uniquely for himself, but in such a way that he can be related to others without the contradictions which arise from the division between public and private characteristics of modern civil societies. The goal of Rousseau's educational project is to create a person who is good for himself and good for others. This involves, as he claims, the education of a natural man.

Yet how can we create a natural man through education if we can only preserve the natural order of the sentiments at the cost of introducing an irreparable and morally debilitating division within the self? The answer to this, and to our original problem of how man can reconstitute his original nature in society while at the same time be de-natured, lies in Rousseau's conception of nature at this stage of his argument. His educational program is not intended to produce natural man in his original form, an amoral and exceedingly limited being, whose natural passions relate everything to himself. It is intended rather to produce a natural being who is nonetheless capable of living in society. This involves denaturing the pupil, because in society he can no longer live entirely for himself alone; but the de-naturing will be done in such a way as to preserve his natural being to the greatest possible extent. This is accomplished by fostering the natural other-regarding passions of pity, love, and presumably under the right circumstances patriotism, so that they may serve, in the form of a moral conscience, as the basis of the pupil's moral will. These passions are natural in the sense that they arise with the initial forms of social life (see Chapter 4), and yet because they are other-regarding, they can serve as an adequate basis for moral relations in a way that self-love cannot. The Vicar's argument proceeds with an attempt to link his conception of moral conscience with man's freedom. This, as we shall see, produces a conception of liberty which is meant to reconcile freedom and virtue, and thus nature and society. In this sense the *Profession de foi du Vicaire Savoyard* supplies one answer to the moral problem raised by man's evolution from nature to society. It gives us an account of how the subject can be free in society, and despite a somewhat different emphasis, is consistent with Rousseau's conception of freedom as he articulates it in the rest of **Emile** and in **du Contrat social**. The problem of freedom is for the Vicar what it is for natural man: how to maintain the capacity for self-determination in the context of social relations which make him dependent and corrupt. The Vicar's answer combines his natural faculty of free will with a fully authentic expression of his natural feeling for the good. As the Vicar conceives it, the new social consciousness must be a form of individual self-legislation, but the ground of this autonomy (what motivates us to act upon our self-willed maxims) can only be found in what links us with Providential nature: man's innate moral conscience.

It might be objected here that Rousseau is simply contradicting himself by asserting that we have natural disposition towards the good in the context of civil society. In the *Discours sur l'inégalité* he argues forcefully that our natural sentiments of self-love and pity are completely distorted in civil society. Furthermore, both are fundamentally self-referential, and so in no way undermine the isolated equilibrium of natural man's consciousness. Yet conscience is said to be both natural and something we experience while engaged in relations with others. It is a feeling about how we ought to be related to others, and yet it must have, as nature's "voice" within, some connection with original nature, which would seem to preclude it being a relative sentiment. The contradiction implied is only problematic if one accepts the radical distinction between nature and society I discussed in the introduction to this Chapter. For Rousseau, conscience is a natural impulse to do good grounded in passions antecedent to the acquisition of reason and the development of social life; yet it only becomes manifest in the context of social relations. In this sense it has the same character as the faculty of *perfectibilité*: without *perfectibilité* human beings would have no history; without an innate sense of the good they would be incapable of morality.[69] It is a relative sentiment in that it is only felt when the

The Metaphysics of Freedom 163

subject is related to others socially, but it is nonetheless natural because it "speaks" for the higher, natural self, against the artificial passions engendered by *amour-propre*. Rousseau seems to sense a tension in his argument when he has the Vicar state that some relative sentiments must be natural.

> Mais si, comme on n'en peut douter, l'homme est sociable par sa nature, ou du moins fait pour devenir, il ne peut l'être que par d'autres sentimens innés, relatifs à son espèce; car à ne considérer que le besoin physique, il doit certainement disperser les hommes, au lieu de les rapprocher. Or c'est du sistême moral forme par ce double rapport à soi-même et à ses semblables que naît l'impulsion de la conscience.[70]

Like pity, and love, the conscience is a natural moral sentiment which makes it possible for human beings to be related to one another in a way that does not betray their natural potential to become free and virtuous persons. Originally, these sentiments are possessed in potential form, but once the frequency of contact between natural men increases they become determinate, and in turn advance the species' progress towards full socialization. We saw above the role that sexuality and love play in the species' initial acquisition of moral and social relations.[71] This is what Rousseau means when he claims, above, that man can only become sociable by means of innate sentiments which he possesses relative to his species. These sentiments remain innate or natural to the self, despite their widespread suppression in civil society, and Rousseau's solution to the moral problem of dependence and alienation requires that they be given expression. The conscience provides a motivation to do the good, which when combined with the other innate faculty of free-will, yields moral autonomy.

5.5 Moral Freedom

The Vicar's attempt to find a certain basis for moral truth is completed with a discussion of the practical (i.e. moral) implications of what he has discovered about his own subjectivity. This involves an account of how the subject's natural potential for freedom and virtue can be realized on the basis of the characteristics of selfhood already outlined. The conception of freedom developed in the *Profession de foi* is important, because it derives directly from Rousseau's conception of the self, and therefore makes the epistemological basis of his moral theory explicit. This of course presumes that the notion of freedom voiced by the Vicar is consistent with Rousseau's other formulations of the concept. My claim is that given the consistency of his underlying conception of the self, we must conclude that it is. The Vicar's notion of autonomy is an account of man's moral freedom; it represents the moral end appropriate to man in the last stage of his species' evolution, and is therefore the highest and most complete form of moral life. It also, in this sense, represents man's return to himself or his original nature, because it constitutes the potential inherent in that nature in determinate form. The self, it turns out, has moral freedom as its natural end.

The Vicar's account of freedom involves three conceptually distinct attributes of the subject's nature: free will, natural sentiment and active reason. Each attribute is made manifest during a different stage of the species' evolution, and each implies a different conception of what the subject's freedom involves. Free will is evident in human consciousness and action from its earliest stage. Natural man was negatively free, that is, free to respond in an undetermined way to his natural desires. There is of course nothing moral in this, it means only that he was capable of choosing between his natural desires. Certain natural sentiments are also inherent in the species's original nature, but they only become manifest in the primitive social relations of the Golden Age. These sentiments presuppose an awareness of oneself relative to others with whom one identifies and has feelings for, but when combined with self-sufficient production and expressive language, they enable the subject to relate to others in a transparent and therefore authentic way. He is incapable of masking his intentions and feelings. Independence is preserved at this stage by the primitives uninhibited, and largely unreflective expression of their feelings for others. What they are for themselves is identical to what they are for others, and as a consequence *amour-propre* has no adverse effect on their relations. Active reason, finally, is an acquired attribute which is at the same time something that only human beings, in virtue of their natural faculty of *perfectibilité*, can acquire. Possession of it implies moral freedom as the appropriate end for persons, because only persons are able to direct their own lives independent of the needs and passions produced in them by their environment. Active reason or judgement gives the subject responsibility for his actions, and thus makes him a being capable of morality.[72] Insofar as his actions emanate from reason, or at least, conform to what reason accurately identifies as the good, the subject is at once free and acting in accordance with his higher, authentic nature.

This brings us to the crucial claim made in the Vicar's derivation of his moral freedom, which is that it entails both the mastery of self made possible by the acquisition of active reason, and the authentic expression of the natural sentiment of conscience. Rousseau's conception of moral freedom in the *Profession de foi* represents an attempted synthesis of the two earlier and more primitive forms of freedom outlined in the *Discours sur l'inégalité*. It combines a capacity to direct oneself, to choose between courses of action, which of itself bears no moral implication, with a natural feeling for the good which can motivate us to act so as to achieve it. These are then combined with active reason or judgement, which Rousseau regards as the necessary though not sufficient condition of moral action. When combined with freedom of the will reason gives us responsibility for our actions, but it is conceptually distinct from a motive to act.

> Connoitre le bien, ce n'est pas l'aimer, l'homme n'en a pas la connoisance inné mais sitôt que sa raison le lui fait connoitre, sa conscience le porte a l'aimer: c'est ce sentiment qui est inné.[73]

The natural sentiment of conscience is thus crucial to moral freedom, and the Vicar's somewhat rhapsodic eulogy to the conscience testifies to this:

> Conscience, conscience! instinct divin, immortelle et céleste voix, guide assure d'un être ignorant et borne, mais intelligent et libre; juge infaillible du bien et due mal, qui rends l'homme semblable à Dieu; c'est toi qui fais l'excellence de sa nature et la moralité de ses actions; sans toi je ne sens rien en moi qui m'élêve au dessus des bêtes, que le triste privilège de m'égarer d'erreurs en erreurs à l'aide d'un entendement sans régle, et d'une raison sans principe.[74]

Rousseau's conception of autonomy attempts to combine our freedom to act on self-determined principles, with a self-conscious sentiment of our actions being authentic expressions of our essential or higher nature. To feel oneself to be in good conscience in the sense Rousseau uses it here, means to present to one's authentic nature as a human being. The conscience is a natural and therefore universal human attribute,[75] and it is meant to be linked to freedom as the ground of our capacity to will moral principles and act upon them. Being in good conscience overcomes the alienation of those for whom being and appearance are not the same thing. It reconstitutes man as a unified being in the sense that he acts wholly in accordance with his true nature, yet at the same time it allows him to retain his freedom, because his actions are determined by his active reason and freely chosen.

This raises again the problem noted above, which is that it is difficult to see how we can be free if our actions are based upon passions or sentiments. One answer to this is that Rousseau does not define freedom in opposition to inclination and passion per se, but rather to inclinations and passions induced in us by the corrupt form of *amour-propre*. Because the conscience is an innate, natural sentiment, an "inner voice", actions based upon it do not deny our free will. It gives moral content to a will which is itself morally neutral, i.e. capable of choosing any course of action, good or bad. The conscience ensures that social man's will is morally free because it enables him to master those passions he acquires from a corrupt social world. In this sense it preserves his authenticity (he acts in accordance with his original nature), and ensures that the principles governing his conduct are self-generated.

There is nevertheless a problem with this account of the relation between natural sentiment and the will, which stems from Rousseau's attempt to integrate rationalism and sensationalism into a conception of subjectivity. The distinction Rousseau employs between higher and lower self does not correspond, as we have noted, to the Kantian distinction between noumenal and phenomenal self. However, insofar as Rousseau retains a view of the self as the simple subject of experience, he must offer an account of how that self can act in the world of experience which it is *ex-hypothesi* not affected by. The Vicar is motivated to act by his natural passions, and although they are said to be innate, they must nevertheless be conditioned by others, or by events which arise in the world of experience. To have a moral feeling the Vicar must feel something in relation to someone other than himself, and it is clear that this is what Rousseau has in mind when he claims that we need these passions to guide both active reason and will. They are the natural characteristics which define the human subject (remember that reason is made possible by *perfectibilité*), but in themselves they bear no specific implications for our moral behaviour. The problem is that both have to be given expression through a concrete or phenomenal self, whose personality, intelligence, and interests, are all formed in his experience of the social world.

This problem arises, as I have been arguing, from Rousseau's attempt to reconcile two fundamentally opposed accounts of subjectivity. Each satisfies a different, necessary, and yet seemingly contradictory intuition about the self. The empiricist paradigm allows us to see the subject as the product of his experience, and so allows Rousseau to explain man's dependence and corruption in terms of the social structures in which he lives. The rationalist/Cartesian paradigm allows us to see the self as something pure in its essence and therefore untouched by its experience, and thus allows Rousseau to argue that our essential humanity consists in the freedom to determine ourselves as moral beings. Both views are basic to Rousseau's moral theory, and yet they cannot be adequately reconciled within the framework he employs.

In his defence I think it can be said that he is careful to stress that the moral passions are natural and therefore innate. They are therefore not dependent, like those arising from *amour-propre*, upon the opinions, status, and intentions of others. This allows him to put the problem of freedom in terms of the opposition between nature and culture; between a self which is naturally capable of generating moral rules for itself to live by, independent of the corrupt self-referential interests it acquires in society, and a self which is dependent upon the wills, intentions and opinions of others. The autonomy of moral freedom is natural in the sense that it represents the fullest realization of man's natural potential for freedom and virtue. However, it is simply arbitrary to claim that there is a congruence of natural passion, active reason, and free will, because the passions cannot be autonomous in the sense that reason and will are autonomous. They must be formed in relation to others, and thus in the world of experience.

Rousseau's version of moral autonomy combines the subject's natural potential for expressive authenticity with the rationalist notion that freedom consists in the subject's mastery of itself through reason. In this sense it is meant to reconcile nature to culture and freedom to virtue. Natural sentiments are held to be the source of our capacity to seek the good in our relations with others, and they are therefore grounded in and represent original nature. Active reason is, as it were, socially produced, but it is also the condition of our knowing the good and being able to pose it to ourselves as an end to pursue. Thus, both attributes are necessary if moral life is going to take place. Moral action or virtue presupposes freedom, because it is only freely willed actions which can be said to be our own, and for which we can bear moral responsibility. Yet the potential to freely choose an end implied by active reason is only realized if the end chosen is a moral one. For it is only in choosing the good that the subject triumphs over his socially determined nature and the other-dependent passions which dominate it.

5.6 Conclusion

There can be no doubt that Rousseau's account of moral freedom *Profession de foi* is an individualistic one. It affirms the sovereignty of the individual over his moral world by asserting that the intellectual and emotional make-up of the self is sufficient to generate moral rules which will ensure his freedom and his virtue. The Vicar discovers the source of moral certainty in himself; the laws or rule he finds it possible to generate on the basis of his own autonomy have a legitimacy for him that the old authorities: revelation, custom and prejudice, simply cannot have.[76] Yet considering its individualistic implication, we may ask whether or not this conception of freedom will enable us to be adequately related to others? In nature, freedom had meant the individual's complete psychological and physical independence, at least until its later stages. In society, as we have seen, this kind of independence can only be reconstituted by one's treating others merely as abstract extensions of oneself. However, by its own criteria moral freedom must involve acting virtuously in our relations with others, and this entails recognizing their needs and aspirations as having a moral value. The question is whether this can be done without compromising the capacity for self-determination?

The Profession de foi du Vicaire Savoyard provides no detailed answer to this question. The capacity to act morally or virtuously must of course entail a recognition of others' basic moral value, and yet according to Rousseau's analysis in the *Discours sur l'inégalité*, this induces an immediate propensity to dependence in the form of an obsessive concern for our own value relative to others. The key to avoiding this dependence, and the alienation it entails, is to remain obedient to one's authentic nature, which can only be done by acting in accordance with one's natural moral sentiments. When the conscience animates our active reason and will, we can transcend the corrupt passions induced by inequality and dependence. It is in a similar sense that Rousseau invokes the natural passions of pity and love as adequate bases for moral relations. For Rousseau, the subject's capacity to be related to others in a way which does not contradict his natural potential for freedom and virtue depends on his capacity to live according to his innate and universal impulse towards the good. It is our natural sentiments which link us to our original nature, and as a consequence they must be at the centre of a social consciousness which attempts to reconstitute original nature. It is in this sense then, that authenticity of sentiment is crucial to freedom. Without the authenticity or integrity of natural sentiment we lack the impulsion to do good; and without the impulsion to do good our freedom is meaningless. We will turn now to a consideration of Rousseau's answer to the problem of how the individual can be related to others in society without compromising his capacity for self-determination. The educational program of *Emile* is meant to answer this.

Endnotes

1. See Chapter 3 above for a fuller discussion of Rousseau's account of natural man.

2. Jacques Derrida, "La linguistique de Rousseau", in *Revue international de philosophie*, 1967, #82, pp. 454-56. For an unusually lucid discussion of Derrida's "strategy" for reading Rousseau, and the paradoxical character of his conclusions, see Paul de Man, "The Rhetoric of Blindness" in *Blindness and Insight: Essays in the Rhetoric of Contemporary Criticism*, (Oxford: Oxford University Press, 1971), pp. 102-141.

3. Derrida, *De la grammatologie*, pp. 345.

4. John Charvet, "The Social Problem", p. 36.

5. *Ibid.*, pp. 91-93.

6. O.C. IV, p. 503.

7. Charvet, *The Social Problem*, pp. 92-93.

8. *Ibid.*, p. 94-96.

9. O.C. III, p. 171.

10. O.C. IV, p. 251.

11. Here I mean relations between persons who recognize each other as self-conscious and self-valuing.

12. O.C., III, p. 174.
See also O.C. IV, pp. 966 67, where Rousseau underlines the importance of language to the unity of being and appearance in the *Lettre à Christophe de Beaumont.*

Sitôt que je fus en état d'observer les hommes, je les regardois faire, et je les écoutois parler; puis, voyant que leurs actions ne ressembloient point à discours, je cherchai la raison de cette dissemblance, et je trouvai qu'être et paroitre étant pour eux deux choses aussi différentes qu'agir et parler, cette deuxième différence étoit la cause de l'autre, et avoit elle-même une cause qui me restoit à chercher.

Je la trouvai dan notre ordre social....

13. Bronislaw Baczko, *Rousseau: Solitude et Communauté*, (Paris: Mouton & Co., 1974), pp. 208, 212-13; see also, Henri Gouhier, "Ce que le Vicaire doit à Descartes" in *Annales de la Société de Jean-Jacques Rousseau*, pp. 142.

14. O.C., IV, pp. 567-70.

15. Baczko, *Solitude et Communauté*, p. 208.

16. O.C., IV, pp. 567.

17. Charles Taylor, *Hegel*, (London: Cambridge University Press, 1976), part I.

18. O.C. IV., pp. 570, 596. "Rentrons en nous-mêmes, O mon jeune ami!"

19. *Ibid.*, pp. 585-86, 594, 598-601.

20. O.C. III, pp. 141-42.

21. O.C. IV, p. 570.

22. *Ibid.*, p. 570-71. It is instructive to compare the Vicar's first question (doubt) with Condillac's definition of the self in the *Traite des Sensation*:

    Son moi n'est que la collection des sensations qu'elle éprouvé et de celles que la mémoire lui rappel. En un mot, c'est tout à fois la conscience de ce qu'elle est la souvenir de ce qu'elle à été.

    Condillac, *Oeuvres Philosophique*, ed. Georges Le Roy, (Paris: Presses Universitaires de France, 1949-51), vol. I, Part I, Chapter II, §2. This resolves Hume's dilemma by ignoring it, and it left Rousseau dissatisfied for the same reason he was dissatisfied with Condillac's account of the origin of language: because it does not explain precisely what needs to be explained, the origin of the active powers of the mind.

23. David Hume, *A Treatise on Human Nature*, edited by Lindsay, I, IV, 6. Hume wrote:

    When I enter most intimately into what I call myself, I always stumble on some particular perception or another...I can never catch myself at any time without a perception, and never even observe anything but the perception...I may venture to affirm to the rest of mankind that they are nothing but a bundle or collection of different perceptions, which succeed each other with inconceivable rapidity, and are Perpetual flux and movement."

24. Rene Descartes. Oeuvres de Descartes, C. Adam and Paul Tannery, eds.), vol. VII, p. 81 ff.

25. O.C. IV, p. 571.

26. Derek Parfit, "Later Selves and Moral Relations" in Alan Montifiore ed., *Philosophy and Personal Relations*, (London: Routledge, 1973), p. 140. It will be seen below that Rousseau's conception of the self involves a distinction between the simple, subject of experience which is defined by its innate freedom and faculty of *perfectibilité*, and the particular characteristics of its concrete or phenomenal identity. As subjects of experience human beings are identical, defined in terms of the same innate faculties. As persons with concrete or particular personal histories and personalities, they obviously vary widely in character. The great difficulty, on the simple view of the self, is to give an account of how the two are related in human action.

27. *Ibid.*, pp. 142-43.

28. *Ibid.*, p. 141.

29. O.C. IV, p. 571.

30. By *passive* Rousseau means a being who only experiences sensation ("l'être purement sensitif"), and who is therefore determined by them.

31. See above: Chapter 2; also Taylor, *Hegel*, pp. 5-8. Also, Michel Foucault, *The Order of Things*, (London: Tavistock, 1970), pp. 59-60.

32. O.C., IV, pp. 571.

33. *Ibid.*, p. 573.

34. *Ibid.*, p. 574.

35. *Ibid.*, p. 576.

36. It should be noted that Rousseau does not say that we can know the self directly, which would contradict his contention that we are always affected by our sensations.

What he does refer to is his "sentiment de l'existance"; a feeling that he exists independent of what he senses, as an inherently free and actively intelligent being. In Rousseau's metaphysic, it is feeling and not reason which is innate, and consequently he considered feeling a more fundamental criteria for determining the truth about the self. (see O.C. IV, pp. 570, 574.)

37. I borrow the phrase "radically situated" from Michael J. Sandel, *Liberalism and the Limits of Justice*, (New York: C.U.P., 1982), pp. 20-21, who refers to the "radically situated subject", i.e. an account of the subject which does not recognize the self as an identity independent of its experience. The distinction he makes is between an account of the self which possesses its attributes, experiences and so on and an account of the self which is, in any given moment, its attributes, experiences, etc. The latter is radically situated in the manner of Hume, unable "to distinguish what is me from what is mine." Rousseau was clearly wanted to avoid this conclusion, but it is a consequence of his dualism that he ends up asserting that the self is distinct from its sensations as the subject of experience -- a simple unchanging self -- while at the same time formed by them as a person with a particular or distinct character. As a subject he is therefore both separate from and situated within his experience.

38. O.C. III, pp. 142.

39. *Ibid.*, pp. 219-20.

40. O.C. IV, pp. 583, 585-86.

41. O.C. IV, pp. 571 73, 581 82; O.C. III, pp. 141-42.

42. O.C. IV, p. 573.

43. See above Chapter III, and Rousseau's discussion in the *Discours sur l'inégalité*, O.C. III, pp. 147-50.

44. O.C. IV, p. 571.

45. O.C. III, p. 149.

46. O.C. IV, pp. 576, 578.

47. *Ibid.*, pp. 580. See also Ronald Grimsley, *The Philosophy of Rousseau*,(Oxford: Clarendon Press, 1973), pp. 58-59. Grimsley argues that Rousseau was influenced by the Deistic implications of Descartes' and Newton's view of the universe as a

rational order governed by laws of cause and effect, and explicable in terms of physics and mathematics. In both cases the implication is that though God creates and sets in motion this rational order, he does not intervene in its operation.

48. O.C. IV, pp. 588. The Vicar proclaims:
"Homme, ne cherche plus l'auteur du mal, cet auteur c'est toi-meme. Il n'existe point d'autre mal que celui que tu fais ou que tu souffres et l'un et l'autre te vient de toi... Otez nos funestes progrès, otez nos erreurs et nos vices,otez l'ouvrage de l'homme, et tout est bien."

49. *Ibid.*, p. 584.

50. *Ibid.*, pp. 1536, 1540. See also **Correspondance Générale**, vol. IV., pp. 64-65, 92.

51. *Ibid.*, p. 582.

52. Descartes, **Principes de la philosophie**, I, 53.

53. *Ibid.*, p. 583; also St. Paul, Epistle to the Romans, VII, 19; and O.C. II, p. 344.

54. O.C. IV, p. 584-85. Further on in the note he refers to the materialists. Burgelin claims that this note was added after Rousseau's reading of Helvétius.

55. See above, pp. 26-29, Ch. II, also Ch. I. See also Rousseau, *Essai sur l'origine des langues*, ed., Porset, p. 39.

56. Helvétius, **De l'Esprit**, I. 4, quoted in O.C. IV, p. 1542.

57. O.C. IV, pp. 590. "Il est très simple que durant ma vie corporelle, n'apercevant rien que par mes sens, ce qui ne leur est soumis m'échape.

58. *Ibid.*, p. 585.

59. *Ibid.*, p. 586-87.

60. We mean by this that natural man is both free and integrated into the natural order. He responds to his natural impulses in an undetermined way, thus while these actions are in the strict sense free, they establish no breach with nature. He imposes no order of his own upon nature, but his responses to it are not, like an animal's, predetermined by genetically coded instinct.

61. It is important to note that although Rousseau is quite obviously a dualist in his

conception of the self, and therefore concerned to distinguish between the two primary substances of matter and spirit, this is not identical to Kant's distinction, in his moral theory, between reason and inclination. The distinction between the higher and lower self is not a distinction between pure practical reason identified with mind, and inclination identified with the body. The attributes of the higher spiritual self include active reason (if properly motivated), freedom of the will, and the natural passions of pity and love as they are represented by conscience. These are opposed to the passions inspired or corrupted by *amour-propre*, such as jealousy, envy, and vindictiveness. The crucial element of the higher, spiritual self is its freedom. This is not negated, in Rousseau's mind, by the assertion that natural passions supply the motivation behind our morally free actions. The reason for this is that Rousseau did not conceive the self as transcendental. He views it as simple and unchanging, but not as absent from the world of phenomenal reality. The tendency here is to identify the spirit/body distinction with the mind/body distinction, and in doing so to assimilate Rousseau's dualism to Kant, and the post-Kantian problem of how mind conceived as a noumenal self can act upon or cause action in a phenomenal world. This can lead one to view Rousseau's moral theory in too Kantian a light. It may indeed be the case that Rousseau would have done better to have grasped the problem in more Kantian terms, though this is debatable. However, it would be absurd to criticize Rousseau for not having produced a Kantian solution to the difficulties his conception of the self had led him to. His insight was to see that the sensationalist paradigm could not account for the conception of agency presupposed by our moral activity, and he attempted to modify that position by reconciling it with the Cartesian account of the self as a spiritual substance.

62. O.C. IV, p 598

63. *Ibid.*, p. 594-95.

Nous croyons suivre l'impulsion de la nature et nous lui résistons: en écoutant ce qu'elle dit à nos sens nous méprisons ce qu'elle dit à nous coeurs; l'être actif obéit, l'être passif commande. La conscience est la voix de l'ame, les passions sont la voix du corps...[and further]...la conscience ne trompe jamais, elle est le vrai guide de l'homme; elle est à l'ame ce que l'instinct est au corps...

64. *Ibid.*, p. 595.

65. *Ibid.*, p. 597.

66. *Ibid.*, p. 599; also Troisième Dialogue, O.C. I, p. 972.

67. O.C. IV, pp. 249-50.

68. *Ibid.*, p. 250.

69. *Ibid.*, p. 599.

70. *Ibid.*, p. 600.

71. See above, Chapter 4.2

72. O.C. IV, p. 545, "Tout le moralité de nos actions est dans le jugement que nous en portons nous-mêmes".

73. *Ibid.*, p. 600.

74. *Ibid.*, p. 600-601.

75. *Ibid.*, p, 601.

76. Baczko, *Solitude et Communauté*, p. 223.

6

An Education According to Nature

6.1 Introduction

My argument thus far, as will be apparent from the previous chapter, presumes that the *Discours sur l'inégalité* and *Emile* are theoretically consistent. Rousseau is concerned in *Emile* to offer one kind of solution to the dependence and corruption he identified in the *Discours* as the pervading problem of modern civil societies. But as the solutions developed there represent only one approach to solving the social problem, we ought not to expect them to be comprehensive, nor in every respect consistent with the solutions he develops in his other works. What we can expect however is some underlying conceptual consistency, and this, I think, Rousseau provides. *Emile* is primarily a work of prescriptive moral theory, which attempts to outline the proper development of an individual's moral psychology.[1]

It provides an account of how a person might be educated with the intention of nurturing his natural potential for freedom and virtue. As such it cannot be a comprehensive solution to the social problem as Rousseau conceives it, for insofar as the origin or cause of this problem lies in the general structure of civil society, in the relations engendered by private property and inequality, no one person could ever be educated successfully. He or she must always live in some form of corrupt society, and this will inevitably undermine the effects of their education. This is one reason Rousseau takes care to outline the principles of political right towards the end of Book V,[2] and to encourage Emile and Sophie to remain in the rustic simplicity of their country retreat, avoiding at all costs the intensely corrupt cities.[3] It can also be seen as the inspiration behind the unhappy denouement to *Emile*, the fragment *Emile et Sophie: ou les solitaires*. Here Emile's trust in Sophie collapses as a result of her infidelity, and he abandons her. He is captured by the Algerian Sultan while crossing the Mediterranean and made a slave, albeit a rather successful one, and although he is said to retain his freedom, he retains it within the context of his complete subjection to another.[4] However, it does not follow from Emile's apparent alienation from existing civil societies that he would be fit for no form of social life, or that every form of political activity would necessarily compromise his freedom and his virtue. The moral consciousness he develops through his education allows him to be related to others without becoming dependent upon them, and so without being corrupted by them. This is crucial to his own well-being, which consists above all else in living according to his nature; but it is also the condition of his being a good citizen, because citizenship requires him to put the good of the community ahead of his own good, something he cannot do if he has been corrupted by dependence upon the wills of others. This is to say then that the prescriptive moral theory of *Emile* is, at least in principle, consistent with both the social criticism of the *Discours sur l'inégalité* and the principles of political right as they are outlined in *du Contrat social*.[5]

The question of the overall consistency of Rousseau's thought arises from any interpretation which views *Emile* as a solution to the social problem identified in the *Discours sur l'inégalité*. To claim that *Emile* offers only one kind of answer or solution is not to diminish its importance, nor to fudge the issue of Rousseau's claim to overall coherence. It is rather to suggest that the consistency of his moral and political theory arises largely out of the way he conceives the problem of the subject's existence in society, and that while he treats this problem from different perspectives (e.g. moral, political, autobiographical), he does not alter his fundamental conception of it. It is this, rather than an architectonic system of ideas, which gives the prescriptive dimension of his thought its consistency. In this respect, Emile's psychological and moral development is a kind of phylogenetic recapitulation of the species' evolution from nature to culture. He undergoes the same fundamental transition, and so faces the same fundamental problem, that is, how to retain his natural potential for freedom and virtue in a society which tends him towards the opposite.[6]

The underlying conceptual consistency between *Emile* and the *Discours sur l'inégalité* is evident from the conception of subjectivity informing both works. In each the self is assumed to have an essential, "simple" nature, defined by its capacity for freedom and self improvement. But equally, in both, the simple subject of experience is shown to acquire a "thick" or concrete character through its experience of the natural and social world. The moral problem in *Emile* is to form this "thick" or concrete character such that the individual does not experience the radical self-division characteristic of most civilized persons. Civilized man is always torn between his duty and his inclinations, neither good for himself nor good for others.[7] Emile's education aims at a moral consciousness which unites freedom and virtue, and thus overcomes the division between higher and lower self, and duty and inclination. The natural freedom which was said to define man in the *Discours sur l'inégalité* is to be reconstituted within a social environment that requires the individual's consciousness and will be developed in relation to others. Insofar as it accomplishes this, it reconciles the conflicting requirements of nature and culture.

Rousseau claims at the beginning of Book I that there are two forms of instruction found in civil societies: "l'une public et commune, l'autre particulière et domestique."[8] These in turn derive from the conflicting demands of nature and society; the individual is torn between his natural self-interest (*amour de soi-même*) and the duties imposed upon him by society, which require that he place the public interest ahead of his own. The two forms of education tend him towards conflicting ends, and so cancel each other out,

An Education According to Nature

leaving social man, as we noted, neither good for himself nor good for others. As an antidote to this confusion, Rousseau proposes a domestic or natural education, one that will raise the individual uniquely for himself, yet with the intention of making him at the same time good for others. The new education will attempt to create a natural being fit for life in a civil society.[9]

The problem posed in *Emile*, of how to educate a person to be good for himself and yet good for others, reproduces the fundamental social problem posed by the *Discours sur l'inégalité*, of how to reconstitute man's original nature in a form appropriate to his existence in society. The irrevocable loss of original nature means that man cannot be educated for himself alone. He must be denatured, because the species' evolution has placed him in a situation in which his will has to be constituted in relation to the wills of others. The educational program proposed in *Emile* attempts to achieve its "double object" of uniting the private and the public (and thus the natural and the social) in one, by reconciling them. The child is educated to live for himself, which means essentially that he is raised so as to ensure that his natural independence becomes a capacity for self-determination once he enters society. And yet he is also educated to virtue, which means that his natural moral passions are to be nurtured so that they can become the basis of his capacity to accept the needs and interests of others to be of equal or, in some instances, of even greater value than his own. He is denatured to the extent that the natural order of his passions is reversed. In his moral relations, self-love is to be as far as possible subordinated to compassion and love of others. Yet at the same time his original nature is to the greatest extent possible preserved; he is to remain free, both in the negative sense of being free from the corrupting other-dependence engendered by the artificial passions of *amour-propre*, and in the more positive sense of being free to determine the principles informing his own moral conduct.[10] The success or failure of Rousseau's moral and educational theory depends on his ability to achieve this synthesis of original and social nature.

An alternative view of the intent and significance of Rousseau's moral theory is presented by Judith Shklar.[11] Shklar argues that Rousseau's moral and political theory is not prescriptive in any practical sense, but rather Utopian, and thus not concerned to offer any actual solution to the opposition between nature and society. In Shklar's view, Rousseau's thought is dominated by two irreconcilable Utopian visions: ancient Sparta and the Age of Gold. The former is a form of community which completely denatures man, wholly subordinating his private, domestic life to his life as citizen. The latter is based on the isolated and self-sufficient family, whose rustic circumstances and natural emotional bonds preserve original nature to the greatest extent possible. In Shklar's view, Rousseau offers a council of despair because he recognizes no possibility of conciliation between these two diametrically opposed ideals. All our self-created miseries stem from our mixed condition, our half natural and half social state. A healthy man, the model for any system of education, would have to adhere consistently to either a natural or civic mode of life.[12] She concludes that Rousseau's project was resolutely critical, that his utopias were designed to show the impossibility of an adequate form of human association. Shklar finds an amenable view of politics and morality in this pessimism, which is that the fundamental values of moral and political life are, in principle, incommensurable. The conflicting requirements of nature and culture are not reconcilable: we must opt for one or the other, knowing always that in choosing one we incur the loss of the other and, beyond this that neither can ever be fully achieved.

There are a number of problems raised by Shklar's argument, notably in respect of her account of the Age of Gold, but I want only to take issue with her more general thesis that Rousseau makes no attempt to offer either a practically realizable or theoretically consistent solution to the opposition between nature and society. It does not follow from the impracticality of Rousseau's moral and political philosophy or, as one might otherwise describe it, its theoretical character, that he regarded the problem to which he consistently directed it as insoluble. Still less does it follow that this supposed insolubility is his fundamental point. If Shklar were correct, Rousseau would not have asked the question, "what will a man raised uniquely for himself be for others?", much less undertake to explain how "the double object we set for ourselves could be joined in one by removing the contradictions of man".[13] That Rousseau was prepared to undertake this kind of enterprise indicates he believed a solution to the contradiction between natural and social existence possible, at least in principle. The "double object" is crucial to his project because man can no longer live as he did in nature, and yet he cannot be denatured to the extent necessary to completely overcome his self-division in society. By viewing him as entirely Utopian, Shklar pushes aside the most problematic, but arguably important aspect of his thought: its prescriptive dimension. Rousseau's solution to the social problem may not be entirely coherent, but it cannot be separated from the body of his ideas as though it were ironic, peripheral, or in Shklar's words, Utopian. It is entailed in his critique of civil society, and if this critique is to be engaged as important for understanding social and political life, the solutions arising out of it must also be so engaged. In portraying him as a Utopian, Shklar merely postpones this.

6.2 The Pre-moral Education

Rousseau's program for educating Emile can be divided into two parts. The first three books describe his pre-moral education to the age of fifteen, when he enters puberty. The last two books chart his induction into civil society, together constituting the moral education of an innocent savage who is drawn naturally into moral relations with others by his awakening sexuality. Rousseau claims his education program follows the child's natural development. At each stage it focuses upon the natural capacities of the pupil, thus ensuring that his development is as far as possible in accordance with nature.[14] In the first three books Emile is educated to live for himself alone. Prior to puberty, neither his passions nor his reason are sufficiently developed to warrant a moral education. Accordingly, Rousseau controls his environment so as to avoid all situations that could make him aware that others possess wills which conflict with his own. Instead, the initial part of Emile's education focuses upon the development of what Rousseau calls his sensual or childish reason.[15] This involves learning to reason naturally, first on the basis of sensory perceptions alone, and then gradually in relation to his immediate or palpable self-interest. In Rousseau's view the initial stages of the child's education reproduce the tutelage of nature. His development from infancy through childhood can therefore be compared to the species' development from the original state of nature to the nascent society of the Golden Age. Like natural man, the child acquires the capacity to reason prudentially and a consciousness which, while necessarily entailing that he distinguish himself from other self-conscious beings, remains wholly concerned with his immediate self-interest. The child is to live for himself alone, taking no interest in the needs or opinions of others. Rousseau writes of him:

> Il n'exige rien de personne et ne croit rien devoir à personne: il est seul dans la société humaine, il ne compte que sur lui seul. Il a droit aussi plus qu'un autre de compter sur lui-même; car il est tout ce qu'on peut être à son âge.[16]

At age fifteen Emile is a savage man. He has reached his potential as a natural being ("tout ce qu'on peut être à son âge"), and so ideally prepared for life in civil society.[17]

The primary goal of the pre-moral education is to preserve the child's natural independence, which consists in maintaining an equilibrium between his desires and his capacity to satisfy them. But in attempting to reproduce the tutelage of nature, Rousseau's educational program faces the same paradox which confronted his account of the species' evolution beyond the original state of nature. On the one hand the child must develop self-consciousness and rationality, which are the basic preconditions of a social life; yet on the other he must do so without becoming dependent upon others, To accomplish this Rousseau proposes a radically new kind of education. The child's environment is to be completely controlled so that while he acquires these attributes he has the illusion of perfect self-reliance. To this end Rousseau stipulates four basic maxims. One, the child is to be allowed to develop his natural strength, by which Rousseau means he will not be artificially protected from the elements, but rather allowed to engage the natural world almost from birth. Two, his strength will be supplemented to enable him to meet his physical (i.e. natural) needs. Three, all assistance given the child will be limited to what is useful to him, which is to say that should not be helped to satisfy his whims. And four, the child's language should be studied carefully so that the tutor can distinguish between those needs which come from nature and those which come from opinion.[18] From our perspective the child's independence is obviously an illusion because Rousseau controls his environment completely. Yet from the child's own perspective, in Rousseau's view the one that counts, he is perfectly free because the only limitation upon his will is his own lack of strength. All obstacles to it appear to him as natural necessities, and as a result he never acquires the sense of being dependent upon anyone.[19] By limiting his needs to those he can satisfy himself, the pre-moral education aims at re-creating the natural liberty of man in his original state. At age fifteen Emile is an analogue to natural man, "un sauvage fait pour habiter les villes".[20]

6.3 The Infant Self

In the first three or so years the child's education is geared towards developing his physical faculties and preserving him from any sense that he can control or even affect the behaviour of others. Rousseau inveighs against many of the child-rearing practices of his time, such as swaddling, and farming children out to nursemaids. His general point about infants is consistent with the first maxim of his education program: they must be allowed the freedom to develop their natural strength to the greatest extent possible. Spoiling a child by unnecessarily protecting him from the elements has the effect of weakening him, and in doing so unnecessarily predisposes him to dependence upon others. Allowing the child the freedom to experience the physical world has the twofold advantage of enabling him to grow strong, while at the same time introducing him to the force of natural necessity. Both are crucial to the more complicated problem of educating him to psychological independence. A weak child will become dependent upon others, and begin because of this to attempt to manipulate them for his own benefit.

The argument that children should be allowed to experience the natural world from birth follows from Rousseau's account of the infant self, which he outlines in Book I. The child is said to be born with a potential capacity to learn (like all other humans he has the innate faculty of *perfectibilité*), but at birth he is not capable of knowing or willing anything. His organs are not fully formed and he has no sense of its own existence.[21] Rousseau intends here to establish a parallel between the infant subject and the subjectivity of the species in its original state. Both are conceived as *tabula rasa* whose consciousness is wholly determined by passive sense perception, and yet both are capable of self-improvement. The difference is of course that natural man has a sentiment of his own existence and a limited awareness of his own will. However, the contradiction here is only apparent. The infant has no sense of self because his organs are not fully formed. Rousseau therefore asks us to imagine an infant consciousness enclosed in a fully developed human body, and claims that this being's level of cognitive development is comparable to that of natural man.[22]

Rousseau invokes this analogy to establish the connection between his program for an education according to nature and his account of the species' natural development in the **Discours sur l'inégalité**. Emile is to be made a savage fit for living in cities, but he can only become this if his education reproduces the natural evolution of the species. The validity of the analogy, and thus in a larger sense the education itself, rests upon his being able to conceive the child's original nature as substantially equivalent to that of natural man. He must begin from the same point, and follow the same course of development. It is in this sense that his account of subjectivity works as a unifying idea in his thought. His account of the infant self is meant to be consistent with the accounts of subjectivity in both the **Discours sur l'inégalité** and the *Profession du foi de Vicaire Savoyard*. It establishes the framework for his education by delineating the subject's natural capacities, and this enables the tutor to structure his environment so that they may be developed properly.

The man/child Rousseau imagines is initially little more than an automaton. He has sensations, and a sentiment of his existence, but he does not distinguish between himself as a subject of experience and the sensations he has of the objects outside his mind. He exists as a *commun sensorium*, a reservoir of sensations over which he has no innate capacity to exert control, or to order. His self-consciousness, if it can be called that at all, is as immediate and primitive as possible. He is for himself just whatever sensation he is feeling at the moment. The basic point Rousseau wants to make with his account of the infant self is that all consciousness begins in, and develops as a consequence of sensation. This is true of all conscious beings, of animals as much as of humans.[23] Rousseau consistently holds to this point. In the **Discours sur l'inégalité** he claims that animals acquire knowledge as a consequence of sensation, and in this differ from humans only in a matter of degree. However, where humans do differ from animals is in the character of their will, which is free, and also in their consciousness of it.[24] The man/child is not therefore identical to natural man, at least initially, because he is aware neither of the distinction between himself and the objects he senses (of himself as a subject of experience), nor of his own will. These two attributes are acquired from his experience of the world, in particular through the sensation of touch.[25] In Rousseau's view, the subject's original consciousness consists of the passive experience of sensation and a sentiment of his own existence.[26]

The second important point on which Rousseau's account of the infant self is consistent with his account of natural man is in respect of the faculty of *perfectibilité*. In the **Discours sur l'inégalité** he claims that with freedom, *perfectibilité* is the distinguishing feature of natural man. He echoes this in his discussion of the infant self when he claims that: "Nous ignorons ce que notre nature nous permet d'être; nul de nous n'a mesure la distance qui peut se trouver entre un homme et un autre homme."[27] In both cases the faculty is merely a potential for development, but in both this potential is understood to be open-ended, and in both it is the condition of the subject's acquisition of language.

Rousseau's conception of the infant self establishes the framework for his education program. At the pre-linguistic or pre-rational stage of cognitive development, knowledge is accumulated as a mechanical consequence of sensation. The child is therefore allowed to experience the physical world as much as possible. His innate desire for self-preservation encourages him to do this, and the knowledge he acquires in the process is natural as a result. He is not however allowed to acquire habits which could give rise to artificial needs, nor is he allowed to find resistance in other wills. Both tend to weaken the child; disposing him towards dependence upon others, while at the same time engendering a corresponding desire for domination.[28] The initial education of the child strengthens his sense of self by allowing him to experience the world in a manner consistent with his nature. The education is in this sense largely negative. Rousseau controls his environment so that he can develop in the manner prescribed by his nature as a subject, as a sense-perceiving being who relates everything to himself.

6.4 The Acquisition of Language

The acquisition of language marks the next important stage of the infant's development. We have seen that for Rousseau, acquiring language is a necessary condition of becoming a fully developed human consciousness. It enables the subject to escape the sense-bound and therefore passive consciousness of natural man, and so begin to exert some control over nature and himself. But it is also a social institution, and so involves the subject in relations with others. As a consequence the child's first linguistic experience must be governed very closely. Like the education program in general, Rousseau's account of Emile's linguistic development reflects the principles of his anthropology. At first, the child's language bears a greater resemblance to the language of primitive men than it does to our own. In its original or natural form it is rich in accentuation and feeling, while being correspondingly devoid of precision and complexity.[29] In Rousseau's view, human language is most natural when it is passionate, because our initial impulsion to communicate is linked to feeling.[30] Emile's linguistic training is geared towards preserving both his physical and psychological independence. To this end the proposals Rousseau makes are based upon one fundamental principle, that the child's language should not mediate his relations with either nature or other persons in such a way as to make him dependent.

The influence of language upon our relations with others is obviously very great, as it is the medium through which they occur. In Rousseau's view language can easily be used as a means of dominating others; indeed in civil society, he regards this as its most pervasive function. Emile's linguistic training is meant to inhibit his capacity to do this. He is encouraged, first of all, to preserve the natural (i.e. passionate) character of his speech. Rousseau believes this will ensure that he retains his natural authenticity in his relations with others, which is to say that he will appear to others (in speech), exactly as he is for himself. In Rousseau's view, original or natural languages are based in our feelings because passion is prior to reason in this species' development. Children and unsophisticated country peasants accentuate strongly when they speak, because their consciousness and their language are closer to nature. Thus Rousseau writes:

> L'accent est l'ame du discours; il lui donne le sentiment et la vérité. L'accent ment moins que la parole; c'est peut-être pour cela que les gens bien élevés le craignent tant. C'est de l'usage de tout dire sur le même ton qu'est venu celui de persifler les gens sans qu'ils le sentent.[31]

The stress on accentuation invokes a parallel between the child's language and the passionate languages of *le siècle d'or*. We saw above that these original languages acted as a restraint upon the propensity towards corruption latent in the first social relations of primitive men. Their passionate, poetical character arose from each speaker's attempt to imitate the feelings motivating him to speak. They were in this sense transparent mediums which denied primitive men the capacity to deceive or manipulate others. Emile is to be encouraged to accentuate so that he will appear to others exactly as he is for himself. Accentuation denies him the means to pretence and irony, and in doing so preserves him from any concern for what others think of him. It also fosters the uninhibited growth of his natural passions, which of their nature require full and unrestricted expression. As a medium or vehicle for the expression of natural feeling, Emile's language is more likely to preserve his natural independence than the sophisticated, prolix languages taught to most children.

Language must also not be allowed to mediate the child's experience of nature. Rousseau insists that children should be allowed to acquire language at their own pace. Teaching them to speak too early, and loading them with verbiage they have not the intellectual facility to grasp, distorts their natural cognitive development.[32] Emile is not rushed into learning his native language, and he is positively discouraged from learning other languages. The basis of Rousseau's contempt for educators who force their charges to learn Cicero, or to dispute upon matters of ancient history, is that the knowledge children acquire through such exercises is not related to their immediate, palpable interest, and therefore both useless to them and beyond their understanding.[33] In Rousseau's view, the proper use of signs to represent ideas presupposes that one has a clear understanding of what is being represented. The natural order of the child's intellectual development requires first that he gain a clear and distinct understanding of the objects of his knowledge, and only secondarily that he learn to represent his ideas of them in language. He must first experience the world through sensation, which his self-love (*amour de soi-même*) naturally motivates him to do; and once he has a sure understanding of the source of his ideas and their use to him, he is in a position to make accurate judgements about how they are related to one another. Teaching a child to recite poetry, or to read history, is to give him a complex system of signs that can have no bearing upon his own experience, and therefore no meaning for him. In fact the likely effect of such exercises

An Education According to Nature 191

is to teach the child that facility in language is a means of eliciting approbation of others.

> Que sert d'inscrire dans leur tête un catalogue de signes qui ne réprésentant rien pour eux? En apprenant les choses n'apprendront-ils pas les signes? ...C'est du prémier mot dont l'enfant se paye, c'est de la prémiére chose qu'il apprend sur la parole d'autrui sans en voir l'utilité lui-même que son jugement est perdu: il aura longtemps à briller aux yeux des sots avant que qu'il réparé une telle perte.[34]

The child's early linguistic training is largely negative, and so consistent with the general principles of Rousseau's education program. Emile is allowed to acquire language at his own, natural pace, which is to say only insofar as it is useful to him. By limiting his utterances to expressions of feeling and to representations of his direct experience of nature, the potentially corruptive effect of language is forestalled and his natural independence preserved.

6.5 Natural Liberty

Independence, as we have seen, is the primary goal of the child's pre-moral education. Rousseau defines this as a condition of self-sufficiency in which the child's desires are matched by his capacity to satisfy them.

> Le seul qui fait sa volonté est celui qui n'a pas besoins pour la faire de mettre les bras d'une autre au bout des siens; d'où il suit que le prémier de tous les biens n'est pas l'autorité mais la liberté. L'homme vraiment libre veut que ce qu'il peut et fait ce qu'il lui plaît. Voila ma maxime fondamentale. Il ne s'agit que de d'appliquer a l'enfance, et tous les régles de l'éducation vont en découler.[35]

It follows from this that the rest of the child's education should be designed to increase his strength and limit the growth of his desires. He cannot of course be independent in the manner described because he is incapable of producing even the barest necessities of subsistence, and so totally dependent upon those around him. But Rousseau's aim is not that he be independent in the actual sense, rather that he regard himself as such because he is ignorant of the provisions made for him by others. The crucial point here is that the child remain unaware of the existence of other wills that could have a direct bearing upon his own. In Rousseau's view a child's weakness stems not so much from the frailty of his constitution, as from the possession of desires he can only fulfil with the aid of others.[36] Yet even Rousseau must admit that there are very few desires a child can satisfy independently. That this is the case does not strike him as contradictory, because he makes a distinction between two types of dependence, one natural and the other social. The former he describes as dependence on things, which he regards as natural, non-moral, and incapable of engendering any vices. The latter is dependence on men, the social phenomena which is the source of all our corruption.[37] The child's dependence on others can therefore only serve as an obstacle to his natural development if he is aware of it. To counter this Rousseau restricts his knowledge as far as possible to those physical objects which are of immediate use to him, and helps him surreptitiously to obtain them. In those situations where it is impossible to disguise his need of others, the child is to see the will which chooses to assist him as self-regarding and in no sense beholden to him (i.e. as free). In this way the child's relations with others duplicates his relations with the natural world. Rousseau wants Emile to regard other persons in the same way that he regards things, as instruments to his satisfaction whose existence is relevant to his own only insofar as he needs something from them. Seeing others in this way preserves his independence, because it denies him the opportunity to conceive the assistance of others as something he can control, and hence to acquire desires he is incapable of satisfying himself.[38]

The instrumental and hence amoral character of the child's relations with others is illustrated by his encounter with the gardener Robert. Rousseau admits that he cannot preserve his charge entirely from knowledge of human relations and the moral problems inherent in them. But he does not regard this as a problem as long as Emile is preserved from this knowledge until it becomes unavoidable, and then as long as the motivation

An Education According to Nature

behind his interest in others is restricted to his immediate utility. He is introduced to the principle of mutual respect for property rights by being made to see the use this principle has for him. To Rousseau's mind, this accords entirely with nature.

> Nos prémiers devoirs sont envers nous; nos sentiments primitifs se concentrent en nous mêmes; tous nos mouvements naturels se rapportent d'abord à notre conservation et à notre bien-être. Ainsi le prémier sentiment de la justice ne nous vient pas de celle que nous devons, mais de celle que nous est due.[39]

Emile is therefore given a plot of land and some seeds to sow, though by design he is given land already sown by Robert. Rousseau introduces him to his property rights in a classically Lockean manner. The child is encouraged to see his labour as the ground of right of ownership. He finds one day however that his plot has been destroyed, and as he has been given to understand that it belongs to him, he is indignant and aggrieved. In the ensuing confrontation with Robert, Emile is given a moral lesson appropriate to his natural intellectual development. He is told that it is he who has acted wrongly, because Robert had already planted melon seeds in the plot, and in virtue of this possessed a right to the fruits of his labour. Robert says to him: "Personne ne touche au jardin de son voisin; chacun respecte le travail des autres afin que le sien soit en sûreté."[40] The moral lesson, or principle, is presented in terms of its immediate palpable advantage for Emile. The child is made to see his obligation in the same way he sees everything else, in terms of its use for him. Rousseau's point here is that this is the only way a child can be made to understand and accept an obligation at this stage of his life. His reasoning is as yet entirely prudential, and his natural passions motivate him to relate everything to his own needs. To give him a moral command (e.g. you *must* respect the property rights of others) is tantamount to inviting him to lie. The child's intellect is too limited to enable him to foresee the future consequences of his action, or indeed the consequences it will have for others. If he cannot be made to believe that the principle is always in his interest, it will seem abstract to him, and he will simply lie to get around it.

The important implication of this argument is that morality contradicts nature,

Emile does not become a moral being when he is first introduced to moral relations because he retains the natural order of his passions; his self-love continues to dominate his behaviour, and he retains his natural indifference toward others. The goal of preserving the child's natural independence requires that he retain the natural character of his self-love. It should be, as it was for natural man, the single most dominant passion in his life. As long as this is the case, he will need no one else (at least to his knowledge), and therefore remain self-sufficient. Once the child enters society, the natural order of his passions will have to be reversed, but prior to this, morality has no place in his life. It might be objected here that the result of such an enterprise would be to make the child into a self-obsessed little brat, but in Rousseau's view this is to miss the point. The child is not to be judged from the standpoint of how he would fit or behave in a social context. He is to be judged relative to his original nature, which Rousseau believes he has preserved intact. Natural self-love preserves his independence by limiting his needs to those he can satisfy with his own resources. It has no adverse affect upon others because it is a natural sentiment. If it causes him to relate everything to himself, it also denies him the capacity to harm others.

> Posons pour maxime incontestable que les premiers mouvements de la nature son toujours droits: il n'y a point de perversité originelle dans le coeur humaine... La seule passion naturelle à l'homme est l'amour de soi-même ou l'amour-propre pris dans un sens étendu. Cet amour-propre en soi ou relativement à nous est bon et utile, et comme il n'a point de rapport nécessaire à autrui, il est à cet égard naturellement indifférent; il ne devient bon ou mauvais que par l'application qu'on en fait et les relations qu'on lui donne. Jusqu'à ce que le guide de l'amour-propre qui est la raison puisse naître, il importe donc qu'un enfant ne fasse rien parce qu'il est vu ou étendu, rien en un mot par rapport aux autres, mais seulement ce que la nature lui demande, et alors il ne fera rien que de bien.[41]

Amour-propre and *amour de soi-même* are identical in the original nature of the child. This unity is broken only when the self-conscious intentions of others become part of his experience, and he begins to determine his identity and his will in relation to the expectations of others. As long as the child's interest in the intentions of others is

An Education According to Nature 195

restricted solely to their affect upon his own self-preservation, the natural order of his passions will be maintained and will preserve him from vice. It is in this sense that the pre-moral education is purely negative. "Elle consiste, non point à enseigner la vertu ni la vérité, mais a garantir le coeur du vice et l'esprit de l'erreur."[42]

6.6 The Acquisition of Judgement

The last stage of Emile's pre-moral education consists in the refinement of his faculty of active judgement, and marks the final preparation for his entry into civil society. As he approaches puberty and the passions which will force him to seek out moral relations with others, he reaches the stage in his natural development when sound judgement will be necessary for him to avoid corruption and dependence. He will have to judge himself and his relations with others accurately if he is to retain his freedom in society. In Rousseau's view the best and most natural method of forming a sound udgement is through a "scientific" education, in which the child investigates nature by determining the use physical objects have for him. His curiosity is natural if it stems from his innate desire for well-being, and it follows that both the knowledge and the judgement he acquires from his investigations into the utility of things is also natural.[43] From about age twelve to fifteen then, Emile is encouraged to develop his judgement through an active investigation of nature.

Rousseau's discussion of this process rests on the assumption that reason and feeling are distinct faculties of the self. This assumption is important to his account of Emile's development, because he wants to maintain that the formation and refinement of his capacity to reflect upon himself and his relations with things will not lead him to reflect upon his standing relative to others, and so compromise his independence. What is to be refined is his capacity to reason instrumentally about physical nature, and in Rousseau's view this cannot lead him to consider himself in relation to other persons unless it is given motivation to do so by his passions.

Rousseau's conception of the faculty of judgement is based upon the Lockean/sensationalist account of thought as the mind's capacity to associate the simple ideas received in sensation into complex ideas or judgements, which are neither determined nor implied by the sensations themselves.⁴⁴ This is contrasted with passive judgement, which is experienced in sensation, and consists simply in affirming what one senses.

> Dans la sensation, le jugement est purement passif, il affirme qu'on sent ce qu'on sent. Dans la perception ou ideé, le jugement est actif; il rapproche, il compare, il déterminé des rapports que le sens ne déterminé pas. Voila toute la différence, mais elle est grande. Jamais la nature ne nous trompe; c'est toujours nous qui nous tompons.⁴⁵

The acquisition of judgement marks a break with nature in one sense, because it frees the child's consciousness from determination by its sensations. It's greatest potential danger is that it creates the possibility of error, therefore it must be confined as near as possible to the association of simple ideas that can be verified directly through the senses.⁴⁶ For Rousseau, sound judgement consists in making accurate associations between the various impressions we experience through sensation. Thus the greater our familiarity with the objects of sensation about which we make judgements, the better and more accurate our judgements and the knowledge that accrues from them. Emile's judgement is therefore developed through an active investigation of physical nature. He is taught to verify his inductions as far as possible through direct observation and examination, and his curiosity is limited, as we have seen, to those objects or phenomena that seem to have a direct bearing on his well-being. Limiting the scope of his judgement in this way serves three purposes in the education program. It preserves him from knowledge of moral relations, of which he has no experience and thus no capacity to make sound judgements. It teaches him to reason accurately within the limits imposed on him by nature, that is, in respect of what contributes to his well-being. But most importantly, it inculcates him with the habit of reasoning independently, so that he does not rely upon the authority or opinions of others when judging or determining courses of action for himself.[47]

Each of these attributes prepares Emile for the proper use of his reason in moral relations. Once he enters the society of others, his identity will come to be constituted in relation to them. To avoid becoming dependent and corrupt, his active reason will have to guide his passions and his will to their proper moral end. A sound judgement, in Rousseau's terms one that reasons independently and accurately within the limits of its experience, is a necessary condition of his moral freedom.[48] However, the initial discussion of reason raises a difficult problem for Rousseau's account of the child's natural development. If Emile is able to make active judgements about his relations with the physical world -- to interpret and so ascribe meaning to his sensory experience, and to form courses of action intended to satisfy his desires -- it is not immediately clear why he would be unable to do this with respect to the behaviour and intentions of others. There is nothing in the character of instrumental judgements that precludes consideration of others' intentions and standing relative to oneself. And given that the child is meant to become very adept at judging things relative to himself, it would seem obvious for him to conclude, at very least, that he is dependent upon his tutor for his well-being. As his tutor, Rousseau must at various times possess things the child desires, as well as the means to deny him access to those things. Thus it would seem obvious for the child to conclude that he is, at least in certain situations, both weaker than and dependent upon his tutor.[49] Yet this is the very conclusion Rousseau wants him to avoid.

In answer to this Rousseau could argue that while the child is capable of judging his weakness relative to his tutor, this gives him no sense of dependence or resentment because he regards his tutor's will as a natural force, as non-intentional and necessary. The child does not consider the tutor's reasons for denying him what he wants because he has no experience of the intentions of others. He has nothing with which to compare his tutor's denial, except the natural physical obstacles to his subsistence he has already experienced, and so he quite naturally assumes that his tutor's will is like them, a natural force. Similarly, Rousseau is careful to stipulate that all punishment should appear to the child as a natural consequence of his behaviour, and not as a consequence of someone else's authority over him. As long as this is the case he will remain ignorant of his dependence on others, and his natural independence will be preserved. This argument rests on the assumption, crucial to Rousseau's philosophical anthropology, that reason and feeling are separate faculties of the self. Rousseau believed that reason could be developed or refined independent of the passions, without causing any necessary acceleration of their development, though it should be noted that he did not think the reverse true, i.e. that the passions can develop without causing a corresponding progress in the subject's capacity to reason.[50] The capacity for active reason does not of itself motivate us to do or be interested in anything. As long as the subject is dominated by his self-love (*amour de soi-même*), his thought will naturally be confined to judgements about the use things have for him. Some passion for others (e.g. sexuality) is required before his judgement can be naturally directed towards the question of how their intentions affect him. This is why, in both the ***Discours sur l'inégalité*** and *Emile*, the transition from nature to society is marked by relations involving moral passions. The child's active but wholly prudential reason then, has no affect upon the natural order of his passions, and for this reason preserves his natural independence while at the same time preparing him for moral relations.

6.7 Natural Consciousness and Moral Relations

The question of course is whether the argument that the child's intellectual development has no affect upon his emotional development is at all plausible? The answer to this has implications beyond Rousseau's discussion of the formation of the child's judgement. If it is not plausible, it is difficult to see how one can take seriously what he claims to accomplish with his pre-moral education, the formation of a savage fit for living

An Education According to Nature

in society. Rousseau's cognitive portrait of Emile at age fifteen has him bearing a remarkable resemblance to natural man just as he entered *le siècle d'or*. He is intellectually better developed than natural man, but this is irrelevant to the analogy because he is self-sufficient for the same reason: each is entirely concerned with himself.

> Emile n'a que des connoissance naturelles et purement physiques. Il ne sait pas même le nom de l'histoire, ni ce que c'est que métaphysique et morale. Il connoit les rapports essentiels de l'homme aux choses, mais nul des rapports moraux de l'homme àl'homme. Il sait peu généraliser d'idés, peu faire d'abstractions...Il ne cherche point à connoitre les choses par leur nature, mais seulement par les relations qui l'intéressant. Il n'estime ce qui lui est étranger que par rapport à lui; mais cette estimation est exacte et sûre. La fantaisie, la convention n'y entrent pour rien. Il fait plus de cas de ce qui lui est plus utile, et ne se départant jamais de cette maniére d'apprécier, il ne donne rien à l'opinion.[51]

The difficulty is that this rests on the assumption that the child has no feeling for his tutor beyond regarding him as useful. If he felt love or hatred, fear or affection, he would not remain independent because his active judgement would be directed towards a consideration of the tutor's value as a subject, and so to how that value compares with his own.

The plausibility of this has been attacked elsewhere,[52] but it would seem necessary to reiterate that it is the least convincing aspect of Rousseau's pre-moral education. It is highly unlikely that the child could have no feeling for Rousseau given the amount of time they spend together and the nature of their relationship. Rousseau admits that the child will feel pleasure in his company, and see him as "son ami, son camarade";[53] but he does not believe this constitutes affection of a degree necessary to make the child need his tutor's company for its own sake, or to devise ways to obtain it. Yet why not? If the company of a specific person gives one pleasure, it contributes to one's well being, and so would seem to constitute a natural need in Rousseau's own terms. But need of a particular person will, in Rousseau's view, inevitably give rise to the question, "why do I need this person and not another?", which in turn raises the question, "does this person need me?" These are moral questions, and would indicate that the child's self-love had taken on a relative aspect. The same point can be made in respect of the child's need for security. When Rousseau allows him to go out on his own as a form of punishment he feels frightened, but the next day in his tutor's company he feels secure, even confident.[54] The feeling of security a child has in the company of a parent or any trusted adult no doubt finds its source in the instinct to self-preservation, but its immediate cause is the child's knowledge or sense of its own weakness relative to others. Again, the feeling of security would seem to have a natural source, but it must undermine the child's independence because it is based on his awareness of his need of another's intention to protect him. Beyond these two examples it would seem obvious that the entire program of instruction, despite being made to appear self-directed, rests on a trust between Emile and Rousseau. Why otherwise would the child be so eager to adopt all his tutor's suggestions? The point being that none of these feelings -- affection, friendship, a sense of security or trust--are consistent with Rousseau's claim that the child will only see his tutor as an instrument to the satisfaction of his natural desires. Insofar as they derive from his innate desire for well-being such sentiments would seem natural enough; yet they put him in need of another person's good will, and so compromise the foundation of Rousseau's claim that the child can be related to others without becoming dependent upon them.

The problems in Rousseau's portrait of Emile as natural man point once again to the fundamental concern between his conceptions of nature and society. The pre-moral education is a contradictory enterprise. It must preserve the child's original nature, yet prepare him for society (the "double object" of which Rousseau wrote at the beginning), and the two seem exclusive of each other. Moral life, as we have seen, requires that one's active reason be capable of guiding the passions and the will to their proper end; to prepare Emile for it, Rousseau must form his faculty of judgement, yet he must do so according to nature, which means without giving the child any concern for his status relative to others, and this seems implausible.

Rousseau's account of Emile at age fifteen remains too loosely tied to his account of natural man to be convincing. It is impossible to believe that a child, however carefully raised, could reach puberty without having felt any emotional attachment towards another; and as I have tried to show, Rousseau's own description of his relationship with Emile belies his claim. But even if we grant this on the grounds that practicality is not part of his enterprise, the account still remains problematic. Rousseau wants to show that the child has a natural development which does not undermine the natural order of his passions; that he can be constituted as a recognizably human subject by nature, without at the same time acquiring any need for the society of others. This, as we saw in Chapter 3, is entailed in the assumption that man is naturally good. Rousseau needs an account of the subject outside society in order to make good his claim that our corruption and dependence are acquired within it. Yet he can only do this by insisting that the child has no passions or feelings for others; and the question this raises is what relation his pre-moral nature bears to his nature as it is constituted in society. The pre-moral education has both a practical and a critical dimension. It is meant in a straightforward sense to prepare the child for his moral education (and thus his induction into society), by developing his active reason and otherwise preserving him from vice. It is also meant to serve as a standard of good, as representative of what nature has made us, and therefore the extent to which we are distorted and alienated in society. Both dimensions point to the same underlying problem in Rousseau's educational program. There would seem to be nothing in his account of Emile's natural education that either prepares him for social life or makes likely the possibility of his retaining his original nature in society.

In claiming that the pre-moral education prepares Emile for social life, Rousseau assumes he has made it possible for Emile to find his own way of reconciling the conflicting demands of nature and culture by preserving him from vice. He is ready to acquire the social or moral virtues, and so to retain some continuity with the constituent elements of his original nature in the context of society. "En un mot Emile a de la vertu tout ce qui se rapporte à lui-même. Pour avoir aussi les vertus sociales, il lui manque uniquement de connoitre les rélations qui les éxigent, il lui manque uniquement des lumiéres que son esprit est tout prêt à recevoir."[55] Yet is difficult to see how this could be true. The natural education has fostered a consciousness for which everything external to the self is either useful or irrelevant. This leaves the child no basis upon which to develop a moral consciousness which must, by definition, find a way of recognizing and respecting the autonomy of other self-conscious wills. Knowledge of things moral, as Rousseau admits elsewhere, is not sufficient ground for his capacity to do this; and neither are the passions he has acquired thus far, for they are wholly self-referential, and therefore cannot motivate him to identify with the interests of others. By nature, Emile is anything but fit for relations with others. His self-sufficiency is founded solely upon his natural egoism, and this places him outside and in opposition to all forms of social life.

Rousseau's account of the child's natural education entails an ambiguous conception of nature. On the one hand, the natural state is identified with a consciousness based solely upon satisfying the physical needs of the self. Yet insofar as this is meant to prepare him for society, the education program presupposes a conception of social nature, wherein the self has a natural development despite being subject to the relativized form of self-love (*amour-propre*) that arises of necessity from intersubjective relations with others. The child's natural consciousness is entirely dominated by desires arising from his physical existence, and the realization of his natural potential consists in achieving a condition in which he has more than enough strength to satisfy them. This wholly negative or non-moral form of freedom is the concrete determination of Rousseau's claim that man is naturally free. His natural development also ensures that he is capable of improvement, for it entails the acquisition of language and rationality, which is the condition of his being able to improve beyond his natural state. Yet at the same time the condition of realizing both these innate attributes, freedom and *perfectibilité*, is the absence of social relations. As such it is not clear what form they could take in society, and thus how they could serve as the basis of his social nature.

The apparent discontinuity between these two conceptions of nature reflects the difficulty of attempting to define man's nature independent of society, and then explain how he can develop naturally within it. It stems from the contradiction inherent in the conception of subjectivity underlying the entire project of reconciling a natural being to the demands of moral and social life. On the one hand the self is conceived as a simple unity, possessed of a natural essence which it must realize if it is to be happy, virtuous, and free. Yet on the other nothing can be said of this natural essence save that it consists in the purely formal or unrealized potential to become these things. If the natural self has no moral attributes, it cannot serve as a guide to the acquisition of such attributes in society. Rousseau took from Descartes the idea that the self must be a simple unity, a subject of experience defined by an essential principle which holds true regardless of context. He locates this essence in the subject's conscious capacity for choice, and so equates freedom with humanity, and the loss of freedom with alienation of humanity. Yet at the same time he attempted to graft this notion of essence onto a sensationalist theory of consciousness, according to which the subject's concrete character, its emotional and cognitive attributes, are acquired through its sensory experience of its environment. This allows him, as we have seen, to view the moral problem of human nature historically, as a product of the species' largely self-created circumstances, rather than any limitations intrinsic to it. But it also yields a contradiction. If the self is essentially free, it must be shown to be so independent of the circumstances which have led to the loss of its freedom, and this means outside society. But in nature the subject's freedom can have no moral content, he has a capacity to choose, but only between impulsions, or self-referential desires, and never while considering the needs or the intentions of others. Rousseau believed this natural freedom would be the only basis upon which a child could realize its potential for moral freedom. Yet insofar as such freedom is predicated upon the child's complete indifference to others, it would seem profoundly opposed to the basic requirements of moral life.

Endnotes

1. This is not of course to deny the importance of its critical dimension, most notably the discussions of educational theory, materialism, and existing civil societies. The two modes of writing, prescriptive moral theory and social criticism, entail rather than preclude one another.

2. O.C. VI, pp. 833-53.

3. *Ibid.*, p. 859. After his travels, Emile comes to the conclusion that there is no state worthy of his active allegiance and participation. Rousseau replies that freedom is to be found in the heart of the free man, and that it can be taken anywhere. He goes on to exhort Emile to live in the country, and imagines a rustic community reminiscent of the golden age growing up around them.

   "On traitte l'age d'or de chimère, et c'en sera toujours une pour quiconque a le coeur et le goût gâtés. Il n'est pas même vrai qu'on le regrette, puisque ces regrets sont toujours vains. Que faudroit-il donc pour le faire renaître? Une seule chose mais impossible; ce seroit de l'aimer."

4. O.C. IV, pp. 881-924.

5. Rousseau claimed at various points that his writings formed a consistent whole. He writes in the ***Lettre à Christophe de Beaumont*** that his writings have always been consistent in terms of their basic principles. "J'ai écrit sur divers sujets mais toujours dans les mêmes maximes, et, si l'on veut, les mêmes principes; toujours la même morale, la mêmes opinions." (O.C. IV., p. 928) See also, ***Rousseau Juge de Jean-Jacques*** (O.C.I., p. 930), and ***Lettre à Malesherbes***, 12 Janvier, 1762 in *Correspondance générale*, edited by Ralph Leigh, etc.).

6. In a letter to Philibert Cramer (14 Octobre, 1764), Rousseau claims: "Vous dites très bien qu'il est impossible de faire un Emile. Mais je ne puis croire que vous teniez le livre pour un vrai traite d'éducation. C'est un ouvrage assez philosophique sur ce principe avance pas l'auteur dans d'autres écrits, que l'homme est naturellement bons. Pour accorder ce principe avec cette autres vérité non moins certaine que les hommes sont méchants, il fallait dans l'histoire du coeur humaine montrer l'origine des tous les vices. C'est ce que j'ai fait dans ce livre, souvent avec justesse et quelquefois avec sagacité."

7. O.C. IV, pp. 249-50.

8. *Ibid.*, p. 250.

9. *Ibid.*, p. 251.

10. *Ibid.*, p. 311. As Rousseau claims in *Emile*, a civil society that could give to its laws the same inflexibility nature gives to hers, could unite the advantages of the civil state with those of nature, and "on joindroit à la liberté qui maintient l'homme exempt de vices la moralité qui l'élevé à la vertu." His conception of moral freedom contains both a negative and a positive element because it attempts to reconcile original and social nature.

11. Judith Shklar, "Rousseau's Two Models: Sparta and the Age of Gold", in *Political Science Quarterly*, vol. LXXXI. March, 1966, pp. 25-51; *Men and Citizens*, (London: Cambridge University Press, 1969), Chapter 1.

12. *Ibid.*, p. 29.

13. O.C. IV, p. 251.

14. O.C. IV, pp. 302-04, 316-18, 424.

    Rousseau insists throughout *Emile* that a natural education will not burden the child with concepts (specifically moral ideas) he is incapable of understanding. His reason is to be allowed to develop naturally, first through his experience of the natural or physical world, and then later, once his sexuality gives him a natural impulsion towards it, through his experience of the social world. Rousseau quite rightly regarded this as a radical departure from traditional forms of education.

15. *Ibid.*, p. 417.

16. *Ibid.*, p. 488.

17. *Ibid.*, p. 484.

18. *Ibid.*, p. 290.

19. *Ibid.*, p. 311. The significance of the distinction between dependence on things and dependence on men will be discussed below.

20. *Ibid.*, p. 484.

21. *Ibid.*, pp. 279-80.

22. *Ibid.*, pp. 280-81.

23. *Ibid.*, pp. 281-82.

24. O.C. III, p. 141.

25. O.C. IV, p. 284.   See also Condillac, *Traites des sensations*, II, xii, § 2-3, in *Oeuvres Philosophiques*, edited by LeRoy, Vol. I.

26. *Ibid.*, p, 570-71. Rousseau also makes this point in the *Profession du foi*, where the Vicar claims as his first indubitable premise: "J'existe et j'ai des sens par lesquelles je suis affecte". He concludes from this that he must be a subject of experience separate from his sensations, because he cannot control their occurrence. The child cannot make this judgement at birth, but he discovers it through the repeated experience of touching objects.

27. *Ibid.*, p. 281.

28. *Ibid.*, pp. 282, 287-88.

29. *Ibid.*, p. 285, and also pp. 293-98, and E.O.L., p. 55.

30. See Chapter 4.4.

31. O.C. VI, p. 296.

32. *Ibid.*, pp. 298-99.

33. *Ibid.*, p. 343.

34. *Ibid.*, p. 350.

35. *Ibid.*, p. 309; compare O.C. III, pp. 153, 159-60, 214.

36. *Ibid.*, p. 310.

37. *Ibid.*, p. 311.

38. *Ibid.*, p. 320.

39. *Ibid.*, p. 329.

40. *Ibid.*, p, 332.

41. *Ibid.*, p. 322. See also O.C. III. p. 219; where Rousseau distinguishes between "l'amour de soi-même est un sentiment naturel qui porte tout animal a veiller à sa propre conservation et qui, dirigé dans l'homme par la raison et modifie la pitié, produit l'humanité et la vertu, (and) L'amour-propre . . . un sentiment relatif, factice, et né dans la société, qui porte chaque individu à faire plus cas de soi que de tout autre, qui inspire aux hommes tous les maux qu'ils se font mutuellement, et qui est la véritable source de l'honneur."

42. *Ibid.*, p. 323.

43. *Ibid.*, pp. 428-29.

44. See Chapters 1 and 2.

45. *Ibid.*, p. 481.

46. *Ibid.*, pp. 430, 483.

47. *Ibid.*, pp. 442, 487.

48. *Ibid.*, p. 600. Here Rousseau describes moral autonomy as active reason determining the good, and the innate moral sentiment of conscience motivating him to will it.

49. *Ibid.*, pp. 333-34, 367-68. In both stories the child has a direct experience of his tutor's relatively greater strength, and the authority which issues from it.

50. O.C. III, p. 143; O.C. IV, p. 481.

51. O.C. IV, p. 487.

52. Charvet, *Social Problem*, pp. 65-67.

53. O.C. IV, p. 419.

54. *Ibid.*, p. 368.

55. *Ibid.*, p. 488.

7

A Moral Education

7.1 Introduction

If Rousseau's education program is to resolve the contradictions between natural and social existence, it must show that the child's pre-moral education, what he has become "according to nature", has some bearing upon his development in society. But given the decidedly asocial character of Emile's original nature, this imposes some conflicting requirements upon his moral education. First, Rousseau must argue that the child has a natural inclination to seek the company of others, even though the first fifteen years of his education has been directed at maintaining his natural isolation. He must argue this to establish some continuity between the child's existence in nature and his existence in society. If Emile had to be forced to live in society because he lacked the natural impulse to do so, there would be no hope of reconciling his original nature to social life. He would become as the product of a social education, a self-divided and artificial being, and thus always torn between his natural egoism (*amour de soi-même,*) and his moral duties. Second, while the link with society must be natural, the moral education must also show that the child can be denatured. If Emile is to become a moral being,

A Moral Education

he must shed his natural egoism so that he can accept the needs and interests of others as bearing a value equal to his own. This requires that the natural order of his passions be reversed; that *amour de soi-même* be replaced as the motivating force behind his actions by passions such as love and pity, which arise from his recognition of others as self-valuing subjects like himself. Emile is to be denatured, and the instrument of this denaturation is to be the passions that arise naturally in his contact with others.

The emergence of his sexual drive provides Emile with a natural desire that can only be satisfied in association with others, and it provides Rousseau with a point of departure for the second stage of his education program. Here again, his account of Emile's development tracks his earlier account of the species' evolution. The passions arising from the birth of his sexuality become the natural instruments of his socialization, just as they did for the primitive savages of *le siècle d'or*. The importance of the child's nascent sexuality is that it gives him needs he can only satisfy in association with others. Rousseau assumes that the inevitable consequence of this for Emile will be his coming to value, and therefore need, others. Unlike natural man he must develop within a social milieu, and this ensures that the passions arising from his sexuality become the reason for his transition from nature to society. The child's entrance into society is therefore natural within his specific circumstances.

> Sitôt que l'homme a besoin d'une compagne, il n'est plus un être isolé! son coeur n'est plus seul. Toutes ses relations avec son espèce, toutes les affections de son âme naissent avec celle-là. Sa prémiére passion fait bientôt fermenter les autres.[1]

However, this desire itself, as we saw in the ***Discours sur l'inégalité***, is purely physical in its natural form. As such it has no specific implications for the child's moral development, it simply ensures that he will be drawn into moral relations. "Le penchant de l'instinct est indéterminé. Un sexe est attire ver l'autre, viola le mouvement de la nature."[2] It is only once the desire begins to be focused upon one particular person that the subject's moral passions are aroused, and the absolute self-unity of his natural egoism is disrupted. The inevitability of this is ensured by the child's environment, and so requires that his self-consciousness be reconstituted by a moral education which teaches him to be related to others without compromising his natural potential for freedom and virtue. Thus Rousseau writes: "quand il commence à sentir son être moral, il doit s'étudier par ses rapports avec les hommes,"[3] Since the emergence of sexuality in a social milieu makes the natural self-sufficiency and isolation of childhood impossible to sustain, the problem becomes how to lose these natural characteristics without succumbing to the corrupt passions that stem from *amour-propre*. The new self-consciousness necessary for moral life opens the self to a potential for both virtue and vice, as Rousseau's analysis of sexuality makes clear. He argues here, as he did in both the *Essai* and the *Discours*, that as a passion born of society, the moral dimension of our sexuality (love) has a double character. On the one hand it is a moral sentiment, because it gives us a reason to regard others as having a value for us that is not merely instrumental. Yet on the other, it produces anxiety about one's standing in the affections of the beloved, and so initiates the relativization of self-love. When Emile begins to focus his sexual desire upon one person, he will have to reconstitute his conception of himself relative to others.

As a child Emile judged the value of others in terms of their use for him. He accorded them a value that was derivative of, and hence secondary to his own. There was nothing malicious in this, as we saw, and it had the salutary effect of preserving him from relative judgements. However, when he does find a lover her value for him will not be derivative or secondary in the same sense. For Rousseau a condition of feeling romantic love is the recognition of the other as a value in her own right. This introduces a need for reciprocity that is not present in the instrumental relations of childhood. The moment Emile begins to love, as opposed to simply desire, he begins to need the love of his beloved. Her preference and esteem, her love for him, now begin to have a bearing upon his self-evaluations in a way that someone's refusal to assist him during childhood never could.

In an instrumental relation what is at stake is the satisfaction of a need. As long as one seeks to satisfy a need independently, success or failure at finding the means to

A Moral Education

do this will only be incidental to one's self-evaluations. However, in love relations one seeks the love of the other, and this has a direct bearing upon one's self-evaluation. Once he loves, Emile can never be certain that his love and the preference and esteem this entails will be reciprocated. He cannot control the affections of his beloved, and so can never be sure of his standing relative to others. When he falls in love then, Emile becomes dependent upon his beloved for his conception of his own value, and this dependence entails an inescapable anxiety about his standing relative to others. In Rousseau's view both the need to be preferred and the anxiety it entails are soon generalized to the lover's relations with all persons. *Amour-propre* demands that the value one accords to oneself be substantiated by the opinions of others, yet no one can be certain that the recognition he receives is given sincerely.

> La preference qu'on accorde on veut l'obtenir; l'amour doit être réciproque. Pour être aimé, il faut se rendre aimable; pour être préféré, il faut se rendre plus aimable qu'un autre, plus aimable que tout autre, au moins aux yeux de l'objet aimé. De là les prémiers regards sur ses semblables; de là les premières comparaisons avec eux; de la l'émulation, les rivalités, la jalousie... Avec l'amour et l'amitié naissent les dissentions, l'inimitié, la haine. Du sein de tant de passions diverses je vois l'opinion s'élever un trône inébranlable, et les stupides mortels asservis à son empire ne fonder leur propre existence que sur les jugemens d'autrui.[4]

As Rousseau puts it here, a successful denaturing of the child will be difficult to achieve, because all relations where the other is recognized as a self-conscious subject would seem to entail *amour-propre* to some degree, and therefore the potential for corruption and dependence. This is why the natural order of the passions must now be reversed. If Emile continues to be dominated by self-love once he enters society, his nature will be lost to the corrupt passions that arise from its relativization. Rousseau's central moral and pedagogic problem is to achieve this reversal. His attempt is based upon his anthropology of the species' transition from nature to culture in the ***Discours sur l'inégalité*** and the ***Essai sur l'origine des langues***. In both these works he argues that the passions initiate the species' socialization.[5] They motivate the subject to take an interest in the self-conscious intentions of others, and yet enable him to accept their needs and interests as constituting a value for him. They do this by displacing natural self-love and yet not, at least immediately, allowing the self to be dominated by *amour-propre*.

In Rousseau's view, compassion and love represent natural emotional responses to the circumstances of social life.[6] They are natural in the sense that they are part of the subject's innate potentiality; and they are given expression within the specific conditions of social life. Thus in both the *Essai* and the *Discours*, natural man's response to increased contact with his fellows (brought on by causes external to his nature), is an increase in the range of his feelings, which in turn draws him into moral relations with them. Emile repeats this process. His new circumstances give rise to natural feelings: first to pity, and then to love, which force his self-consciousness to be constituted in relation to others. Rousseau re-states his view of the role of the passions in the transition from nature to society in the *Profession du foi* when he claims:

> Mais si, comme on n'en peut douter, l'homme est sociable par sa nature, ou du moins pour le devenir, il ne peut l'être que par d'autres sentimens innés (i.e. moral passions), rélatifs à son espèce; car à ne considérer que le besoin physique, il doit certainement disperser les hommes, au lieu de la rapprocher.[7]

The moral education is thus aimed at denaturing the subject while preserving the greatest possible continuity with its original nature. This continuity is possible because the self has innate moral passions, which enable it to be related to others without at the same time being subject to relativized self-love. The moral education posits the passions of love and pity as the basis of Emile's capacity for morally acceptable relations. Emile must develop his natural potential for both if he is to be completed as a moral being. But the two sentiments are of different character, and they are meant to serve as the basis of different types of moral relation. Pity is meant to be the basis of relations with people who would not, except for their suffering, constitute as value for him; while love is meant to serve as the basis of Emile's relation with someone who constitutes a much more intense and specific value for him, his wife Sophie. The development of these natural moral

A Moral Education 213

sentiments constitutes the formation of Emile's conscience: an innate sense of the good which nature instills in us, and which we saw in the previous chapter to be the ground of Rousseau's conception of moral freedom. A good deal hangs on Rousseau's account of the development and effect of Emile's moral passions. They are meant to establish the link between his natural freedom and his capacity for virtue.

7.2 The Doctrine of Pity

In Rousseau's view pity, rather than love, is the "premier sentiment relatif qui touche le coeur humain selon l'ordre de la nature".[8] The reason for this would appear to be that by nature, sexual need develops much more slowly than we are accustomed as social beings to suppose. By nature Emile develops feelings first for his species in general (or at least those around him), and for the female gender second.[9] But more importantly, as a sentiment pity is closer to nature because it involves a direct extension of natural self-love to include the suffering other. Emile's compassion is predicated on his being able to identify with another's suffering, experiencing it as it were, by proxy. As Rousseau puts it: "C'est n'est pas dans nous, c'est dans lui que nous souffrons."[10] Pity allows Emile to be related to others without requiring him to make a radical departure from the unified and self-sufficient egoism of his natural consciousness. It is therefore less prone to *amour-propre* than romantic love, which as we have seen entails a certain degree of anxiety about one's value relative to others.

Rousseau's account of moral relations based on natural Pity has been subject to much debate. He has been accused of both inconsistency and incoherence in respect of it,[11] and while both these charges are in some measure unfair (in particular the first), it is not overall very compelling as a moral theory. In my discussion of it I want to make two specific arguments. First, that his account of natural pity and its importance for moral relations is consistent if understood in terms of his conception of subjectivity. And second, that while moral relations based on pity cannot be comprehensive enough to serve as the basis of a general moral theory, they do satisfy a number of important moral criteria, and as such cannot be ruled out as the basis for every kind of moral relation.

However, I also want to claim that an analysis of the doctrine of pity does reveal a problem in Rousseau's moral strategy of reversing the natural order of the passions. In his attempt to forestall the corrupt passions arising from *amour-propre*, Rousseau constructs a conception of compassion too closely tied to natural egoism to be convincing as the basis of a moral standpoint. On Rousseau's argument natural compassion can only motivate us to altruism in the absence of all other emotions that might arise from our relations with the person suffering. It is predicated on indifference, and while it may allow us to account for a certain type of moral relation, it hardly represents a very compelling vision of morally fulfilling relations.

7.3 The Consistency of Rousseau's Doctrine of Pity

The charge of inconsistency has been made by a number of commentators, Starobinski most notable among them. In a note to the Pléiade edition of the *Discours sur l'inégalité* Starobinski argues that the account of pity in the *Essai sur l'origine des langues* contradicts the account given in the *Discours*. "Dans l'Essai, Rousseau n'admet pas la possibilité d'un élan de sympathie irréfléchie, et parait plus enclin a soutenir l'idée Hobbienne de la guerre de tous contre tous."[12] In the *Discours* Rousseau presents pity as a natural sentiment that precedes all reflection, which occasionally moderates the ardour with which the original humans pursued their well being.[13] However, in the *Essai* Rousseau presents a rather different picture. He claims there that natural men were ferocious because they were weak; that though they had little conflict, what they had was

A Moral Education 215

terrible. He also claims that the social feelings necessary to abate such conflict only develop once the species acquires imagination (and reason), and he gives pity as an example.

> La pitié, bien que naturelle au coeur de l'homme, resteroit éternellement inactive sans l'imagination qui la met en jeu. Comment nous laissons-nous émouvoir à la pitié? En nous transportant hors de nous-mêmes; en nous indentifiant avec l'être souffront.[14]

This account of pity varies from the account in the *Discours*, where natural men are presented as peaceful and capable of spontaneous, pre-reflexive pity. It is closer to the account of pity in *Emile*, in which the subject is said to make an imaginative identification with the other. It would seem then that there is some inconsistency in Rousseau's doctrine of pity.

Two important questions are raised by Starobinski's note. The first has to do with dating the composition of the *Essai*, which has implications for the importance of this work in Rousseau's thought. This question has received a good deal of attention, and has produced a wide and confusing range of arguments.[15] The second question has to do with the charge of inconsistency itself, and here I think Starobinski is simply wrong. There is no necessary contradiction between the claim made in the *Discours sur l'inégalité* that pity is a natural sentiment which precedes all reflection, and the arguments he makes in the *Essai* and *Emile*, where pity is said to involve an imaginative identification with the sufferer, and so to depend upon the subject's having acquired both imagination and reason. In the *Discours sur l'inégalité* pity is described as a natural or innate repugnance at the suffering of those similar to us. The impulse is so deeply imbedded in nature that even animals are said to possess it in some measure.[16] However, while it does moderate the conflict between natural men and so contribute to the well being of the species as a whole, it is merely an impulse, a distaste for suffering wherever it is sensed. It is not a positive moral attribute in the sense that it allows us to recognize the other as a particular subject like ourselves, whose suffering we ought to alleviate. It can only become a moral attribute in this sense when it is experienced by a person with an imagination, because imagination is necessary to appropriate the other's suffering as one's own. In the *Discours* the acquisition of imagination is linked to the acquisition of reason and language,[17] which indicates that Rousseau held consistently to the view that pity could only become a moral attribute once the a subject has entered society.

In each of the three texts we have been discussing he refers to it as a natural or innate feeling, and in both the ***Discours sur l'inégalité*** and ***Emile*** he claims that no depravity induced by society can completely destroy it.[18] Thus for Rousseau its being a natural sentiment is not inconsistent with its becoming a moral attribute in society. As a natural sentiment it is linked to our innate or defining potential as human beings. Our natural capacity to feel compassion for the suffering of others gives our distinctively human attributes, freedom and *perfectibilité*, a determinate moral potential. Once we acquire the cognitive attributes necessary for moral relations, the natural sentiment of pity gives us a motivation upon which to build relations that do not entail the immediate relativization of self-love. Rousseau, then, finds the source of our capacity to be moral in natural sentiment.

> Si c'en etoit ici le liez, j'essayerois de montrer comment des prémiéres mouvemens du coeur s'élevent les premieres vois de la conscience... Je ferois voir que *justice et bonté* ne sont point seulement des mots abstraits, de puis êtres moraux formés par l'entendement; mais de véritables affections de l'âme éclairée par la raison, et qui ne sont qu'un progrès ordonné de nos affections primitives...[19]

The doctrine of pity is therefore consistent when understood in the context of Rousseau's developmental conception of subjectivity. It is, with love, the basis of the conscience; what Rousseau refers to as the voice of nature within us. When linked with active reason and freedom of the will, these natural sentiments become the ground of the subject's moral freedom.

A Moral Education   217

7.4 The Coherence of the Doctrine of Pity

The charge that Rousseau's account of moral relations based on natural pity is incoherent, is most forcefully made by John Charvet in *The Social Problem in the Philosophy of Rousseau*. Charvet does not think the opposition between nature and society in Rousseau's thought can be resolved because of the way Rousseau conceives natural man. He argues that Rousseau's view of what defines man in nature, his natural self-sufficiency, "existing entirely for himself alone and needing no relation to another", cannot be reproduced in society without denying humans satisfactory moral and political relations. In order to retain natural liberty (self-sufficiency) in society, the individual can only relate to others as abstract and undifferentiated extensions of himself.[20]

His critique of natural pity as the basis of moral relations illustrates this general point. He claims that the conception of pity which draws Emile into sympathetic relations with others denies the subjective character of their suffering. Rousseau asserts that the person who pities identifies with the other, but only because of their common identity as sufferers, and not because of any particular characteristics the other may possess as a person. The sympathizer appropriates the other's suffering as his own, and because of this is able to sympathize with it.[21] It is consequently irrelevant to Emile who the specific person suffering is, or what the particular the nature of his suffering involves. To preserve the natural principle of self-sufficiency, the particular characteristics of the other cannot be accepted as a value for one, and so the sufferer is de-personalized. The specific character and distinctiveness of his subjectivity are simply appropriated, and denied, by Emile's projection of himself into him.[22]

Charvet ties pity to the impossible project of retaining man's natural independence in society; and as a result, moral relations based on it appear to involve a kind of imperialism of the self. The subject extends himself into others by an act of imagination which displaces the otherness of that person. This displacement is the condition of our capacity to feel pity for the other and at the same time preserve ourselves from the corrupting influence of *amour-propre*. In Charvet's view, to feel pity for someone, for the unique and specific character of both his person and his suffering, is to subordinate one's own value to the value of the other, and to make his pleasure (or relief) the focus of one's concern. But from Rousseau's standpoint, the problem with this is that it requires the subject to judge himself relative to another; that he regard the other's need as a value for him, equal to or even greater than his own. And regarding another's needs in this way draws one's own value into question. It raises the doubt that one is valued in the same way, thus subjecting one to the judgements of others, and to *amour-propre*. By regarding natural compassion as an extension of *amour de soi-même*, Rousseau is able to avoid the relativization of self-love implicit in a relation where the other is regarded as a value in his or her own right. But, as Charvet argues, when this occurs " . . . what has taken place is not an identification between myself and his suffering self, but rather a separation of his needs as suffering body from himself as a person and then the appropriation of these needs as mine."[23] Understood in this way, relations based on pity are merely an extension of our natural egoism, and attempt to displace the other with ourselves.

Charvet is undoubtedly correct in his general point that Rousseau's account of moral relations based on natural compassion abstracts from the particular characteristics of the sufferer, and this is at least partly because Rousseau wishes to avoid the relativization of self-love. Yet it does not follow from this that Rousseau's account of pity amounts to a parody of real compassion. It is possible to distinguish between two types of compassion: compassion as it is felt for a loved one or friend who suffers; and compassion in a more general sense, a general disposition of sympathy towards the suffering of others, which could in certain circumstances lead one to act so as to relieve another person's suffering. The two are not identical, but neither are they contradictory. The first would be the sort of compassion Charvet regards as impossible on Rousseau's argument: sympathy based in the specific value for one, of the person one pities. The second would seem to be closer to what Rousseau has in mind when he writes of natural

A Moral Education

compassion as the basis of moral relations, a general disposition of sympathy towards all suffering human beings which enables us to recognize the equal value of their needs and our own.

But while it is correct to argue that Rousseau's analysis of *amour-propre* precludes (or at least makes highly unlikely) the first form of pity, this does not exhaust all forms of compassion. Indeed, compassion based in the unique value another has for one is a relatively restrictive instance of this form of moral relation. It is the sort of feeling one would have for a friend or loved one, as we noted, but because of this it would seem to be dependent upon one's feeling something other than a common identity based on a mutual capacity for suffering. The value the other has for one in such an instance derives from a more intense form of identification, and would normally be based on something other than feeling pity itself, such as love or affection. Compassion in this sense would be mixed with, even contingent upon other emotional commitments. But one can also imagine feeling compassion for a person towards whom one is entirely indifferent, except for the fact of their suffering. In this sort of relationship, what is important is not the specific characteristics of the person's suffering but the mere fact that he is suffering. One identifies with the other wholly in terms of the objectively given fact of his pain. Such an identification abstracts from the subjective characteristics of the person suffering, but it does so in this case because there is no other basis for the relation, not because it is necessary to in some way destroy the other's subjectivity.

Rousseau begins his discussion of pity by claiming that it is our common weakness or capacity for suffering that makes us sociable, "qui portent nos coeurs à l'humanité". He also argues that Emile should be taught to pity and to love mankind, but not to allow this general disposition towards his species to be complicated (or corrupted) by personal feelings.[24] He opts for the more general or abstract account of pity because of the individualist bias built into his conception of the natural consciousness. As Emile emerges from his natural state, he has no natural motivations, other than his sexuality and this general feeling of compassion, to consider the needs or interests of others. As a child, it must be remembered, he has formed no profound attachments. The danger he faces as he enters society is that in recognizing others as valuers of themselves, his self-love will be transformed into *amour-propre*, and then that he will acquire a whole range of artificial reasons for being interested in them. To ensure that his denaturing is as consistent as possible with original nature, his new relations must preserve his independence while at the same enabling him to accept the needs of others as having a value for him.

Given this standpoint there are some good reasons for conceiving of compassion as a general disposition to sympathize with the suffering of others. First, it meets the important requirement that moral values be impersonal, that their hold on us not depend upon our likes and dislikes, upon our having some additional motivation to uphold a value beyond that value itself. Relief from pain and suffering can be conceived in this way. They are something that every person, regardless of social status or natural attribute, considers evil. They give persons a concrete common basis for identifying with each others' needs, and perhaps more controversially, they give each a reason to desire the cessation of pain quite apart from whomever is experiencing it. (Though obviously, if it is one's own pain, one's reasons for wishing its cessation are likely to be greater than they would be for another person's pain. But this too would be subject to qualifications: e.g. who the other is, the degree of pain, etc.)[25] One need neither know nor care about the sufferer to feel the desire to relieve his suffering, and this is an important reason why Rousseau puts compassion forward as a basis for certain kinds of moral relations. A second reason (following from this) Rousseau conceives of compassion in this way, is that he wants to ground our capacity to be moral in nature. Some capacity to feel compassion is at least arguably a natural fact about us, especially if it can be linked to self-love. Regarding pain as evil for ourselves would seem to entail the view that it is also evil for those we identify with. If it is a feeling we all share, at least potentially, it can lead us to recognize the fundamental moral equality of all persons, the recognition of which Rousseau regards as a necessary condition of any adequate form of moral or social life.[26] And thirdly of course, compassion in the general sense preserves us from the relativization of self-love. It

A Moral Education 221

displaces (i.e. renders irrelevant) any particular characteristics of the sufferer (his physiognomy or character for example), and doing so preserves our independence from his judgements of us. It can even give us, Rousseau writes, a sentiment of pleasure. We feel contentment both because we feel pity and because we do not suffer.[27]

What then are we to make of Rousseau's strategy of reversing the natural order of the passions by attempting to derive an objective moral principle or rule (that one ought to relieve the suffering of others) from a subjective feeling (that one's pain is evil and requires relief)? Charvet argues in another text that given the unity of the subjective and objective ego in Rousseau's account of the natural consciousness, the subject has only two options once other self-valuing persons appear on the scene. He can attempt to reconstitute his natural egoism by attempting to make all values accord with his own, i.e. dominate others; or he can subjugate his subjective needs to the objective demand for equality, i.e. that we are all equal in terms of our capacity to suffer.[28] In his view these two options highlight the contradiction in Rousseau's moral theory between subjective and objective personality. To treat others morally, one must impose the objective ego or self upon the other in such a way as to abstract completely from his subjective needs and characteristics as an individual person.

It would seem however that this argument proposes misleading alternatives. Rousseau's project is the denaturing of the self, not the recovery of its original egoism in the form of a compassion which consists in an arbitrary extension of the self into others. Denaturing involves, as I have argued, allowing self-consciousness to be reconstituted in relation to others without at the same time incurring the radical relativization of self-love. The central question of Rousseau's moral theory is thus not whether we can retain our natural egoism in moral relations, but whether we can acquire a moral standpoint which does not substantively contradict our natural independence.

To this end Rousseau produces an account of compassion as a disposition to act in accordance with the general moral principle that one ought to relieve pain and suffering. The principle is derived from our natural being in two senses. It is an innate sentiment, something we feel even in nature, though it has no moral significance until we become aware of other self-conscious beings like ourselves. And it is also consistent with self-love, which is to say that the general form of compassion Rousseau argues for does not draw one's own value into question, because it establishes a unity of interests between the persons involved. Rousseau writes:

> quand la force d'une âme expansive m'identifié avec mon semblable et que je me sens pour ainsi dire en lui, c'est pour ne pas souffrir que je ne veux pas qu'il souffre; je m'intéresse à lui pour l'amour de moi, et la raison du précepte est dans la Nature elle-même, qui m'inspire le désir de mon bien-être en quelque lieu que je me sente exister.[29]

This does not assert that the other's suffering is irrelevant, but rather that the condition of one's capacity to act according to the moral principle of compassion is the ability to generalize a subjective, self-referring value (one's desire not to suffer) into an objective, universal one (the feeling of compassion for another). The suffering of others, or to be more precise our recognition of it, provides the occasion for this generalization. We could imagine other occasions and other sentiments inspiring us to accord a value to the needs of others (e.g. love, friendship, even self-interest), but in the case where one has no other kind of emotional or social commitment to the other person, the generalization of one's aversion to pain could be sufficient explanation. It has the important advantage, as we have seen, of establishing a common moral ground on the basis of universal human value, avoiding pain. To accomplish this it relies on the assumption that pain or suffering is intrinsically evil, that it should be got rid of whoever is experiencing it. This gives us an objective moral rule to follow, one that is not based upon subjective preferences formed in society. That it makes no reference to the sufferer's particular characteristics in this instance (i.e. when no other common ground exists between them), does not deny its character as a moral relation, nor demean or deny the identity and value of the other. On the contrary it gives us a reason to value others regardless of what constitutes their identity; to accord them an equal value as suffering persons which is not subJect to the vagaries of subjective preference.[30]

It is not of course to be assumed that this type of compassion exhausts the range of moral relations possible between human beings, or even that it represents a particularly edifying or fulfilling kind of moral relation. What it does represent is a moral relation appropriate to Emile's development at this stage of his education program. In cultivating this natural disposition of sympathy towards the suffering of others Rousseau believes he is nurturing the development of the conscience while at the same time forestalling the development of the artificial passions associated with *amour-propre*. The moral relations based on pity are abstract. But they are this way because Rousseau wanted his project of denaturing Emile by reversing the natural order of his passions to retain as much continuity with original nature as possible, and not because he wished to recapture original nature in society. With the expansion of his knowledge and the refinement of his reason, and as well with the development of his capacity to love, natural compassion becomes a crucial aspect of Emile's moral psychology. It becomes part of the emotive structure upon which his moral freedom is based.

Relations based on pity mark Emile's entrance into the moral order. They elevate him to the possibility of virtue, and in doing so create the need for moral instruction. If he is to achieve his potential as a moral being, Emile must acquire knowledge of his fellows and his place among them. His new relations require him to compare himself with others (at least to some degree), and consequently they open his psyche to the influence of *amour-propre*. To forestall the adverse effects of this new awareness of others his judgements of them must be sound, and his moral instruction is intended to give him the basis for this. "Il faut étudier la société parles hommes, et les hommes par la société."[31] The education which follows involves two basic subjects, history and religion, though of course it touches upon other branches of knowledge, in particular metaphysics. The religious/metaphysical education was discussed in some detail in Chapter 5, and will be discussed again below. The historical education is of interest to us for its affect on the process of denaturation. Rousseau claims that history is the suitable subject of study for Emile at this stage of his development, because it allows him to study men from afar, to cultivate a standpoint of detachment from which to judge them.

> Voila le moment de l'histoire: c'est par elle qu'il lira dans les coeurs sans les leçons de la philosophie; c'est par elle qu'il les verra, simple spectateur, sans intérêt et sans passions, comme leur juge, non leur complice, ni comme leur accusateur.[32]

The point of developing this disinterested standpoint is to enable Emile to generalize his capacity for pity to the entire species; into, as Rousseau views it, a principle of justice. This will prepare him for the next stage of his denaturation, his courtship and marriage to Sophie.

As Emile is taught history, it is a catalogue of facts demonstrating the vanity and cruelty and misery of men. He is given no theories to explain this, no heroes to identify with nor villains to despise. He is simply shown human corruption for what it is, and allowed to compare himself to those he has studied. Rousseau is confident that his charge's response will be to pity them. Emile is healthy, moderate and free, and consequently in comparing himself to others Rousseau believes he will come to regard himself as better off than most, and that he will pity them for their servitude and their misery.[33] This in turn raises the problem of *amour-propre*, which is to say that in pitying others Emile might also begin to despise them for their largely self-inflicted misery. Now that he has entered the moral order, *amour-propre* has become a permanent feature of his existence. His self-love is now necessarily relative to others to some degree.

As an antidote to this, Rousseau suggests that both *amour-propre* and pity can be generalized. The extension of *amour-propre* to other beings is said to transform it into a virtue, by abstracting self-love from one's particular interest and extending it to a recognition of the equality of interests among all persons. Such equality limits the competitiveness latent in comparative self-evaluations because it recognizes that each has an equal claim to respect in moral relations, and consequently does not require one to consider (or compare oneself with) the specific characteristics of other persons. We have seen that it was possible to extend *amour-propre* in Emile's childhood, because the

A Moral Education

intentions of others were no part of his experience. For the child, *amour-propre* and *amour de soi-même* were identical. In the moral order however, this is no longer possible. Emile must find a way of generalizing his self-love so that he can be related to others without becoming dependent, or seeking to dominate them. Rousseau's answer to this, as we have seen, is the generalization of natural compassion.

> Pour empêcher la pitié de degenerer en foiblesse il faut donc la généraliser, et l'étendre sur tout le genre humain. Alors on ne s'y livre qu'autant qu'elle est d'accord avec la justice, parce que: de toutes les vertus la justice est celle qui concourt le plus au bien commun des hommes. Il faut par raison, par amour pour nous, avoir pitié de notre espèce encore plus que de notre prochain, et c'est une très grande cruauté envers les hommes que la pitié pour les mechans.[34]

Pity becomes a principle of justice when it is applied equally to all persons. It cannot be contingent upon the subjective preferences of individuals, no matter how virtuous; "...mais ne souffrons jamais en lui de preference aveugle fondée uniquement sur des acceptions de personnes ou sur d'injustes préventions."[35] At this stage of his development Emile is neither emotionally nor intellectually ready for relations in which the particular needs and interests of the other become a value for him. His historical education teaches him to pity his species, and is therefore important in two ways: it gives him a basis for being related to others in whom he has no particular interest, and it prepares him (by forestalling the dependency and competitiveness associated with *amour-propre*) for the more complex moral relations based upon romantic love.

7.5 The Moral Contract

His historical and religious instruction complete, Emile is ready to enter the last stage of his moral development. He has acquired some knowledge of both his species and his relationship with God; and with these a general disposition of compassion towards the suffering of other individuals or humanity in general. In Rousseau's view he is well prepared to enter the social world. He has also reached the stage where his sexuality can no longer be sublimated into other activities, such as education, or into other feelings, such as pity. It now demands fulfilment in more intense and immediate forms of relation. As a consequence of this he begins to strain against his tutor's authority, his inclinations drive him beyond the protective shell of their relationship towards the social world. Sexuality is in this sense the cause of Emile's last break with the natural consciousness. In relations based on pity, some elements of the natural consciousness are preserved because Emile is not required to consider the subjective characteristics of others in his moral judgements. With love Emile becomes a fully fledged moral being who must take responsibility for his own actions, which is to say, become master of himself. "Je n'ai donc plus qu'un parti raisonnable à prendre; c'est de le rendre comptable de ses actions à lui-même".[36]

But this does not mean Emile is to be left to fend for himself just as he is about to enter fully fledged moral relations. He has come to the stage where he must take responsibility for himself, yet he is not capable of doing so. As Rousseau conceives him at this stage, Emile is still in some respects an analogue of the savages of *le siècle d'or*. He will resist the restraints imposed on him by his tutor, their interests will conflict, but this will not inflame his *amour-propre*. He cannot but express himself authentically.

> Au moment même où les fureurs du temperament l'entraînant et où revolté contre la main qui l'arrête il se débat et commence à m'échaper, dans ses agitations, dans ses emportemens je retrouve encore sa prémiére simplicité; son coeur aussi pur que son corps ne connoit pas plus le déguisement que le vice; les reproches ni le mépris ne l'ont point, rendu lâche, jamais la vile crainte ne lui apprit à se déguiser: il a toute l'indiscretion de l'innocence, il est naïf sans scrupule; il ne sait encore à quoi sert de tromper. Il ne se passe pas un mouvement dans son âme que sa bouche ou ses yeux ne le disent, et souvent les sentimens qu'il éprouvé me sont connus plus tôt qu'à lui.[37]

But while Emile's innocence will ensure that his socialization is not prejudiced from the start, it will not enable him to ascend immediately to moral autonomy. Neither his passions nor his reason are sufficiently developed for him to govern himself. Rousseau's solution to this is a kind of moral contract. Emile proposes, of his own free will, that his tutor not

A Moral Education

relinquish his authority. He begs Rousseau to become his legislator; to force him to be free.

> O mon ami, mon protecteur, mon maître! reprenez l'autorité que vous voulez déposer au moment qu'il m'importe le plus qu'elle vous reste... Je veux obéir à vos loix, je le veux toujours, c'est ma volonté constante; si jamais je vous désobéis ce sera malgré moi; rendez-moi libre en me protègent contre mes passions qui me font violence; empêchez-moi d'être leur esclave et forcez-moi d'être mon propre maître en n'obéissant point à mes sens, mais à ma raison.[38]

Emile will make the last crucial step in the transition from nature to culture under Rousseau's tutelage. The fact that he has recognized and accepted his dependence upon Rousseau indicates that their relation is now a moral one, and this is why its continuance is contingent upon a contract. As a moral being, Emile must consent to all authority exercised over him. His contract with Rousseau bears some affinity to the contract in *Du contrat social*, in particular as it is discussed in the chapter on the Legislator. In both works the transition from nature to culture can only be accomplished successfully with the aid of a beneficent external force. The problem is that in nature we are too limited to legislate for ourselves, and in society we are already too corrupt. We need a legislator to break out of the circle. Rousseau will do for Emile what the laws laid down by the Legislator in *Du contrat social* do for natural man. He will make Emile free by completing his development as a moral being. He will make Emile fall in love, and in so doing complete his denaturation by reversing the natural order of the passions dominating his moral psychology. This will provide him with the basis for his moral freedom: the capacity both to know the good, and to will it.

7.6 Sexuality and Love

Rousseau believed our sexuality was amoral in the state of nature. Natural men and women were promiscuous and indiscriminate in their sexual life, and initially at least, the relations they formed through desire had no effect upon their moral development. However, transferred into the social context, sexuality poses the problem of dependence in an acute form. It puts us in need of others, necessarily exciting *amour-propre*. The first problem Rousseau faces is transforming Emile's natural (and therefore indiscriminate) sexual drive into a moral passion. We know from the *Discours sur l'inégalité* that this involves focusing desire upon a specific lover,[39] which is precisely Rousseau's strategy in *Emile*. He claims to make Emile moderate (i.e. to protect him from the radical dependence and corruption of promiscuity), by sublimating his sexual desire into love for an imaginary woman: his future fiance and wife Sophie. "En lui faisant sentir quel charme ajoûte à l'attrait des sens l'union des coeurs je dégouterai du libertinage, et je le rendrai sage en le rendant amoureux."[140]

The sublimation of natural sexual drive into love has three advantageous effects upon Emile's moral development. First, it gives him a standard by which to reject the other women he encounters, who would almost certainly corrupt him. Second, it imposes a moral structure upon his imagination. This is important because under the influence of *amour-propre*, his imagination would create needs far beyond his power to satisfy, and infuse him with a desire for domination. Focusing his desire upon an ideal woman enables his imagination to suppress his senses (his natural, indiscriminate desire), and immunizes him to the opinions of others.[41] Finally, by focusing Emile's desire upon an ideal woman, or at least someone whose qualities of virtue are very rare, Rousseau links that desire to a moral object in a manner which recalls Plato's conception of the philosophic eros.[42] In loving Sophie, Emile loves an embodiment of moral virtue, of the good. The qualities he loves in her have value quite apart from the fact that she possesses them, but they are

A Moral Education 229

made more compelling for him by being made the object of his eros. His love for her as a specific embodiment of these virtues constitutes at the same time a love of the good. He cannot love her without loving virtue.

Rousseau maintains throughout the education program that Emile is not fit to live alone, and an implication of this is that Emile's fulfilment as a moral being is tied to his relations with others. Emile will become dependent upon Sophie, but this is natural in the context of a love relation, and will not necessarily contradict his autonomy. In Rousseau's view men and women are naturally different: in both physical and moral terms. The physical differences, which were said to be insignificant in the state of nature, take on profound moral implications in society. They prescribe that men and women have different moral characteristics, which naturally compliment each other in moral relations. As long, that is, as each contributes according to his or her natural attributes.

> Dans l'union des sexes chacun concourt également à l'objet commun, mais non pas de la même manière. De cette diversité naît la première différences assignable entre les rapports moraux de l'un et l'autre. L'un doit être actif et fort, l'autre passif et foible; il faut necessairement que l'un veuille et puisse; il suffit que l'autre resiste peu.[43]

Men are stronger beings who are suited to self-sufficiency virtue of their strength. Women are naturally dependent on men in virtue of their weakness, and so stand in greater need of men than they of women. The differences create a mutual dependence between the sexes. As Rousseau conceives it men are stronger, and therefore ought and do seek to dominate women both sexually and morally. Another way and perhaps more accurate way of putting this is that Rousseau thought men are natural sexual aggressors, and therefore have a natural right to rule in the context of the sexual relationship. But at the same time, Rousseau believes they can only do this if women assist them. This is particularly evident, he argues, in sexual relations, where men are always dependent on women for a feeling of mastery that is crucial to their sexual competence. This is due to

> une invariable loi de la nature, qui, donnant à la femme plus de facilité d'exciter les désirs qu'à l'homme de les satisfaire, fait dépendre celui-ci malgré qu'il en ait du bon plaisir de l'autre, et le contraint de chercher à son tour à lui plaire pour

obtenir qu'elle consente à le laisser être le plus fort.⁴⁴

The natural differences have another important implication, which is that women naturally seek to make men dependent upon them because of their weakness. Their lack of power puts them in need of men to supplement their strength; and it also ensures that they must satisfy this need largely by duplicitous means, through what Rousseau imagines to be natural feminine wiles. These wiles compensate women for their lack of strength by enabling them to capture men in a web of psychological and emotional dependence.

> Cette addresse particuliére donnée au sexe est un dédommagement très équitable de la force qu'il a de moins, sans quoi la femme ne seroit pas le compagne de l'homme, elle seroit son esclave; c'est par cette supériorité de talent qu'elle se maintient son égale et qu'elle le gouverne en lui obéissant.⁴⁵

Women are therefore crucial to the process of male denaturation. They are naturally more sociable than men because their well-being depends upon the social conventions of romantic love and the nuclear family. For their part, men are susceptible to female domination for natural reasons, but also because of *amour-propre*. They need women to satisfy their sexual drives, but this need is more than simply physical, because male sexuality cannot reconcile its performance to its conception of itself without female assistance. The master is thus dependant on the slave: "le maitre en apparence et dependre en effet du plus foible". There is also, as we saw above, an emotional dependence established. The male's love for a female is necessarily tinged with anxiety about the degree to which she reciprocates, because the passions of *amour-propre* have become an ever present danger. Ordinary men and women, as Rousseau insists Emile and Sophie are, cannot escape the mutual dependence of romantic/sexual relations. This is natural in the sense that it is the natural outcome of our physical and emotional development as subjects, but at the same time, as I have argued, it poses the problem of dependence and alienation in an acute way. In love relations, as Rousseau conceives them, men stand to lose their potential for moral autonomy to the natural weakness of women.⁴⁶

A Moral Education

Given the dependence entailed in this type of relationship, we must ask why and in what way Rousseau thinks it necessary to the acquisition of a moral consciousness suitable to freedom? The answer should be evident; Rousseau regards love as integral to the development of the moral psychology necessary for moral freedom. His relationship with Sophie is therefore crucial to his education. If it is possible to keep Emile's *amour-propre* from dominating his moral passions, Sophie's life and virtue must be put in the service of his moral autonomy. She must, paradoxically, make him dependent on her so that she can make him free. Thus despite their dependence on men and the will to power that grows out of it, women can have a beneficial effect upon male moral development.[47] The mutual dependence of men and women can in Rousseau's view, contribute to their mutual moral fulfilment.

> La rélation sociale des séxes est admirable. De cette société résulte une persone moral dont la femme est l'oeil et l'homme le bras, mais avec une telle dépendance l'une de l'autre que c'est de l'homme que la femme apprend ce qu'il faut voir et de la femme que l'homme apprend ce qu'il faire... dans l'harmonie qui régne entre eux tout tend à la fin commune, on ne sait lequel met le plus du sien; chacun suit l'impulsion de l'autre, chacun obéit et tous deux sont les maitres.[48]

The success of the partnership depends on Sophie's virtue; when she is loved for her virtue, her influence upon her lover cannot but be to the advantage of his morals.[49] In Rousseau's view, the chief virtue of women is chastity, which he equates with self-mastery. Chastity gives women control over both themselves and others. It gives them self-esteem independent of what others think of them, which is a form of self-mastery; and at the same time it receives the respect and admiration of others, especially of men. Rousseau values chastity for women because he believes that by nature their virtue, contrary to that of males, is founded upon opinion. "L'homme en bien faisant ne dépend que de lui-même et peut braver le jugement public, mais la femme en bien faisant n'a fait que la moitié de sa tâche, et ce que l'on pense d'elle ne lui importe pas moins que ce qu'elle est en effet."[50] The reason for this is that women are naturally dependent on the good opinion of men for their well-being. If a women is not chaste (or thought to be chaste) the effect will be to create insecurity over her husband's paternity. This will undermine her husband's virtue by subjecting him to anxiety about being perceived as a cuckhold, and as a consequence will likely undermine her own well-being. Sophie will be chaste, she will also be obedient and patient. She will possess all the virtues appropriate to her nature, and be loved by Emile for them. As such their relationship will have a beneficial effect upon his moral psychology. Insofar as Emile seeks to be esteemed by his beloved, which given the psychological dynamic of love he must do, he will seek to be esteemed for being good, which is as much as to say for being himself.[51]

Their relationship itself, as Rousseau describes it, is marked by three stages: their courtship, a separation, and their final reunification. The first stage is akin to the relations Rousseau describes in *le siècle d'or*. The lovers achieve a passionate unity of feeling in which their dominant moral characteristic is their innocence or transparency. When they meet, Emile is a torrent of emotion which he is incapable of hiding. Sophie is more modest, but it soon becomes clear that she too is experiencing feelings she cannot hide. The two of them are like the savages of the Golden Age, their emotions are powerful and yet completely lacking in anxiety about the opinions of others. Emile "il se livre avec confiance, avec raison même, au plus charmant délire, sans crainte, sans regret, sans remord, sans autre inquiétude que celle dont le sentiment du bonheur est inséparable."[52] Even when Sophie seems to spurn Emile because of her fears over money, he does not succumb to *amour-propre*. His passion remains simple and strong, and he regains her love by the purity of his sentiments. Rousseau's point in these passages is to show the effects of his moral education on Emile. The natural order of his passions has now been reversed to the extent that his emotions are completely dominated by his feelings for another person, yet there has been no radical rupture with nature. He and Sophie have become dependent on one another without becoming corrupt and without losing their freedom. In this sense their romance is a recapitulation of the species' history.[53]

But just as the species could not remain in *le siècle d'or*, Emile and Sophie are not able to remain in the idyllic innocence of their courtship. The reason for this is that the

A Moral Education

emotional unity upon which their initial relations are based is too all-encompassing, too powerful, to allow Emile to achieve moral autonomy. His moral passion has made him dependent by subjecting him to new range of needs which he cannot hope to satisfy. He needs not only his own well-being, but Sophie's as well. Thus even though his new desires arise from a moral passion, they begin to give rise to anxiety over things Emile cannot control, and hence to deny his freedom.[54]

This is as we have seen consistent with the nature of the passion. As his legislator, Rousseau compels Emile to leave Sophie by arguing that he has become too dependent on her. His temporary abandonment of her is the last step in his progress towards the realization of his potential for freedom. Until this point, Rousseau claims, he has not felt the full yoke of moral virtue. His education has carefully protected his from all corrupt forms of dependence, consequently he has not yet achieved full self-mastery. He has been good, but not virtuous. To achieve autonomy he must overcome the dependence that arises out of his passions, even his moral passions. In forcing Emile to leave Sophie, Rousseau hopes Emile will recapture his sense of self. This is crucial to his moral freedom, and he is in danger of losing it to his love for Sophie. This is not a denial of the moral value of love, but it is an assertion that morality cannot be based upon passion alone. Thus Rousseau writes:

> Qu'est-ce donc que l'homme vertueux? C'est celui que sait vaincre ses affections. Car alors il suit sa raison, sa conscience, il fait son devoir, il se tient dans l'ordre et rien ne l'en peut écarter. Jusqu'ici tu n'étios libre qu'en apparence; tu n'avois que la liberté précaire d'un esclave à qui l'on n'a rien commande. Maintenant sois libre en effet; apprends a devenir ton propre maître; commande à ton coeur, ô Emile, et tu seras vertueux.[55]

7.7 Conclusion: Moral Freedom

The moral autonomy Emile achieves first by leaving Sophie in order to master his passions, and then finally returning to her a morally complete, free man, accords substantially with Rousseau's account of moral freedom in the *Profession de foi du Vicaire Savoyard*. I argued in Chapter 5 that Rousseau's strategy in the *Profession* was to elaborate the natural ground of the subject's freedom. This was said to involve denaturing man through the development of his moral passions, which is to say reversing the natural order of his passions so that he becomes capable of recognizing the needs of others as a value for him. The problem of freedom is the same for the Vicar as it is for Emile. Each must realize their natural potential for self-determination in the context of relations which induce in them needs that cannot be satisfied independently, and anxieties that make them neurotically dependent on others. We can see from the above quotation that for Rousseau freedom and morality are inextricably bound up with one another. Without freedom in the sense of self-mastery there can be no true moral virtue, because the individual can only be said to be responsible for his actions insofar as he alone wills them. Yet in the context of society there can be no freedom without moral virtue, for without it the individual is always subject to *amour propre*, and therefore to passions that make him intensely dependent on others. Rousseau's moral and educational strategy aims at combining the subject's natural capacity for free choice with a fully authentic expression of his natural feeling for the good. Thus both Emile and the Vicar are said to be free when they will the moral ends prescribed by their active judgement, and follow them because of their natural moral sentiments.

One might object to this that, at least on the basis of the quotation at the end of the last section, Rousseau ends up asserting a conception of moral freedom that involves suppressing the passions. "Qu'est-ce donc que l'homme vertueux? C'est celui que sait vaincre ses affections." However, this should not be seen as an abnegation of the passions.

A Moral Education 235

In asserting his independence from the passions engendered by his love, Emile is not denying his love for Sophie, nor the importance it has for his moral life. He is on the contrary trying to preserve that passion in the form in which it originally arose, by preserving his independence from the impulsion towards dependence latent in it. Rousseau believed that the moral passions were natural and should therefore constitute a central part of the moral psychology of freedom, but he nevertheless saw in them a propensity for dependence which could lead to their corruption. This is why he asserts that they always require the guidance of reason. The question of course is whether his account of moral freedom manages to achieve a harmony between the moral will and our moral sentiment?

Rousseau saw in his contemporaries a radical division between their natural potential and what they had become under the influence of social structure; and his analysis of this alienation remains, for all its self-righteousness, one of the most compelling aspects of his thought. Rousseau's diagnosis of the social problem entailed a new and important insight into the nature of the human subject, which was that what we commonly refer to as human nature is something acquired largely under the influence of society. This insight led him to an account of subjectivity which required a synthesis of the two dominant epistemological traditions of his period. As a Cartesian, he was able to regard the self as having an essential character (its freedom and *perfectibilité*), which gives its development some moral significance. Yet as an empiricist he was able to conceive the problem of original sin as a problem of morality and politics. Human consciousness and action is constituted by its social environment. As a consequence of this Rousseau conceived of the self in two senses: as a simple subject of experience defined by its innate potential for freedom and improvement, and as a complex subject with a concrete identity (i.e. talents, passions, dispositions, etc.) constituted by its experience of the natural and social worlds.

For Rousseau freedom in a social context requires a synthesis of these two selves, which involves the expression of our innate potential for freedom and virtue through the concrete identity we have acquired in society. Such a synthesis is obviously difficult to conceive, for it is difficult to see how the simple self, which is *ex hypothesi* independent of experience, can receive expression through the identity we form in our experience. Rousseau attempts to link the two by arguing that the moral passions which are the basis of our motivation to act morally are of a double character. They are natural in that they derive from our innate potentiality as persons, yet they can only be acquired though our experience of the social world. In this sense they mediate between the natural characteristics of the subject, in particular his natural capacity for free choice, and his experience in society. They give us reasons to choose the good, but these reasons are not simply contingent upon our whims or dispositions and therefore arbitrary, because they arise from our natural (and thus in Rousseau's mind morally correct) responses to social experience (e.g. love, or pity, or patriotism).

Acceptance of this account of moral freedom depends on our being able to accept the idea that there are universal moral passions which can, given the proper circumstances, constitute our will in such a way as not to compromise our capacity for free choice. But it is in part I think because of the power of Kant's moral theory that we have great difficulty in accepting any individualist account of liberty which attempts to link free will with moral virtue via the passions. The division between synthetic and heteronomous judgements makes any coincidence between the moral will and moral feeling seem wholly fortuitous and arbitrary. Nevertheless, this coincidence must occur if we wish to avoid intolerable self-division. In a coherent conception of moral freedom reason and feeling must be integrated. In *Emile* Rousseau attempts to overcome the division between reason and feeling by arguing that a properly educated person will acquire moral passions which can give his natural free will moral content. The importance of this argument is that it draws our attention to the constitutive affect of social life upon the evolution of our subjectivity. To realize their natural potential individuals must be constituted within a social environment (or an education program), which will nurture the development of these passions. The problem is of course that Rousseau does not really convince us (or indeed himself) that the passions Emile acquires under his tutelage can serve as adequate motivation to will the good. They seem arbitrary because he has simply tried to run the two conceptions of self together. However, Rousseau's argument underlines the need to ground our moral and political theory upon a conception of the self which in some manner integrates the simple and complex accounts of subjectivity. To do this we must, as Rousseau did, conceive the self developmentally or historically: as constituting itself through the construction of various forms of social organization, which in turn must be judged according to the extent to which they promote and help to realize human potential.

Endnotes

1. *Ibid.*, p. 493.

2. *Ibid.*, p. 493; see also O.C. III, pp. 147, 157-58.
   It should be noted that what is inevitable here is not that sexuality automatically leads Emile to a proper form of love relation, but rather that it leads him to relations with others who are recognized as values in their own right, and who as a consequence cannot be treated by the child simply as instruments to his satisfaction. When he begins to need others, they take on a value for him and at the same time draw his own value into question, thus relativizing his self-love. Sexuality gives him a new awareness of others, which simply precludes the natural indifference of his childhood.

3. *Ibid.*, p. 493.

4. *Ibid.*, p. 494; see also O.C. III, p. 169, for the double character of romantic love.

5. O.C. III, pp. 143, 168-69; E.O.L., pp. 41-43.

6. O.C. IV, p. 1121. In his *Notes sur De l'Esprit de l'Helvètius*, Rousseau distinguishes between "les impressions purement organiques et locales des impressions universelles qui affectent tout l'individu. Les prémiéres ne sont que de simples sensations, les autres sont des sentimens.

7. O.C. IV, p. 600. See also p. 503, where Rousseau argues that God is the only self sufficient being. He claims that humans must love to be happy, which assumes that the species has evolved to a point at which natural self-sufficiency is no longer possible.

8. *Ibid.*, p. 505.

9. *Ibid.*, pp. 495, 502.

10. *Ibid.*, pp. 505-06, 523.

11. See Jean Starobinski's note (#2) to O.C. III, p. 154, for the charge that Rousseau is inconsistent in his conception of pity. See also Charvet, *Social Problem*, pp. 74-84, for the charge that he is incoherent.

12. O.C. III, pp. 1330-31.

13. *Ibid.*, p. 154.

14. E.O.L., p. 93.

15. Robert Wokler, *L'Essai sur l'origine des langues en tant que fragment du Discours sur l'inégalité; Rousseau et ses "mauvaises" interprets*, en *Rousseau et Voltaire en 1978*, Actes du Colloque International de Nice, Juin, 1978, (Genève-Paris: Éditions Slatkine, 1981), pp. 145-64.

    The question of when Rousseau actually composed Chapter IX of the *Essai* is a difficult one. There would seem to be evidence that it was composed prior to the *Discours sur l'inégalité*, but also evidence that it was composed after. Those who support the earlier dating, have argued that Rousseau must have changed his mind on the issue while writing the *Discours*, and have concluded that the *Essai* is an early and peripheral work. This view is attributed to Starobinski by Porset (*Essai sur l'origine des langues*, p. 18; and also by Derrida, *Of Grammatology*, p.181) However, the significance of its date of composition is dependent on the question of whether or not Rousseau is consistent in his treatment of the subject. On this issue I will argue that there are no serious inconsistencies in Rousseau's various discussions of pity, from which it follows that the date of composition of the *Essai* is irrelevant to the question of its importance on this subject.

16. O.C. III, p. 154.

17. *Ibid.*, p. 174.

18. *Ibid.*, p. 155; O.C. IV, p. 597; E.O.L., p. 93.

19. O.C. IV, pp. 522-23.

20. Charvet, *Social Problem*, pp. 92-93.

21. O.C. IV, pp. 503-06.

22. Charvet, *Social Problem*, pp. 92-93.

23. *Ibid.*, p. 92.

24. O.C. IV, pp. 503, 510.

25. Thomas Nagel, *The View From Nowhere*, (New York: Oxford University Press, 1986), pp. 161, 167-68.

26. Baczko, *Solitude ou communauté*, p. 218; O.C. IV, pp. 509, 524.

27. O.C. IV, p. 514.

28. John Charvet, *Rousseau and the Ideal of Community*, in **The History of Political Thought**, vol. I. #1. 1980, pp. 69-80.

29. O.C. IV, p. 523.

30. Nagel, *Nowhere*, p. 161.

    "My objective attitude toward pain is rightly taken over from the immediate attitude of the subject, and naturally takes the form of an evaluation of the pain itself, rather than merely a judgement of what would be reasonable for its victim to want: "This experience ought not to go on, whoever is having it." To regard pain as impersonally from the objective standpoint does not involve the illegitimate suppression of an essential reference to the identity of its victim. In its most primitive form, the fact that it is mine -- a the concept of myself -- doesn't come into my perception of the badness of my pain."

31. O.C. IV, pp. 523-24,

32. *Ibid.*, pp. 526-536.

33. *Ibid.*, p. 536,

34. *Ibid.*, p. 548.

35. *Ibid.*, p. 548.

36. *Ibid.*, p. 641.

37. *Ibid.*, p. 642.

38. *Ibid.*, pp. 651-52; also O.C. III, pp. 381-84.

39. O.C. III, pp. 157-58.

40. O.C. IV, p. 654.

41. *Ibid.*, pp. 656-57.

A Moral Education 241

42. Plato, *Phaedrus*, Walter Hamilton translator, (Harmondsworth: Penguin Books, 1980), pp. 60-66; also, Plato, *Symposium*, Walter Hamilton translator, (Harmondsworth: Penguin Books, 1980), pp. 106-108.

43. O.C. IV, p. 693.

44. *Ibid.*, pp. 695-96.

45. *Ibid.*, p. 712.

46. It should be noted here that Rousseau regarded female sexuality in general to be one of the greatest threats to male freedom in civil societies. As Rousseau conceived it, the threat arose from women's capacity to inspire unlimited sexual desire in men, and from their ability to undermine men's confidence in their sexuality and their paternity. The former arose from what Rousseau took to be women's ability to control men by exciting in them unlimited and ultimately unfulfilable desires. If female sexuality were left uncontrolled, "men would be tyrannized by women". Men would lose their capacity for self direction to a *libertinage* of uncontrollable sexual desire. (O.C. IV, p. 694). This is why he places modesty and chastity among the first virtues of women. But it is not enough merely that women be modest and chaste, they must also *appear* to be so. Rousseau says of women that "leur honneur n'est pas seulement dans leur conduite mais dans leur réputation..." and further that, "l'opinion est le tombeau de la vertu parmi les hommes, et son trône parmi les femmes." (O.C. IV, pp. 702-03) The reason for this is that women are naturally dependent on men in society, and therefore need male respect to satisfy their needs. If they are not perceived to be chaste, especially when they are wives and mothers, their husbands will feel their sexuality and their paternity threatened. This will in turn excite their husbands' *amour-propre*, intensify their psychological dependence on the opinion of others, and so undermine their capacity for freedom and virtue.

    The upshot of Rousseau's analysis of sexuality is that women's sexuality must be suppressed, or at least strictly controlled, in the interests of male freedom. He seems to regard women's freedom simply as chastity, and has no qualms whatsoever about imposing this upon them. (See for instance the *Lettre à d'Alembert sur les spectacles*, Fuchs, ed., Genève: Libairie Droz, p. 110.) Male freedom, as we have seen, requires mastery over mere bodily or sexual desire, and for Rousseau, the only society in which this is possible is a rigorously patriarchal one. Women must be strictly consigned to the private sphere of the family, and completely subordinated to male authority.

47. Schwartz, *Sexual Politics*, pp. 89-91.

48. O.C. IV, p. 720.

49. *Ibid.*, p. 745.

50. *Ibid.*, p. 702.

51. It will be apparent here that the virtues appropriate to Sophie's virtue are so because they serve the goal of male freedom. Rousseau assumes that in society, their relative physical and intellectual inferiority stipulates that women are by nature suited to the service of men. (O.C. IV, p. 693). This contrasts starkly with his claim, in the ***Discours sur l'inégalité***, that in the pure state of nature men and women were equally promiscuous and independent. (O.C. III, pp. 147, 158-59, 216-18). This reversal allows him to conceive women's moral duties in wholly instrumental terms. This is why chastity is the first virtue for women. It preserves men from dependence on others by protecting them from sexual insecurity, and consigns them to the home where the generally disruptive effects of their sexuality can be subordinated to patriarchal authority. In effect then, Sophie's virtue consists in defining her life solely in terms of what is necessary for Emile's freedom. Her own moral fulfillment as a women, is dictated for Rousseau by the imperatives of male freedom.

52. *Ibid.*, p. 782.

53. *Ibid.*, p. 777.

54. *Ibid.*, p. 815-16.

55. *Ibid.*, p. 818.

Bibiliography

Aarsleff, Hans *From Locke to Saussure: Essays on the Study of Language and Intellectual History*. Minneapolis: University of Minnesota Press, 1982.

Baczko, Bronsilaw. "Rousseau and Social Marginality". *Daedalus*. Summer, 1978.

Baczko, Bronislaw. *Rousseau, solitude et communanté*. Paris: Mouton and Co., 1974.

Berman, Marshall. *The Politics of Authenticity*. New York: Athenaeum, 1970.

Bloom, Allan. "The Education of Democratic Man". *Daedalus*. (Summer, 1978): 135-153.

Bloom, Allan. *The Closing of the American Mind*. New York: Simon and Shuster Inc., 1987.

Buffon, G-L. L. Comte de. *Oeuvres philosophiques de Buffon*. Edited by Jean Priveteau. Paris: Presses Universitaires de France, 1954.

Buffon, G-L. G. Comte de. *De l'homme*. Paris: Francois Maspero, 1871.

Burgelin, Pierre. *La Philosophie de l'existence de Jean-Jacques Rousseau*. Paris: Presses Universitaires de France, 1952.

Cameron, David. *The Social Thought of Rousseau and Burke*. London: Weidenfeld and Nicolson, 1973.

Cassirer, Ernst. *The Philosophy of the Enlightenment*. Trans. Koelln and Pettegrove. Boston: Beacon Press, 1955.

Cassirer, Ernst. *The Question of Jean-Jacques Rousseau*. Trans. Peter Gay. Bloomington: Indiana University Press, 1967.

Charvet, John. "Rousseau and the Ideal of Community", in *The History of Political Thought*. vol. I, No. 1, 1980.

Charvet, John. *The Social Problem in the Philosophy of Rousseau*. Cambridge: Cambridge University Press, 1974.

Chomsky, Noam. *Cartesian Linguistics: A Chapter in the History of Rationalist Thought.* London: Harper and Row, 1966.

Cobban, Alfred. *Rousseau and the Modern State.* London: George Allen & Unwin, 1964.

Cole, G.D.H. *Introduction to the Social Contract and Discourses.* New York: Dutton, 1968.

Colletti, Lucio. *From Rousseau to Lenin: Studies in Ideology and Society.* New York: Monthly Review Press, 1972.

Condillac, Etiénne de Bonnot. *Oeuvres Philosophiques.* Edited by George Le Roy. Paris: Presses Universitaires de France, 1949-51, vols. I-III.

Cranston, Maurice. *Jean-Jacques: The Early Life and Work of Jean-Jacques Rousseau 1712-54.* London: Allen Lane, 1983.

Cranston, Maurice. *Philosophers and Pamphleteers: Political Theorists of the Enlightenment.* Oxford: Oxford University Press, 1986.

de Man, Paul. *Blindness and Insight.* Minneapolis: The University of Minnesota Press, 1983.

Derathé, Robert. *Le Rationalisme de Jean-Jacques Rousseau.* Paris: Presses Universitaires de France, 1948.

Derrida, Jacques. "La Linguistique de Rousseau". *Revue international de philosophie.* 1967/8, No. 82.

Derrida, Jacques. *Of Grammatology.* Trans. G. Spivak. Baltimore: The Johns Hopkins University Press, 1976.

Descartes, Rene. *The Philosophical Works of Descartes.* Trans. Elizabeth Holdane and G.T.R. Ross. Cambridge: Cambridge University Press, 1931.

Duchet, M. and Launay, M. "Synchronie et Diachronie: *L'Essai sur l'origine des langues et le second Discours*". *Revue international de philosophie.* (1966): LXXXII.

Emberley, Peter. "Rousseau and the Management of the Passions". *Interpretation.* vol. 13, No. 2, (May, 1985).

Fellows, Otis. "Buffon and Rousseau: Aspects of a Relationship". *PMLA.* No.75 (1960): 184-86.

Featherstone, Joseph. "Rousseau and Modernity". *Daedalus*. (Summer 1978), 167-92.

Foucault, Michel. *The Order of Things*. Translated by Alan Sheridan. London: Tavistock Institute, 1970.

Freeman, Michael. *Burke and the Critique of Political Radicalism*. Oxford: Basil Blackwell, 1980.

Gay, Peter. *The Enlightenment: An Interpretation*. New York: Norton, 2 vols., 1966.

Gay, Peter. *The Party of Humanity*. New York: Knopf, 1964.

Goldschmidt, Victor. *Anthropologie et politique*. Paris: Librairie Philosophique J. Vrin, 1974.

Gouhier, Henri. "Ce que le vicaire doit à Descartes". *Annales de Jean-Jacques Rousseau*. No. 35, (1959-62): 139-54.

Gouhier, Henri. *Les méditations métaphysiques de Jean-Jacques Rousseau*. Paris Librairie J. Vrin, 1970.

Grimsley, Ronald. *The Philosophy of Rousseau*. London: Oxford University Press, 1973.

Hampson, Norman. *The Enlightenment*. Harmondsworth: Penguin Books, 1968.

Hankins, Thomas L. *Science and the Enlightenment*. Cambridge: Cambridge University Press, 1985.

Hegel, G.W.F. *Phenomenology of Spirit*. Translated by A.V. Miller. Oxford: Clarendon Press, 1977.

Hegel, G.W.F. *Philosophy of Right*. Translated by T.M. Knox. London: Oxford University Press, 1967.

Hobbes, Thomas. *Leviathan*. Edited by C.B. Macpherson. Harmondsworth: Penguin Books, 1968.

Horowitz, Asher. *Rousseau, Nature, History*. Toronto: Toronto University Press, 1987.

Hume, David. *A Treatise of Human Nature*. Edited by L.A. Selby-Biggs. Oxford: Oxford University Press, 1978.

Kavanagh, Thomas M. *Writing and Truth: Authority and Desire in Rousseau*. Berkeley: University of California Press, 1987.

Kelly, G.A. *Idealism, Politics, and History*. Cambridge: Cambridge University Press, 1972.

Keohane, Nannerl O. "But For Her Sex...The Domestication of Sophie". *The University of Ottawa Quarterly*. Vol. 49 (1979).

Knight, Isabel. *The Geometric Spirit*. Princeton: Princeton University Press, 1968.

La Mettrie, *L'homme machine*. Edited by A. Vartanian, Princeton: Princeton University Press, 1960.

Lange, Lynda. "Women and the General Will". *The University of Ottawa Quarterly*. Vol. 49 (1979).

Leigh, Ralph, ed. *Rousseau After Two Hundred Years: Proceedings of the Cambridge Bicentennial Colloquium*. Cambridge: Cambridge University Press, 1978.

Lemos, R.M. *Rousseau's Political Philosophy: An Exposition and Interpretation*. Athens: University of Georgia Press, 1977.

Levine, Andrew. *The Politics of Autonomy: A Kantian Reading of Rousseau's Social Contract*. Amherst: University of Massachussetts Press, 1976.

Levi-Strauss, Claude. "Jean-Jacques Rousseau, fondateur des sciences de l'lhomme". *Jean-Jacques Rousseau*. Neuchatel: Editions de La Baconnière, (1962): 239-48.

Levi-Strauss, Claude. *Le totemisme aujourd'hui*. Paris: Presses Universitaires de France, 1965.

Locke, John. *An Essay Concerning Human Understanding*. Edited by Peter Nidditch. Oxford: Clarendon Press, 1975.

Locke, John. *Two Treatises of Government*. Edited by Peter Laslett. New York: New American Library, 1965.

Lovejoy, A.O. *Essays in the History of Ideas*. Baltimore: Johns Hopkins University Press, 1948.

Lovejoy, A.O. *The Great Chain of Being: A Study of the History of an Idea*. Cambridge, Mass.: Harvard University Press, 1964.

Marshall, T.E. "Rousseau and Enlightenment". *Political Theory,* No. 6 (1978): 421-55.

Masters, Roger D. *The Political Philosophy of Rousseau.* Princeton: Princeton University Press, 1968.

Masters, Roger D. "Jean-Jacques is Alive and Well: Rousseau and Contemporary Sociobiology" *Daedalus.* (Summer 1978): 93-105

Mencken-Spaas, Godelieve. *The Social Anthropology of Rousseau's Emile,* in *Studies on Voltaire and the Eighteenth Century.* No. 132 (1975): 137-81.

Nagel, Thomas. *The View From Nowhere.* New York: Oxford University Press, 1986.

Norris, Christopher. *Derrida.* Cambridge, Mass.: Harvard University Press, 1987.

Parfit, Derek. *Later selves and Moral Relations* **Philosophy and Personal Relations.** Edited by Alan Montifiore. London: Routledge, 1973.

Pateman, Carole. *Participation and Democratic Theory.* Cambridge: Cambridge University Press, 1970.

Plattner, Marc F. *Rousseau's State of Nature: An Interpretation of the Discourse on the Origins of Inequality.* DeKalb: Northern Illinois University Press, 1979.

Plato. *Phaedrus.* Translated by Walter Hamilton. Harmondsworth: Penguin books, 1980.

Plato. *Symposium.* Walter Hamilton. Harmondsworth: Penguin Books, 1980.

Porter, Jean. "Will and Politics". *Unity Plurality and Politics: Essays in Honour of F.M. Barnard.* Edited by J.M. Porter and Richard Vernon. London: Croom Helm, 1986.

Rousseau, Jean-Jacques. *A Discourse on Inequality.* Trans. Maurice Cranston, Harmondsworth: Penguin books, 1985.

Rousseau, Jean-Jacques. *Emile.* Trans. Allan Bloom. New York: Basic Books, 1979.

Rousseau, Jean-Jacques. *Essai sur l'origine des langues.* Edited by Charles Porset. Paris: A.G. Nizet, 1970.

Rousseau, Jean-Jacques. *Oeuvres Complétes.* Edited by Bernard Gagnebin and Marcel Raymond. Paris: Bibliothéque de la Pléiade, 5 vols., 1959-.

Sandel, Michael J. *Liberalism and the Limits of Justice.* New York: Cambridge University Press, 1982.

Schwartz, Joel. *The Sexual Politics of Jean-Jacques Rousseau.* Chicago: The University of Chicago Press, 1984.

Searle, John. "Chomsky's Revolution". *On Noam Chomsky.* Edited by Gilbert Harman. Garden City: Anchor Books, 1974.

Shklar, Judith. *Men and Citizens: A Study of Rousseau's Social Theory.* Cambridge: Cambridge University Press, 1969.

Shklar, Judith. "Jean-Jacques Rousseau and Equality". *Daedalus.* (Summer) 1978: 13-25.

Shklar, Judith. "Rousseau's Two Models: Sparta and the Age of Gold". *Political Science Quarterly.* Vol. LXXXI. (March, 1966).

Skinner, Quentin. "Meaning and Understanding in the History of Ideas." *History and Theory.* No.8 (1969).

Skinner, Quentin. "Motives, Intentions and the Interpretation of Texts". *New Literary History.* No. 3 (1972).

Skinner, Quentin. "Some Problems in the Analysis of Political Thought and Action". *Political Theory.* No. 2 (1974).

Starobinski, Jean. "The Accuser and the Accused" *Daedalus* (Summer 1978): 41-58

Starobinski, Jean. *La Transparence et l'obstacle.* Paris: Editions Gallimard, 1971.

Strauss, Leo. *Natural right and History.* Chicago: University of Chicago Press, 1953.

Talmon, J.L. *The Origins of Totalitarian democracy.* London: Sphere Books, 1970.

Taylor, Charles. *Hegel.* London: Cambridge University Press, 1976.

Taylor, Charles. *Philosophy and the Human Sciences: Philosophical Papers.* Cambridge: Cambridge University Press, 2 vols., 1985.

Tyson, Edward. *Orang-outang, Sive Homo Sylvestris: or, The Anatomy of a Pygmie.* Edited by Ashley Montague. London: Dawsons of Pall Mall, 1966.

Wittgenstein, Ludwig. *Philosophical Investigations.* Translated by Anscombe. Oxford: Basil Blackwell, 1967.

Wokler, Robert. "Essai sur l'origine des langues en tant que fragment des *Discours sur l'inégalité. Rousseau et Voltaire: Acts du colloques International de Nice.* Genéve et Paris: Editions Slatkine, 1981.

Wokler, Robert. "Perfectible Apes in decadent Cultures: Rousseau's Anthropology Revisited." *Daedalus.* (Summer 1978): 107-34.

Wokler, Robert. "Rousseau's Perfectibilian Libertarianism". *The Idea of Freedom.* Edited by Allan Ryan. London: Oxford University Press, 1979.

Wokler, Robert. "Tyson and Buffon" *Studies on Voltaire and the Eighteenth Century.* (1973).

For Product Safety Concerns and Information please contact our EU representative GPSR@taylorandfrancis.com
Taylor & Francis Verlag GmbH, Kaufingerstraße 24, 80331 München, Germany